NONSTOP
SALES
BOOM

POWERFUL STRATEGIES TO DRIVE
CONSISTENT SALES GROWTH
YEAR AFTER YEAR

Colleen Francis

AMACOM AMERICAN MANAGEMENT ASSOCIATION

NEW YORK · ATLANTA · BRUSSELS · CHICAGO · MEXICO CITY
SAN FRANCISCO · SHANGHAI · TOKYO · TORONTO · WASHINGTON, D.C.

This publication is designed to provide accurate and authoritative information in regard to the subject matter covered. It is sold with the understanding that the publisher is not engaged in rendering legal, accounting, or other professional service. If legal advice or other expert assistance is required, the services of a competent professional person should be sought.

Library of Congress Cataloging-in-Publication Data

Francis, Colleen, 1970-
  Nonstop sales boom : powerful strategies to drive consistent sales growth year after year / Colleen Francis. -- 1 Edition.
      pages cm
  Includes index.
  ISBN 978-0-8144-3376-8 — ISBN 0-8144-3376-6 1. Selling. 2. Customer relations. I. Title.
  HF5438.25.F6947 2014
  658.8'101—dc23

                                                    2014005360

About AMA
American Management Association (www.amanet.org) is a world leader in talent development, advancing the skills of individuals to drive business success. Our mission is to support the goals of individuals and organizations through a complete range of products and services, including classroom and virtual seminars, webcasts, webinars, podcasts, conferences, corporate and government solutions, business books and research. AMA's approach to improving performance combines experiential learning—learning through doing—with opportunities for ongoing professional growth at every step of one's career journey.

Printing number
10 9 8 7 6 5 4 3 2

This book is dedicated to all those
who make their living as professional salespeople.
I am extremely proud of the work you do
and am honored to stand alongside you.

Contents

CONTENTS

Acknowledgments

A SPECIAL NOTE OF APPRECIATION: Some of you probably know Alan Weiss, the author of over 50 books in 12 languages, *the* thought leader in solo consulting, often called "the rock star of consulting." It's been my good fortune to be part of his community and be coached by him. In fact, we've often shared drinks (me) and cigars (him) over that time.

I can't begin to thank him enough for his close help in working with me to make this book the best it can be. He helped with parts of the writing, editing, analysis of ideas, and examples. I offered to include his name on the cover after mine with "and" or "with," but he graciously declined.

Yet I do want to recognize his terrific contributions and thank him for both his assistance and friendship in this project and over the years. I have referred countless colleagues in consulting, coaching, and professional services to his world-class guidance. I do the same for you.

....

There are five people in particular without whom this book would not be.

Robert Nirkind. Thank you for proactively reaching out to me to write this book. Your belief in the quality of my work and that sellers needed to hear what I had to say was a driving motivation.

Thank you to my editors Chris Murray and Debbie Posner. Your thoughtful commentary and professional guidance resulted in a book that moves the discussion about selling to a new level of sophistication.

Thank you Casey. Your loyalty to Engage and our clients is second to none. Without you, I would not have been able to simultaneously write this book and continue to do what I love best: serve our clients.

Finally, thank you to my husband and business partner, Chris. Your unwavering support and inspiration motivate everything I do.

A Better Way: A Nonstop Sales Boom

MOST SALES ORGANIZATIONS ARE FAR TOO FAMILIAR with the following scenario: As the end of the quarter approaches, team members are frenetically working to close deals. Some will close those deals and some won't. At the end of the quarter some salespeople have made their target, some haven't. And at the start of that next quarter, almost all of them—those who didn't meet their targets *and* those who did—will be facing insufficient pipelines and spend the next weeks chasing new leads that may or may not close in time.

Feast or famine, boom or bust, apex or nadir—it's a pattern that too many sales organizations regard as a necessary evil. I don't. I see it simply as an evil. This is what compelled me to write *Nonstop Sales Boom*.

Sadly, all too often when teams perform well in one quarter they are more likely to see results collapse in the next. Why? In the all-consuming rush to close deals at the end of the quarter or year, key activities fall by the wayside. And when activities like lead qualification and account management suffer, the seeds are sown for bad results down the line—in effect, creating *a self-imposed vicious cycle where results vary significantly from quarter to quarter.*

For sales leaders, this boom and bust cycle creates enormous uncertainty and inconsistency. Yet it's considered "normal." Do any of the following statements sound familiar?

> ➤ "We always have inconsistent results because our buyers don't buy in the first month of the quarter!"
>
> ➤ "I expect fluctuating individual sales performance! They can't be perfect all the time. If they were, that would show that our targets are too low."
>
> ➤ "It's okay to have a few on the team who underperform. They are balanced out by the overperformers."
>
> ➤ "I'm just in a slump. I'll get over it soon."
>
> ➤ "Our business is *always* seasonal."
>
> ➤ "It's just the typical hockey stick!"
>
> ➤ "It's always been this way. Nothing we can do will change it now."

These are the justifications of poor sales management. And reasons why you should read this book carefully!

However hard you try to justify it, boom–bust revenue production is indicative of a much larger problem: a nonstrategic, boom–bust mentality that somehow manages to adhere like glue to the brains of sales management. I know that sales reliability is highly sought in sales organizations and that reliability continues to be an elusive goal. I also know that the process of chasing it down leaves sales executives (who are dealing with end-of-quarter stress) and individual salespeople (who are trying to establish consistency) completely devoid of the energy they need to do their jobs. A sales vice president I spoke with recently told me sales reliability was also the cause of her gray hair!

While extensive improvement work has been done by experts and well-intentioned companies in specific tactical parts of the sales process, such as cold calling, prospecting, and presenting, never before has a focus been placed on the specific causes of and cures for the roller-coaster boom–bust cycle that most sales organizations endure.

Until now.

Welcome to *Nonstop Sales Boom*. In this book, I will challenge you to reject the typical boom and bust sales cycle where results lurch between highs and lows and the end of each quarter is a mad scramble. Instead, you'll learn the strategies and tactics for creating your own perpetual sales growth quarter after quarter, year after year.

At the heart of these strategies and tactics is a new framework called the *Sales Radar*™ that replaces the step-by-step mindset of traditional sales with a holistic, constantly spinning assessment of all the opportunities for sales that surround you. The Sales Radar mindset is not just focused on *attracting* prospects and closing sales, but also explores the myriad opportunities with and through current customers—from the leads and sales that arise during the implementation or *participation* phase, to bigger sales to current customers looking to *grow* their engagement with your company, to the leads to new, qualified prospects from satisfied customers whose enthusiastic advocacy can be *leveraged* into sales to new clients.

In the pages that follow, you'll learn in detail how the four states of engagement of your Sales Radar—Attraction, Participation, Growth, and Leverage—break the boom and bust sales cycle and instead lead your company to a Nonstop Sales Boom.

I'm sure that some of the stories of success and failure that you'll read in this book may appear to be taken from your own operation. Don't worry, it's not just you. Many sales teams and organizations have been drawn into these never-ending highs and lows. It's time to end the cycle.

PART I

ENGAGEMENT

IN THE FIRST PART OF THE BOOK, we are going to explore in more detail the harrowing roller-coaster ride through the highs and lows of continuous booms and busts that too many sales organizations are willing to endure. While Chapter 1 documents the boom–bust cycles, Chapter 2 shows you the role that tunnel vision plays in creating these vicious cycles, and how the 360° mindset of the Sales Radar cures tunnel vision. The key is to think of prospects and customers as being *continuously engaged* with the company in one way or another.

The Destructive Power of Boom–Bust Cycles

IS IT POSSIBLE to create a perpetually growing, evolving, improving sales organization, in which the alchemy of the talents and strategy create eternal gold? Or is this some crazy search for a mythical philosopher's stone?

Before you answer, read on.

To start, let's examine the current sales environment. Most businesses suffer from inconsistent sales results, and inconsistent responses to them. On top of the lost revenue opportunity, substantial organizational costs are incurred, including:

> ➤ **An overwhelming burden is placed on a few top performers, putting revenues at risk.** Fewer than 25 percent of sales team members produce the largest share of revenue. If just one of those top performers fails to exceed targets, your revenue flow will be undermined. Remember the adage "putting all your eggs in one basket"? When you rely too heavily on a few top performers to produce the entire team's quota, your eggs are going to start breaking rapidly.

> ➤ **Last-minute deals force concessions that ultimately undermine both top and bottom lines.** When a team is in a slump,

and needs to win every opportunity it can, discounts are given that erode company margins and sacrifice future profits with those customers. Once customers have tasted your desperation to get the deal done at any cost to your business, they will always demand that discount (or more) for future business. I call this vicious circle of discounting "eating your young." (Clients call it "waiting for the fire sale.")

> ➤ **Roller-coaster sales results tax an executive's patience and responsiveness and leave investors with a lack of confidence.** When this happens, panicked, expensive, and wrong decisions are made to change markets, pricing, and personnel that are not in the best long-term interests for the company. Sales executives who can't pull their teams out of a sustained bust are always the first to be fired. Investors who witness booms and busts pull their financing or demand cutbacks to maintain profitability, regardless of the revenue attained.

It doesn't have to be this way. Sales booms followed by busts are self-inflicted wounds. Perpetual sales booms are sustained, lasting, and replicable periods of organic sales growth. They occur when your team hits every sales target over a lengthy time frame. This has occurred in a wide variety of companies, including in large, publicly traded organizations such as Apple, Ericsson, and the Royal Bank of Canada, and in smaller, privately held companies such as home healthcare software provider Kinnser Software, sales force automation software maker Infusionsoft, and the temporary staffing company The Placement Office.

So why isn't this the norm for most organizations? Because a fundamental shift in philosophy, moving against the grain, is required. I'm going to tell you how to get there without losing your skin in the process.

KEY CHARACTERISTICS OF BOOMING COMPANIES

Over the last 20 years I have studied top-performing sales teams and companies, and in that research I have noticed that perpetually booming companies share key characteristics. Here are five key characteristics of this very real perpetual boom alchemy at work:

1. **They expand the view of the client beyond the current transaction.** Perpetually booming companies expand the traditional transactional view of the client to attend to both pre-sale and post-sale activities for client development. They are accountable and measured on all phases of the client life cycle, including lead generation, closing, enablement, growth, and leverage. Think of a process, and not an event.

2. **They define and refine performance metrics beyond quota.** Businesses experiencing a perpetual sales boom achieve consistent results month after month by setting specific goals for specific periods. They don't just set one revenue goal but a series of goals that measure both activity and detailed sales results. These refined goals provide the team with valuable information on performance toward targets with sufficient warning to ensure that action can be taken to correct any potential shortfall. A subtle but critical point is that each performance period is treated as stand-alone; there are no "carry forward" credits that can enable the boom and bust behavior.

3. **Their sales teams are managed to ensure 80 percent or more are hitting their targets—and poor performers are coached up or out quickly.** In most companies, sales leaders have learned to manage a team where less than half of the sellers hit their targets on a regular basis. In a Nonstop Sales Boom environment, on the other hand, leaders build an entire team of top performers. To do this, *they get rid of their average sales reps, not merely the underachieving ones.* Their tolerance level is far below what most companies will endure. I call this "Find the best, remove the rest."

4. **Their product and service lines are managed consistently.** Perpetually booming companies do not fall into the trap of becoming overly reliant on one product at the expense of others. For example, companies that launch new products into an existing market and do not train their sellers effectively on these products

run the risk that their sellers will ignore the new products because the older ones are easier to sell; thus they ensure the product launch is a failure. Too often, a seller's unwillingness to sell both product lines in parallel is used as an excuse to avoid learning about new product lines and stay in their comfort zone. This is particularly dangerous because growth (selling new products to existing clients) is a key strategy for booming companies.

5. **They produce results consistent with forecasts.** They can reliably predict the revenue flow from their team to within 5 percent accuracy each month, quarter, and year. In fact, it is not unheard of to see a 2 percent accuracy in the forecast for the quarter.

MOVING TO A PERPETUAL BOOM: TALKSWITCH INC.

Thanks to TalkSwitch Inc.'s then vice president of sales, Tim Welch, the organization exemplified the perpetual sales boom characteristic of consistent revenue attainment. Quarter after quarter, Tim was successful in hitting his numbers, with consistent growth of both sales and market share—but it didn't start out this way. When Tim took over the team, company targets were not being achieved and everyone was performing far below expectations of management. Changes had to be made, and fast.

First, Tim transitioned his sales team from a transaction-based focus to a relationship focus, where the prospect was more than someone with whom to close a deal and move on. Three areas of reseller–client engagement were identified and became the focus of sales efforts: lead generation (cultivating prospects for the channels); client enablement (getting the channels to sell the product); and client growth, including using clients as centers of influence to bring in new prospects.

A second key to Tim's success was the establishment—for the first time—of a specific growth target unique to each member of his team. The key here was not to establish a single sales target for the company, but to measure multiple variables leading to the required results for the sales team and the company. Specifically, he set revenue goals for:

➤ Each team member

➤ Each service and product line

➤ Each channel partner

➤ Each month and quarter

To track progress toward those goals, Tim established activity-based key performance indicators (KPIs). These served two purposes: to provide an early-warning system so that corrective management activity could be taken in time to impact results, and to provide an ongoing stream of data to refine what activity was precisely required to achieve a particular sale as well as overall sales growth. His KPIs included:

➤ Number of conversations

➤ Number of resellers added

➤ Number of referrals received

➤ Number of new contacts per reseller added

As Tim describes it: "TalkSwitch was your typical high-tech firm run by engineers—an amazing product that needed some sales discipline to get out into the market. Colleen worked extensively with the TalkSwitch sales team as we reshaped the sales process, defined and built KPIs, implemented new tools, and measured our results. Engage Selling even recorded customer calls for us to undertake Quality Assurance and leverage coaching opportunities. Colleen's firm approach and clear interaction with our teams resulted in a program that once built was easy to maintain and reinforce." Tim is too kind. (Though I appreciate it!) And what he's really referring to are the four key principles outlined in this chapter:

1. You must *expand your view of the client beyond the current transaction* in order to create a Nonstop Sales Boom.

2. The best companies *define and refine performance metrics beyond quota* to ensure they can estimate current and future revenue attainment on the team accurately.

3. Top-performing sales teams are *tightly managed to ensure 80 per-*

cent or more are hitting targets (and poor performers are coached up or out quickly).

4. All product and service lines need to be *rigorously and evenly managed* to produce consistent results.

Yet a third approach that Tim took that few businesses undertake was to involve his sales team in setting up revenue and activity targets, and to show how attainment of these goals affected their earnings. Tim involved the team in setting these goals and ensured they understood their impact—both to each other (e.g., how activity metrics relate to the number of sales) and to the team's commissions.

With the rollout of these goals, Tim held his team accountable through one-on-one coaching, regular sales meetings, and executive meetings centered on the KPIs and the sales pipeline. The replacement of a sales automation software with an online CRM tool enabled immediate measurements of the KPIs and pipeline. The power of activity-related metrics is that they provide sales management with early indicators so that remedial action can be taken to either improve results or to identify team members who need to be managed out of the organization.

As the team began achieving their KPIs, revenue started to flow and sizable commissions followed. Their success cemented buy-in from all levels of management and the sales team itself.

The result of this transformation was that within a year, Tim's team consistently achieved their sales targets, month after month, and for two years each successive quarter was their best yet. In short, they had achieved a perpetual sales boom!

ENGAGED SELLING:

Don't assume a roller-coaster effect is inevitable. Assume you are capable of consistent growth. What you talk about informs behavior.

SALES BUST CYCLES

Sales busts are defined as sales failures or flops. They happen when sellers—individuals or teams—fail to hit their expected monthly, quarterly, or annual sales target, and in the most extreme cases cause a company to lose money over a set reporting period. And they most commonly happen immediately following a boom period. Why? Because during the boom, sellers become complacent and ignore all activities required to create future opportunities in favor of closing all the opportunities they can immediately. As a result, a great month is followed by a dismal month, or a record period is followed by a dramatic crash, a *bust*, in revenue.

There are three types of sales bust cycle: *sales cramming, the sales trap,* and *unidentified failing objectives.* Every one of them is invidious and potentially fatal.

Sales Cramming

Remember "cramming" in school? You tried to compress three months of preparatory work into 24 hours of nightmarish tension, and you were lucky to scrape by with a barely passing grade. Why would you subject yourself to that repeatedly as part of your career—constant stress to be mediocre at best?

Sales cramming is caused by a sales team habitually closing little to no revenue in the early stages of a reporting period, and slowly starting to bring in more until a steep revenue jump occurs (see Figure 1–1).

Figure 1–1. Sales Cramming

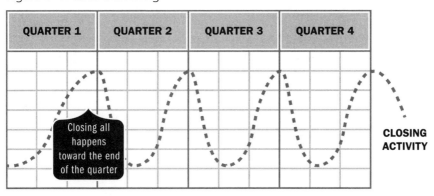

This flat period is caused by sales teams that are:

> **Resting from the busy end of their previous sales period.**
> When members of a team cram in March to make their
> numbers by overworking, they are exhausted and coast for
> the first few weeks of April. Plus, they have come to believe
> that they can "make magic happen" at the end of the quarter,
> so why work now? These people need an energy drink.

> **Processing all the clients from the previous month.** There
> are so many clients needing products, scheduling, and
> services that sellers are distracted by servicing them, rather
> than by their empty pipeline that needs filling. These people
> need calm.

> **Prospecting because their funnel is dry.** At the end of the
> quarter it is common for team members to have nothing left in
> their sales pipelines because everything has been won or lost or
> beaten to death. As a result, the first two months of the next
> quarter are spent finding sales-ready leads to close at the end of
> the period. These people need a compass.

> **On vacation!** Because you can't go away at the end of the period.
> Vacations are more prominent at the beginning of the quarter
> and often disallowed at the end of the quarter. These people
> need better scheduling.

> **Reorganizing, because the start of the period is always a good
> time to reorganize files, territories, desks, pipelines, sales pro-
> cesses, or compensation plans.** These people need organization.

> **In training meetings, account review sessions, quarterly
> business review, and all other internal business meetings that
> were put off because it was the end of the month or quarter
> the previous week.** These people need a break.

As the period lumbers on, revenue trickles in skewing upward as
cramming starts.

One year, during a New Year's Eve dinner party at our house, my best
friend was monitoring her email for deals closing until a minute before

midnight. Our dinner guests applauded her for being a real trouper. I quietly wondered, "Why weren't those deals closed two weeks ago?"

Of course, in another minute she was going to be a "loser" again, far behind her goals on January 1!

The Sales Trap

The Sales Trap is a product of a seller delivering inconsistent revenue production through several reporting periods. Characteristically, a great quarter is followed by a dismal quarter (see Figure 1–2).

As you can see, the seller delivered 130 percent quota attainment one quarter, 50 percent the next, 60 percent in quarter three, and finally back at target (100 percent) in the final quarter of the year.

Aside from inconsistency in revenue production (and commissions), the Sales Trap also leads to a more serious issue because record-setting or on-track reporting periods are followed by several poor performance periods. The reason? It's difficult to dig yourself out of the hole and get forward momentum rolling again.

Quite often in my consulting practice, I see companies deliver a record month followed by a dismal month, a barely surviving month, and a passable month—all before getting back to hitting or exceeding their targets. That inconsistency can be a sales organization killer.

Here's a classic example of the Sales Trap. The company's target was

Figure 1–2. The Sales Trap

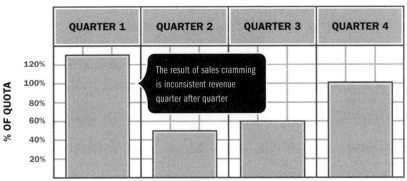

$100,000 per month. If sellers hit the goal each quarter, commissions doubled. The results were as follows:

> ➤ Record January at two times goal
> ➤ Poor February at 10 percent of goal
> ➤ Subpar March at 50 percent of goal
> ➤ Slightly better April at 70 percent of goal
> ➤ May at goal
> ➤ June at goal

Look at the results in Figure 1–3 and compare them to the seller's goals.

For the seller, being behind at the end of June meant the difference between receiving his regular commission and an accelerated commission. Using the numbers above, the seller ultimately earned a 10 percent commission level (i.e., $53,000) rather than the accelerated commission of 20 percent (i.e., $120,000) that would have been received had he achieved his goal for the first six months.

Figure 1–3. The Results of Falling into a Sales Trap

MONTH	ACTUAL SALES PER MONTH	CUMULATIVE QUOTA	DIFFERENCE BETWEEN TARGET AND ACTUAL
January	$200,000	$100,000	+$100,000
February	$ 10,000	$200,000	+$ 10,000
March	$ 50,000	$300,000	−$ 40,000
April	$ 70,000	$400,000	−$ 70,000
May	$100,000	$500,000	−$ 70,000
June	$100,000	$600,000	−$ 70,000
Totals	**$530,000**	**$600,000**	**−$ 70,000**

If you're a seller, you can see why the Sales Trap is troubling. If you're a sales leader, the Sales Trap is potentially deadly for four reasons:

1. **If your team is not hitting its sales goals and making full commissions,** *neither are you!*

2. **Goal attainment is linked to voluntary and involuntary turnover.** A 2008 Sales Executive Council report ("Improving Sales Performance Through Effective Manager Coaching") shows that sales reps achieving 90 percent or less of their sales goal *have a voluntarily turnover rate that is four times higher* than those over 90 percent of goal attainment.

3. **If your sales team is failing, or if you consistently allow them to miss quota, then you're complicit in their failure.** And if your boss believes that you are complicit in your team's failure, you will be replaced. Sales results start at the top. My research shows that the average "nonvoluntary" turnover rate for sales leaders in the United States is 16 months.

4. **If your team is not producing consistent revenue results, resource allocation for sales tools, marketing projects, travel, and events will be held back.** Companies that experience two months in a row or more of lower than anticipated results will routinely ground travel, cancel client events, and shut down marketing programs. *Spending will be held back until the company is confident that it will hit its sales targets.*

Unidentified Failing Objectives

We define the characteristic of unidentified failing objectives, or UFOs, as I like to call them, as inconsistent sales performance, reporting period after reporting period, by individual reps or multiple teams. Essentially, everyone is in the Sales Trap, but never in sync with each other.

Having UFO sales performance is a particularly unique challenge because it can occur even when overall revenue is consistently above target. In other words, a high-performing group may make up for losses in another group. That might not sound like a big problem, but if one group or division is thriving while another is suffering, you will:

> Never meet your total potential.

> Lose sales and market share opportunities in the failing territory or division.

> Create a culture of poor performance that eventually migrates to other divisions.

Companies that display UFO symptoms generally allow languishing people or departments to suffer for too long. The reason for that tolerance is often due to focusing on overall results rather than specific performance metrics. As a result, *underperformers may be hidden and sometimes protected.* This can cause profits to erode, market share to decline, and reputation in the market to be tarnished.

Recently I witnessed the heartbreak of a company discovering too late it was heading for a massive sales bust because of UFO characteristics. The CEO called us in to examine the company's sales situation because he had a hunch something was wrong but could not put his finger on it. For me, the situation was obvious as soon as I opened up his database and took a deep, thorough look at the pipeline.

The company had two lines of business managed by two sales teams and one overall sales leader. Team One had great long-term prospects with large annuity-type deals that were contracted over multiple years. Team Two provided short-term quick revenue with high profit and repeat orders from existing clients.

Team One closed a two-year deal that provided profit to the company, while also building its sales funnel. Team Two had a sales funnel that was half the size required for moderate success, and had not closed a sale in four months. However, the VP of sales had stopped paying attention to that team's results because Team One was more or less funding the company.

Eventually, the VP of sales discovered Team Two's problem, but it was too late to make any progress on the year's revenue attainment. Even worse, when I began working with the CEO to dig into that team's pipeline, we discovered that more than two-thirds of the pipeline was outdated or duplicated. That left only 10 percent of the opportunities that Team Two realistically needed

ENGAGED SELLING:

You can't correct a sales bust unless you know the cause and take the appropriate corrective actions.

to successfully close the year, and it only had three months of selling remaining. In the end, the VP of sales and Team Two lost their jobs and were replaced during a 12-month rebuilding process.

FOURTEEN REASONS WHY BOOM AND BUST CYCLES ARE UNNATURAL AND DAMAGING

Our research and experience has shown that, left unaddressed, boom and bust cycles will negatively impact your company in 14 distinct ways. These cycles are often accepted as "necessary evils," but there is no circumstance under which a company can remain healthy with the following 14 damaging symptoms:

1. **Sales rep stress.** Busts are difficult to recover from because a sales pipeline takes time to replenish and this means time with low or no sales (and, of course, no commissions). *Filling the pipeline takes half the time of the total sales cycle.* So, for a company with a six-month sales cycle, three months are spent filling the pipeline to the point where proposals are sent and forecasts are created. That's 90 days of prospecting work with no commissions being paid!

2. **Sales rep exhaustion.** If the team has been cramming, they will be exhausted. As a result, little work is done, or often even encouraged in the first week of the quarter. Vacation time is encouraged and many sales VPs give extra time off in the first few days of the quarter to ensure a team is well rested after a difficult period. Recently,

I worked with an inside sales leader who gave his whole team a day off the first day back after an exceptional quarter ended. While this seems like a good reward, it put the team almost $25,000 in a revenue hole in one day due to their highly transactional nature. Of course, that revenue had to be made up at the end of the quarter, resulting in cramming.

3. **Administration overload.** Sellers who ignore internal meetings, training sessions, or administration tasks during the last month of the quarter will have to make up for them during the first month of the following quarter. I remember once, as a sales director, walking the floor the first week of the month to find my entire team was engaged in nonsales activities, including filling out lost luggage claim forms, in the middle of the day! Every week that goes by without activity is a week that must be made up in order for the seller to hit targets. That week is usually made up at the end of the quarter through cramming—thus creating the same trend the next quarter.

4. **Emotional contagion.** Sellers who are struggling are contagious because they are louder, talk about their struggles more often, and blame others voraciously. Those who are doing well run the risk of being dragged down by those who are not, and even top performers will eventually be dragged down into poor performance when the bottom performers are allowed to stay in their jobs too long.

5. **Emotional decision making.** Desperate salespeople close desperate business. My first boss in technology sales once said to me, "If you think they are awful to deal with now, just imagine what they will be like after they pay us. Bad prospects do not grow old gracefully!" Most sellers have experienced the gut feeling of "I should not sell to this prospect" at least once in their career but choose to ignore it because they desperately need the business to meet their quota. It is impossible for a seller who is behind to walk away from the only potential close in her pipeline.

Sadly, if the situation is bad enough, salespeople may also lie and cheat the system to get deals done. One of our clients shared with us his past experience:

"One of my first jobs in sales was working as a rep for a large manufacturer of printers. I can still remember the day I made my first sale of a brand new printer to an international organization supporting people with sight disabilities. When I told my manager the particulars of the sale, he ordered me to send the client a used printer instead of a new one because, 'It's the only one we have in stock now that can be counted toward a sale this month and they won't be able to see the difference!' "

6. **Delayed buying decisions.** When sellers are cramming, deep discounts are given to clients to secure deals at the end of the quarter. As a result these buyers know to wait until the end of the next quarter to buy again. You have trained them into this behavior. A vicious and self-inflicted cycle is created because the *discounted price becomes the baseline price for these clients in the future.* If you offered them 20 percent off for buying now, when they reorder next quarter what do they expect? Exactly! Twenty percent off that 20 percent discount. You have just created an unprofitable customer.

7. **Management turnover and firings.** Consistent revenue is critical to consistent profits and shareholder value. If the sales manager cannot provide this, he or she will be fired. My research shows that the average retention of sales management in North America is 16 *months*; you can be sure that senior leadership is scrutinizing every month of revenue to make sure the problem is not at the top. The most likely sales leaders to succeed are those who communicate a plan for consistent revenue, stick to that plan, and hit it with accuracy (or exceed it).

8. **Stock price drops.** If your sales organization fails to produce consistent revenue numbers, sales management and sales team income may be impacted negatively and the company's stock price will likely be devalued. A devalued stock price for most companies means reduction in spending to get profits back on track. When

this happens, travel is curtailed, marketing budgets are frozen, and client events are cancelled.

9. **Internecine conflict.** When personal income is cut due to reduced commissions, the team becomes disheartened and frustrated. While they may know that their behavior and lack of activity is responsible for the reduction, they will blame the company first. Internecine conflict erupts when Sales blames Marketing for poor leads, Accounting for bad billing, Customer Services for angering clients, and Shipping for messing up orders. Once communication breaks down between departments, it can take months to rebuild profitability. At a large Canadian company, the marketing department shut off the flow of leads to an inside sales team due to the internecine conflict that started between a poor-performing sales team and a new marketing VP. It took five months, a structural reorganization, and a new sales manager to restart the sales lead lifeline.

10. **Decreased client onboarding effectiveness.** As customers get stacked up unevenly, it becomes nearly impossible to onboard them smoothly. They "stack up" like logs outside a mill, and often wind up on the same buzz saws.

11. **Reduced client leverage.** Boom and bust cycles will impact the seller's ability to leverage client successes as customers are ignored during busy periods. During busy boom cycles, sellers tend to ignore current clients in favor of the new prospects. Ignoring current customers during a boom cycle, though, is a quick way to create a bust. This lack of attention during the boom time is exactly what leads to attrition. When your customers leave, you not only lose the immediate income but your ability to leverage those clients for use in case studies and for referrals.

12. **Missed opportunities.** During especially busy times, sales reps and their managers tend to bury their heads in the work that feels most urgent. Typically, this means they are solely focused on chasing down leads and closing deals. As a result, they often miss huge future (and longer-term) revenue opportunities.

13. **Lack of long-term planning.** Because bust cycles make it difficult to understand where a seller's successes are coming from and when they are going to be successful, it can be very challenging to plan ahead.

14. **Incredible inefficiency.** Poorly performing resources or team members are often hidden by the top performers. As a result, companies tend to hold on to them, preventing the business from being as efficient or successful as it could be.

Unlike roller coasters, successful sales don't depend on deep troughs to build momentum to climb the next hill. In the next chapter we'll take a look at how to generate speed without taking dips.

ENGAGED SELLING:

Don't tolerate boom and bust mentalities. Focus on the perpetual boom.

CHAPTER 2

The Sales Radar:
How the Continuous Sweep of
Customer Engagement
Destroys Tunnel Vision

BOOM AND BUST cycles are not intentional. No sales organization, sales team, or sales leader sets out at the beginning of the year to generate a euphoric spike in sales to then watch as sales figures tumble off the cliff with no prospects in the pipeline to save the year. And yet, year after year, the same frustrating cycle repeats itself. Why?

After a decade of studying and consulting with sales teams and companies around the world, I discovered the virus causing the disease: the almost invisible culture of tunnel vision. I call it invisible because most companies never realize that they are suffering from tunnel vision. And I call it a culture because *tunnel vision* is more than processes, tactics, or strategies; it's the fundamental way that the team or the company *defines* sales.

THE THREE CATEGORIES OF TUNNEL VISION

Most of us are familiar with the concept tunnel vision. We might call it a "one-track mind," "having blinders on," "a fixation," "myopia," "constricted vision," or "narrow-mindedness." Pick your poison. These phrases are all accurate descriptions of what tunnel vision is inside a sales organization, and it's much more prevalent than you might think.

Tunnel vision is created when you have a myopic view of what your role as a seller is and focus all your time and attention on only one component of the sales process at the expense of all others. Working with troubled sales teams and organizations, I have consistently found that the core root of the problem was tunnel vision manifesting itself in one of three ways:

> ➤ Tunnel vision created by too much prospecting
> ➤ Tunnel vision created by the "always be closing" rallying cry
> ➤ Tunnel vision created by "farming"

Let's look at each of these in closer detail.

Too Much Prospecting: A Pile of Leads but Meager Sales

After hiring me to help turn around its disappointing sales figures, an online warehousing engine for e-retailers admitted that it was too busy to follow up with leads except for one email and one phone call over 30 days. The team was exceptional at sending "thank you for contacting us" emails within 24 hours, but follow-ups stopped there. Their closing ratio was *2 percent*, and included only those leads that respond back with "please sign me up." The sales team consistently received 500 new leads per month and had 20,000 leads in their database—all unqualified, never nurtured.

Companies that focus only on prospecting and attracting leads lack the assertiveness to ask for the sale. They have a pipeline of potential friends but few customers. While they can create an effective lead generation machine, their closing ratios are lower than average.

In other words, a whole lot of sizzle, but no steak.

This is a performance issue, and it can go unchecked for a long time because some business will close regardless of whether your team is asking for the sale. If you bring in enough leads, some will always close on their own. The clients that I have seen with this tunnel vision affliction tend to close about 15 percent of the leads they receive without even trying. Because they are closing *some* leads this affliction goes unchecked for a long time. Often it is masked as a product issue ("We don't have the right features") or a pricing issue ("Our products are too expensive").

Sadly, though, companies that focus too much on prospecting don't live up to their potential—nor can they predict their revenue.

The solution to prospecting tunnel vision is to move some of your effort from prospecting to closing, which includes following up on your leads to get them to sign up or sign on the dotted line. With the addition of a new, proactive sales process I designed for the online warehousing engine, sellers now follow up four times with each new lead and specifically ask: "Would you like to get started?" Also, a monthly company newsletter is sent to every contact in the database of stagnant leads.

As a result, their closing ratio on new leads improved by 15 percent within five days. Over 90 days, new contracts were signed with 1 percent of the leads in the "stagnant" database—that's 200 new customers.

Small changes like these were all it took to eliminate tunnel vision from their business habits. The company is thriving with $500,000 more annual recurring revenue, no increase in head count, and they have implemented a more predicable measurement of future revenue for the company.

Too Much Closing: Quick Wins and Reactive Sales Will Leave You Dry

In David Mamet's play *Glengarry Glen Ross* (which was later adapted for film), Blake is an aggressive motivator who demands that his audience of salesmen adopt his "ABC" or "Always Be Closing" mindset . . . or else! The scene is memorable, but it's worth noting that as the plot develops, the story eventually becomes an indictment of the ABC philosophy.

In sales, I've seen the ABC method play out many times. It seldom ends well for the company. If all you do is focus on closing, you will be doing so at the expense of both the front end and back end of the sales cycle. That includes prospecting and the post-sale account management follow-up. When you are too busy closing to do any prospecting, you are faced with an empty pipeline at the start of each month or each quarter. That's how a sales bust gets started. And it gets worse. Since you are focused on closing above all else, and since your pipeline is so lean, you need to consistently reach an unrealistically high closing percentage, or you won't hit your sales targets. ABC is a tail-chasing dog. Don't be one of those.

There are two kinds of closing tunnel vision behaviors you need to avoid: focusing only on new sales, and focusing only on *reactive* sales.

Focusing Only on Closing New Sales

Sellers who focus on closing new opportunities above all else tend to jump on leads that will produce a quick win with a product that's easy to sell at the lowest price point. They are "hunters," always on the prowl for opportunities to close quickly. They are adrenaline junkies: "fire and forget" sellers who are more interested in a hot new lead than in nurturing existing customers. "If you can't close now, I'll find someone who can" is the hunter's threat to a sales team. This behavior is indicative of tunnel vision, because it focuses all attention on the opportunities coming straight at the sellers and creates blinders to the other opportunities from existing customers, referrals, or marketing leads that are all around them.

Making matters worse, and escalating this tunnel vision are compensation plans that only pay for new business. In this case the organization is creating tunnel vision by telling the seller that nothing else matters except for new business development. Let's face it, if a seller is only going to get paid for net new business, rather than repeat business or incremental sales, she will only focus on the new business and ignore everything else.

For example, a U.S.-based computer chip manufacturer built an effective inside sales team focused on closing new business. They always hit their new business targets and were excellent at finding and closing new projects quickly. They discovered that the fastest deals came from companies looking to test a new design. These test projects were priced below $50,000 and could be contracted quickly.

Moving from opportunity identification to contract often took less than 60 days. After the sale was complete, the newly contracted clients were turned over to the design group for project management. That group did an excellent job servicing their new customer, and repeat sales for new design and testing projects were very high.

It sounds like the sales team for this computer chip manufacturing company was doing everything right, doesn't it? Not so fast. The company eventually learned it was missing all the post-test production runs of the newly designed chips, *which was at least 10 times as valuable as the testing business.*

The company had the facilities for the lucrative production runs. And since it had the testing component, there was a pool of natural production clients looking for a company to take care of production. However, the sales team was not compensated for follow-up business and had moved on to hunting down new clients, and the design team was not equipped to manage the client after the project ended. As a result, no one was asking for the full production run business, and many clients were not even aware they could use their testing company for full production capabilities. Over $3 million in two years was lost from missing project revenue. They were so busy closing that they were leaving money on the table . . . all because of deeply entrenched tunnel vision.

Focusing Only on Closing Reactive Sales

With reactive sales, your team isn't doing much more than taking orders, closing deals that come to them. Often these teams are in mature markets and have very large client bases that call voluntarily to place orders. In addition, they have strong branding in the market, making marketing campaigns highly effective. Complacency takes hold when orders are plentiful, but sales go flat when those orders wind down, because the sales team has lost its momentum and sellers' prospecting skills are no longer as sharp as they need to be. This is one of the greatest vulnerabilities of any sales force: untended clients that can fail to produce, just like untended, fallow fields.

I worked with the Northeast Asia regional offices of an international ships-services company that ran a busy operation with high expectations for sales success. Operating in one of the most economically vibrant regions of the world and in an industry at the heart of global trade, the sales team had highly ambitious sales targets. However, they only yielded mediocre results, because sellers focused on closing the small orders that were coming to them easily rather than expanding their relationships to sell more proactively.

At one point, their average order size was $1,500 and came exclusively from clients calling to place repeat orders. Meanwhile, their competitors were picking up multimillion-dollar contracts because they were managing accounts proactively while vigorously seeking new opportunities with new prospects.

Our contact, the VP of sales for the region, lamented: "We have a long history of losing the national contracts from our existing accounts . . . why?" The answer: because his team's tunnel vision created a culture of order-taking rather than being more aggressive about seeking new opportunities and retaining and growing clients.

Order-taking is especially damaging if a seller is chasing an exceptionally large opportunity—sometimes referred to as *a whale*. That word is a symbol borrowed from Melville's classic tale *Moby Dick*, in which a vengeful sea captain seeks to catch an elusive white whale . . . and in the process dooms his entire crew. In sales, sellers chase a whale of their own making with the same kind of blind fury. They stop following up on smaller orders. They delay calling clients back. They choose not to send quotes and get lazy by not asking for the sale from small accounts. Understandably, things end badly when you do this.

Recently a seller on a team we work with closed a $150,000 sale. As the average deal size for this inside team is $3,500 this "whale" was considered a huge win and the seller was elevated to superstar status immediately. What everyone failed to notice, however, was that it took the entire quarter for this seller to close the deal, and, because of the complexity and time it took to close the deal no attention was paid to the next quarter's pipeline. As a result the next quarter's performance came in at less than half of quota. Last quarter's superstar had crashed back to earth.

I have my own story of experiencing tunnel vision in sales in pursuit of a whale at the expense of other deals. During my first year at London Life as a sales rep, million-dollar insurance policies were my nemesis. I would spend weeks qualifying, nurturing, and planning for this kind of policy and inevitably the prospect would not buy, or would be delayed, or would opt for a much smaller policy. In the meantime, having ignored my sales funnel for too long, there were no fresh prospects to make up for my losses. It took me a year to realize very few "whale" candidates call into an office looking for large insurance policies, much less can afford one. This tunnel vision was one of the main reasons I fell $15,000 behind in my draw account in the first year of my business.

ENGAGED SELLING:

An exclusive focus on the close today will only create more pressure in the future on the close. That just leads to spinning wheels, not advancement.

Too Much Farming: Who Needs New Customers?

There is one more mindset to cover in our study of tunnel vision, and that's related to sellers who find it easier to nurture their existing customers, and repeatedly approach them for new sales, rather than creating new opportunities with brand-new clients. This is a practice that is sometimes referred to pejoratively as "farming." These sellers are focused exclusively on trying to upsell, cross-sell, or sell newly developed products to their existing customer base—essentially farming the land they already own. Busts are created because there is no balance between existing and new clients in their pipelines, and no new clients are added to replace the natural attrition every business undergoes when their clients close, are acquired, or change their focus.

A farming mindset will lead to four specific types of erosions:

Erosion of revenues occurs because companies don't supplement natural attrition with new client acquisitions (just as a farmer faces problems by failing to rotate the fields). A 2011 United States Census Bureau Business Dynamics study shows a 10 percent rate of "business exits" (in other words, business failures). That rate has remained steadily between 9 and 11 percent since 1982. A percentage of those exits are your clients. What are you doing to make up for those losses?

Erosion of profits occurs because it's difficult to successfully launch new pricing for existing products and services in an entrenched legacy client base (just as the farmer faces the risk of exhausted soil that's been depleted of nutrients). For example, I currently enjoy a cell phone contract that has not been offered to new customers for years; my provider is losing money by not billing me for any roaming fees. Because I am grandfathered in, I will not change plans. While the company is keeping me as a client, I will never cancel my contract and renew with additional, new (higher-margin) services.

Erosion of overall market share occurs because your competition swoops in to close the new opportunities you are ignoring (just like the farmer faces a loss of arable land). If you are ignoring your market, you create a vacuum in which the competition can step in to capture the new business and lock you out. In the worst cases, when another company sees the opportunity to grow into your space, you create competition that was not originally viable.

Erosion of personal income occurs because it becomes increasingly difficult to hit your targets with a stagnant client base (just as a farmer contends with lower yields). After all, you can only "go back to the well" so many times! If you don't grow your business you can't grow your commissions!

The likelihood of a farming mindset is greatest with companies that introduce many new products to their existing markets. For example, an industry-leading graphics software company had a newly acquired desktop suite, which it launched intending to reach its existing client base. It was an all-hands-on-deck move: Sales, marketing, development, and customer service resources were all diverted to the new products. Aggressive new targets were established with lucrative bonuses.

Enhancements to the existing graphics products were put on hold and sales requests were only taken reactively. As a result, the graphics suite was ignored and *only customers interested in the new products were nurtured*. Graphics customers fled and the competition swooped in to fill the vacuum, quickly taking over the number one and number two positions in the graphics market. The former leading player was replaced in all marquee accounts and was never able to compensate for the market losses or regain the market position. Eventually, the CEO resigned and the then publicly traded company was sold to a venture capitalist who stripped it to its core product suite to regain profitability, readying it for sales once again.

DISCOVERING YOUR SALES RADAR: SHATTERING THE ONE-DIRECTION BIAS

After more than two decades of studying the business habits of top-ranked sales professionals in organizations of all sizes, I've identified a solution that can put an end to the boom–bust sales cycle: I call it the *Sales Radar*. The concept of the Sales Radar emerges from what I see as the root cause of tunnel vision, which is to frame selling as a step-by-step process.

Conventional thinking about sales tends to be linear, built on the assumption that solving sales problems is like laying railroad tracks across Kansas in a straight line: repeating a series of tasks without paying attention to the changing landscape around you. The temptation of the linear, step-by-step process is that it often prevents a holistic view of the customer's engagement with the company. Remember the example of the computer chip company that manufactured and tested chips—and that ignored the potential for selling the lucrative production runs to its customers? The reason so much money was left on the table was that the chip manufacturer only viewed its customers as needing products for testing. Once the test product had been sold, the manufacturer moved on to new testing customers, instead of exploring with its current customers any other potential collaboration including the full production run of the product that was just tested!

Think of the 19th-century lookout sailor on an ocean clipper. With his hand-held monocular, he could only look in one direction at a time to see if ships were coming on the horizon. Today, sailors use a radar to see an approaching hazard—whether it's an enemy ship or an iceberg. Unlike the one-directional spyglass, a radar continually sweeps the horizon all around the ship, providing a 360° view of the ocean that surrounds it.

The computer chip testing company and the other examples in the previous chapter had their "eyes" stuck to the monocular, looking in one direction only. And while it might seem a simple matter to consciously pivot to other sales opportunities, in the real world, adopting a 360° view is far from intuitive. The salespeople had a chip-testing product that they sold to chip-testing customers. Once the customer bought the product, the salespeople considered the transaction ended.

The Sales Radar introduces three-dimensional thinking that prevents losing opportunities for new business just because they are not directly in your path. For example, let's assume you have just made a large sale to a Fortune 500 company. With that client, your next sale could come from any number of sources: Maybe it's from a client testimonial, or from being introduced to a new division. Maybe it's from a referral to a new buyer in another company. Maybe it's a new lead that comes from your implementation team while they conduct training, installation, or services work. Those are just a few of what could be a long list of possible sources for new sales—and every one of those sales opportunities would show up on your Sales Radar. The reason is that the Sales Radar does not track customers, but rather customer *states of engagement*.

YOUR SALES RADAR AND THE FOUR STATES OF ENGAGEMENT

Imagine that you're selling software systems to small-business clients. In the traditional framework, the potential client is considered a "prospect" until the client buys the software, at which point it becomes a "customer." However, on the Sales Radar (see Figure 2–1), the client is considered in the *Attraction* state of engagement when it is still a prospect. When the deal closes, the client is now engaged at the Sales Radar *Participation* level—that is, there is now an ongoing relationship between you and the client that involves not just service issues, but also training and continuously learning (keeping the client educated on news in its field, for example). The client is also in the *Growth* state of engagement, since the ongoing relationship can potentially lead to new sales to the client. Finally, the same client is in the *Leverage* state of engagement, in which the relationship with the client can be leveraged into sales to new customers through referrals, testimonials, and so forth.

In the rest of this chapter, we will have a look at each one of these states, and in later chapters we will examine in detail how to keep the Sales Radar sweeping continuously through each state to create a Nonstop Sales Boom.

Attraction: So Much More Than Cold Calling

In this state, all prospects and opportunities with a targeted company are new. You have never done business with that company before and they represent new revenue potential for you. Leads are attracted to you by outbound marketing activities, such as awareness campaigns, such as promotional, industry and educational events, or by direct outbound sales campaigns. Most sellers excel at activities in the Attraction state because these tasks embody what is traditionally thought of as sales and marketing. New leads are generated by the sales and marketing teams and put

Figure 2–1. Sales Radar

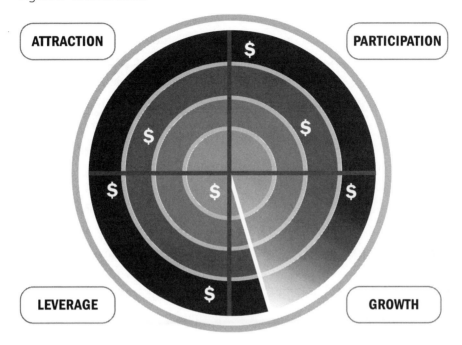

ATTRACTION

PARTICIPATION

LEVERAGE

GROWTH

into the sales funnel to convert prospects into clients. Cold calling and direct mail are also features of the Attraction state.

Kinnser Software, for example, is a home health software company that puts Attraction to work immediately after attending industry-related events (e.g., trade shows and conferences). Each time, its marketing team invites new prospects to attend a subsequent educational event, where they can learn about better practice management for their home health companies. There, prospects also learn about Kinnser's software and receive special pricing offers. After each trade show or other industry event, Kinnser's marketing team documents all leads, enters each one into the sales pipeline, and turns them over to the sales team for conversion. On the strength of the high-quality leads obtained from each event, the sales team closes 50 percent of those that express interest.

Participation: Selling Means Never Saying Good-Bye

In the Participation state, opportunities are being actively pursued and converted into new clients who are now actively using your products. Pay attention to the not-so-subtle difference in how we are defining this concept in the context of the Sales Radar. Most sellers stop selling—and stop participating—once a sale is made. They thank the client for the order, shake hands, and then turn their attention to attracting new clients. With the Sales Radar your work with a client does not stop when you close a sale. It continues until the client is actively using the product.

New opportunities arise during the Participation state, and if you have moved on too soon you could miss out on many of them. For example, many employment agencies routinely send their sellers out to attract new clients and then pass the new clients on to a recruiting team. The recruiter's job is to enable the client by actively filling the open employment position. At the same time, the seller moves on to attract a new lead. Do you see the problem? While the recruiter is focusing on the open position and the seller has moved on to attract new leads, no one is paying attention to the additional opportunities available with this client.

Our client, The Placement Office, missed out on some $900,000 in add-on business from its current clients. Tunnel vision within the recruiting team prevented them from seeing new opportunities with one of their existing clients, and tunnel vision within the sales team distracted them from current clients, focusing instead on new leads in the distance. Once they corrected that behavior, sales grew easily by $900,000 the first year and by over a million dollars again in the next year.

Many large consulting and professional services firms have similar hand-offs from engagement managers to delivery people, abandoning the original client and creating a loss of additional opportunities.

José Laurel Cross from Ericsson is a lead seller on a marquee account. In her sales work, José always insisted she be active in project meetings during project implementation. While you might not think that this is a good use of her selling time, it was during one of those project meetings that she discovered an inefficient process in another department. While her project leaders were blind to the opportunity because it was irrelevant to the current project at hand, José knew better than to ignore the new information. As a result, she closed a new $3 million project in less than 12 months with the client. By paying attention to the Participation state, and being involved in the actual enablement of her client, José found a new deal that was worth half of her target for the following year.

Growth: When Clients Want More!

The Growth state exists with clients who are actively using your product and are clamoring for more. Why does this happen? Perhaps the company is growing and needs more of your products, or it has expanded and has new offices open, or it wants other departments within the company to participate. Growth opportunities have a fast closing trajectory, and that means they appear close to you on your Sales Radar.

Growth protects you from client attrition. While you might not always be able to sell more to every client, you can use the Growth state to better ensure that your clients don't leave you for the competition. A holistic approach is key: The more departments in your company that are involved in a client's success, the longer you will keep the client.

Let's look again at the Kinnser Software example. That company maintains a 98 percent client retention rate, much higher than the industry average. Why? Because the entire company is involved in the success of each client. The sales team completes the sale and partners with training to get the client using the product as quickly and as thoroughly as possible. The development and support teams routinely reach out to clients for enhancement requests and problem solving. Their marketing and sales teams nurture the clients with advisory roles and case studies. Kinnser's structure is set up to deliberately retain as many clients as possible. With just a few exceptions, the only clients they lose are those that go out of business.

The Growth state is also meant to grow revenue from clients who have the capacity to increase purchases from you. The most profitable sale your team can make is a repeat sale to an existing client. Net new sales are always more expensive, simply because of the costs associated with new prospecting and the time it takes to develop a trusting relationship. Once you have an established base of clients who already know you and like you, it's critical you nurture those relationships for additional sales.

Chris Wooley from agricultural products seller Agrimar created a Nonstop Sales Boom in his territory. While his colleagues were overly focused on new client Attraction (falsely assuming existing clients would keep ordering regardless of their lack of communication), Chris set out to nurture the Growth state with the following steps:

- ➤ He added each new client to a special monthly newsletter distribution with updates, specials, and invitations.
- ➤ He arranged special visits from leadership and product specialists to each new client on a regular basis to help them understand and use the products better.
- ➤ He made visits each month to his newer clients, helping them with products and suggesting better ways to grow their business and acquire new clients.

In total, Chris saw or talked to his clients on average twice as much as his colleagues. As a result, his sales soared to the number one position in the company with over two million dollars in growth in one year and the highest contribution margin of all the company's territories.

Leverage: Inspire Clients to Join Your Sales Team

When you have achieved the Leverage state, your clients have been transformed into advocates. They provide testimonials, references, and case studies powerful enough to attract other prospects to you without you asking them to do it. In this way, they become your secret sales force.

The Leverage state can yield an incredible amount of power. Recommendations from peers were cited as the number one decision-making criterion according to a Nielsen Research study on trust in global advertising (www.nielsen.com/us/en/newswire/2009/global-advertising-consumers-trust-real-friends-and-virtual-strangers-the-most.html). Our own client research shows buyers believe buyers first and salespeople second. Furthermore, research from companies such as Yahoo, DemandGen, Marketing Sherpa, and Saga tells us that while 87 percent of people believe reviews they see on websites, fewer than 10 percent of people believe what they read in conventional business-to-consumer marketing products. It's in your interest to leverage your current client's successes to support what you are saying about yourself and your work. When you're successful at this, you build a bridge of trust with your clients—one that is a critical component to creating a Nonstop Sales Boom.

Apple is frequently cited as an example of a company that has mastered this bridge of trust, but there are plenty of other examples, too: Starbucks commands fierce loyalty among coffee drinkers, Nike connects deeply with exercise enthusiasts and athletes, and Amazon is loved deeply by shoppers of everything from books to software.

WHAT MAKES THE SALES RADAR SO UNIQUE?

Keep in mind three key important points about the Sales Radar that underline its unique capacity to create a Nonstop Sales Boom for your organization.

It's a nonlinear process. Clients can skip over states, move forward or backward or diagonally. That's why having a finely tuned Sales Radar is so important. For example, some clients can be leveraged before Participation is complete. Have you ever recommended a product that you just purchased and have not used yet? It's a common occurrence and it shows you just how many new opportunities—of which the competition is not aware—can be present.

Clients can be in more than one state at a time. This is why the radar analogy is so important. Some clients stay in the Participation state for years, because they are implementing complex programs. At the same time, they are growing and being leveraged because of new opportunities. For example, we once worked with a client who needed four years to fully implement a very unique product. At the same time they were in the Participation state they were also in the Growth state (adding new departments to the project). They also were in the Leverage state by acting as a reference site and allowing the sales team to attract and convert new opportunities into new clients.

Each team needs its own Sales Radar. It's important to ensure that nonselling departments be involved both in nurturing client relationships and in spotting new opportunities. Give them their own Sales Radar and let them exercise it from a perspective that might be different from the one you have in sales. The outcome can mean new opportunities, new relationships, and more sales.

EVALUATING YOUR SUCCESS IN EACH OF THE FOUR STATES OF ENGAGEMENT

For many sales organizations, performance measurement is based on traditional quotas, which has limited value in revealing the root causes of a sales team performance—whether poor or satisfactory. In contrast, each of the four states of engagement in the Sales Radar includes a series of key benchmarks that allow the organization to monitor, control, and improve sales performance throughout the year. The benchmarks help you evaluate your success in adopting each element. Mastery of all four is your goal. Let's take a look at key benchmarks for each of the four states, so you can do a preliminary self-evaluation. In later sections of this book, we will provide more detail on how to use these benchmarks to improve your performance.

Your Attraction Metrics

Opportunities are attracted in a variety of ways from a variety of sources, and have many conversion ratios. For this reason, the following measurements are critical to the Attraction state:

➤ Adopt a specific goal for the number of net new clients you want to attract in your current selling year.

➤ Identify the number of leads you can expect from each lead generation activity. Remember that the best sellers in the marketplace use a variety of lead generation sources to attract new clients, including trade shows, social media, direct mail, cold calling, referral programs, educational events, networking, advisory panels, and speaking tours.

➤ Pinpoint your prospect-to-conversion ratio as well as the number of leads that will convert to qualified opportunities. Some ratios will be determined through marketing, others by sales. Use these metrics to guide your goals. This will help you to decide which events to continue or drop, and whether you are ahead or behind in new leads required for new sales. Be precise! The mistake most companies make at this point is that they guess on the ratio and underestimate their new lead requirements.

➤ Zero in on the number of qualified opportunities that are ready for proposals. As you move through the Attraction state, some leads fail while others move to the next stage in their conversion. As a guideline, companies that enjoy a Nonstop Sales Boom convert *50 percent of qualified opportunities to proposals.* The other 50 percent are either delayed or fall out of the pipeline, because they have been disqualified by the buyer or the seller. You should measure your own conversion rates now and set goals to improve if they are not at least at this best practice rate.

➤ Identify the length of time it takes to move from lead to qualified opportunity to proposal, the number of new leads your best sellers can manage at once, as well as the average value of the proposals sent out.

Your Participation Metrics

While you are moving the opportunity along in the Participation state, many deals fall apart if they are not managed carefully. That's why it's essential to adopt the following benchmarks with respect to the Participation state:

- ➤ Identify the number of proposals that are accepted or won, and ensure the accuracy of each proposal (e.g., what was the original proposal price versus the price agreed to on closing?)

- ➤ Know why a proposal fails. This data should be relayed to your leadership regularly, so that each department can fix issues that may be repelling clients. Case in point: The Ritz-Carlton Hotel Company is famous for its daily management sessions where guest issues are brought to the table for discussions. As departmental mistakes and client complaints are discussed, solutions are offered to address each issue identified. As a result, departments learn to avoid making those same mistakes again and guests are treated to an exceptional hotel experience.

- ➤ Identify the most common buyer objections as well as the approaches that your best sellers adopt to overcome these concerns.

- ➤ Pinpoint your win/loss ratio against each of your competitors as well as your overall closing ratios from proposal to close.

- ➤ Identify the average length of a negotiation, the terms most likely to be negotiated, the length of your onboarding process, and the number of calls to your help desk during implementation.

Your Growth Metrics

Opportunities are right under your nose with existing clients. You just have to know where to find them, and of course how to measure your results! Start by taking stock of your top 10 Growth prospects annually and set a goal for them based on historical results. Doing so will ensure you strike a balance between the longer and more risky sale to new clients and the shorter more predicable sale to existing clients. This revenue balance helps to create a Nonstop Sales Boom.

Your Growth state benchmarks should include the following:

- ➤ Identify the average lifetime value per client, the average annual growth per client, as well as the average number of cross-sell and upsell opportunities.
- ➤ Profile the characteristics of your most promising Growth prospects.
- ➤ Ensure that your client's organizational chart is up to date and complete. How many contacts do you have inside the client account? Do you have a trusting relationship with all decision makers, influencers, and feasibility buyers?

Your Leverage Metrics

While managing success in the Growth state is about how much more revenue each client can bring you, managing success in the Leverage state is about the value each client has beyond revenue. To do this successfully, you must pay attention to the following metrics:

- ➤ Ensure that you keep track of Return on Client Relationship. What is the total value of the client's relationship to you? More than measuring the additional sales the client gives you, look at the referrals the client provides and the leverage this creates by attracting new customers (we will cover this in more detail in Chapter 11).
- ➤ Identify the average number of years that a client is loyal to you, as well as the ROI the client receives from working with you, as stated by the client.
- ➤ Examine whether you have developed insider status. In other words, does your leadership team have trusting relationships with your client's leadership team?
- ➤ Identify all referrals, testimonials, or case studies provided by the client, and explore opportunities where a client might be willing to speak on your behalf at networking events (e.g., advisory meetings, trade shows, or webinars).

YOUR SALES RADAR AND THE SALES PIPELINE

The sales pipeline (see Figure 2–2) is one of the most familiar and effective frameworks used by sellers, and it has its place in the context of the Sales Radar. The sales pipeline, however, only represents a portion of the entire Sales Radar.

Let's briefly review the individual stages in the pipeline, before we explore them in more detail in the following chapters. The first two stages of the sales pipeline, discovery and prequalification, are discussed in Part II, which looks at the Attraction state of engagement, while the remainder of the pipeline is discussed in Part III, which looks at the Participation state of engagement.

1. **Discovery.** In this stage the prospect is identified. This includes doing the math and knowing your ideal prospect. The discovery stage is not just finding the prospects, but helping them find you. We cover the discovery stage in chapters 3–5.

Figure 2–2. The Sales Pipeline

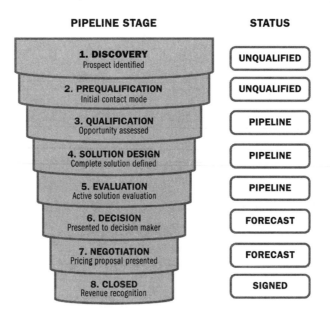

2. **Prequalification.** In this stage, the seller determines whether the prospect is a good fit for the company. But as described in Chapter 3, the discovery stage and the prequalification stage are no longer the distinct stages of the past. The reason: Today, while the seller is discovering and prequalifying prospects, *prospects are discovering and prequalifying sellers!* We cover the prequalification stages (both seller-driven and prospect-driven) in chapters 3–5.

3. **Qualification.** In this stage, the first step of the Participation state of engagement, you are in a dialogue with the prospect to mutually uncover what his objectives are, and whether your products and services are a match for meeting these objectives. The qualification stage is often the longest and most robust stage in the pipeline, involving many people and many conversations. We cover qualification in Chapter 6.

4. **Solution design.** In this stage, you are working with the prospect to define (together) the right solution to meet his objectives. We cover solution design in Chapter 6.

5. **Evaluation.** In this stage, the prospect is evaluating whether he wants to move forward with a formal proposal from you. We cover evaluation in Chapter 7.

6. **Decision.** In this stage, you are presenting a proposal to the prospect for consideration. He has not said yes or no yet. We cover decision in Chapter 7.

7. **Negotiation.** In this stage, you are negotiating your final terms and answering any last objections or questions before the agreement is signed. We cover negotiation in Chapter 7.

8. **Closed.** This is when you have a final signed agreement and the prospect is now a client. We cover closing in Chapter 7.

Once the sale is closed, the prospect is no longer in the sales pipeline. However, the prospect (now customer) has *not* left the Participation state of engagement. Sellers often make the mistake of walking away from the customer once the sale is made. Nonstop Sales Boom sellers, on the other hand, recognize that they need to stay with the customer and help him implement the product or service. The implementation phase is covered in Chapter 8.

. . . .

In the remaining chapters of this book, you will learn how to install your own Sales Radar in your company, never again missing any of the myriad of sales opportunities from prospects and your current clients. From transforming the sales pipeline into a realistic tool for measuring potential revenue, to developing a deep and rich relationship with your clients during the often-squandered Participation state, to fully mining that relationship for extraordinary Growth and Leverage opportunities, the following chapters will shatter the one-direction mindset and culture of your sales organization once and for all.

PART II

ATTRACTION

IN THE FIRST STATE OF CLIENT ENGAGEMENT, sellers are looking to connect with buyers. In the sales pipeline, attraction covers the discovery and prequalification stages.

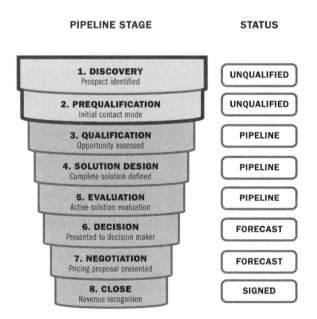

PIPELINE STAGE	STATUS
1. DISCOVERY Prospect identified	UNQUALIFIED
2. PREQUALIFICATION Initial contact mode	UNQUALIFIED
3. QUALIFICATION Opportunity assessed	PIPELINE
4. SOLUTION DESIGN Complete solution defined	PIPELINE
5. EVALUATION Active solution evaluation	PIPELINE
6. DECISION Presented to decision maker	FORECAST
7. NEGOTIATION Pricing proposal presented	FORECAST
8. CLOSE Revenue recognition	SIGNED

In Chapter 3 I describe some of the ways that you, the seller, can identify which prospects are most likely to turn into profitable customers. This chapter covers what you might already know as the traditional prequalification stage of the sales process. But as we shall learn, in today's prospect- and customer-driven world, it's often the buyer who discovers the seller she wants, and not the other way around. Today, the discovery stage is a never-ending process. In chapters 4 and 5, I describe how you can *help prospects to continue to find you* by developing expertise content for a wide variety of platforms.

Before taking any concrete Attraction steps, you need to do some homework and set your attraction targets: specifically, how much money you need to make from new customers, and how many prospects you need to call/contact to make that money. The first part of Chapter 3 will show you how to "do the math."

Of Math and MADness: How to Identify the Most Promising Prospects for Your Pipeline

IT SEEMS THESE DAYS that companies are in a hurry to acquire new clients. The prevailing wisdom has been that the sooner they get more paying customers, the greater the chance they will survive and thrive. But, companies seeking to establish a Nonstop Sales Boom must have a different mindset. Their goal is not to get just any client, but the *right* clients. Or to put it a different way, the question is not "How can we best attract prospects?" but rather "How can we attract the best prospects?"

Attracting the best prospects requires three dynamics:

1. Understanding the *quantity* of leads you need to attract

2. Understanding the *quality* of prospects that suit you best

3. Knowing how to *prequalify* the leads in and out of your attraction funnel including knowing how to spot and attract these new prospects on your radar

A Nonstop Sales Boom is created only when you are clear on your specific sales goals for net new clients, the number of prospects required to hit that goal, and the profile of the best quality prospects. To create a Nonstop Sales Boom you must attract the right *quantity* of the best *quality* of prospects and not waste your time selling to people who either are never going to buy, or those who will become poor clients in the future.

Remember that Attraction is only one quarter of your radar. For a Nonstop Sales Boom you must ensure the clients you attract will participate fully, grow, and be leveraged.

ENGAGED SELLING:

A Nonstop Sales Boom is part art, part science. The art is in designing the right prospects to attract and the science is in knowing exactly how many of those prospects you need to boom!

THINK QUANTITY: SET YOUR PROSPECTING GOALS

There is just no getting around sales math! It's not like high school where you try to avoid calculus. And it's here that I see most sellers with tunnel vision fail. Focused on the other states of engagement, mediocre sellers ignore what is required and always underestimate how much prospecting they must do. They nurture too few new leads and spend too much time with too few prospects, often of poor quality. Yet, the new sales math is easy to do and quick to show results. While twelfth-grade geometry almost cost me my university entrance, I do sales math successfully for top sellers every day!

There are three steps for you to complete the new sales math. They are:

1. **Set your net new revenue goal.** "Net new" refers to revenue that comes from prospects that are not currently clients. (In other words, there are two ways to get revenue: selling to new customers, or selling new and more things to current customers. Net new revenue comes from selling to new customers.) Your net new revenue goal might be $100,000 this year, for example.

2. **Break down your net new revenue goal into the number of required transactions.** Rather than saying, "I need $100,000 from new clients," tell yourself, "I need 10 sales of $10,000 each from new clients."

3. **Calculate the number of attempts needed to achieve your goal.** Knowing your final goal is not enough. To be successful you must know clearly how much activity is required to hit your sales goal.

Let's take a closer look at each of these steps, including the formulas you will need to calculate your goals and activities.

Step #1: Set Your Net New Revenue Goal

The first step is to *understand clearly* how much of your overall sales goal must be met with *net new revenue*. While there is no magic formula, a portion of your revenue should always come from new customers because they are your future growth. Here are some examples:

> ➤ A client with a limited distribution model and limited production capacity only has the ability to manage 5 percent market growth. In this case the sellers will be expected to bring in 95 percent of their revenue targets from existing customers and **5 percent** from new customers.

> ➤ A start-up software company with only 1 percent market share expects its sellers to hit their targets with **80 percent** from new business and 20 percent from existing clients.

> ➤ A mature professional services firm balances its revenue requirements between 60 percent existing and **40 percent** new.

Regardless of what mix is right for your company, it's critical that you set a goal for how much business you want to attract so you can accurately create the activities required to accomplish this goal. Let's say, for example, that your overall revenue goals are $2 million—of which 50 percent must come from new sales. You would thus need $1 million in new sales by the end of the year.

If after one quarter you are well behind or well ahead, you may want to adjust your goals accordingly based on your company's requirements and market conditions.

Step #2: Break Down Your Net New Revenue Goal into the Number of Required Transactions

The second step is to *break down that revenue goal* into the required number of sales or transactions. This sounds like sales 101, but in our studies of perpetually booming companies, we notice that all teams and sellers not only have a clear and documented revenue goal, they also know exactly how many net new customers are required to make that goal. This number is always posted where they can see it.

To calculate your number of net new sales simply take the revenue amount and divide it by the average new customer's first sales revenue. Here is the formula:

Net new sales goal/average first sale per client = # of new clients needed

For example, if your goal is to bring in $500,000 from new customers and your average customer purchases $50,000 from you on his or her first invoice, you will need 10 new customers this year to hit your goal.

Step #3: Calculate the Number of Attempts Needed to Achieve Your Goal

Here's where this math gets interesting! Your third step is to *calculate the number of attempts or activities required* to achieve your target. For a number of reasons, including increases in competition, reduction of corporate budgets, access to increased information, and fear of decision making (on the client's part), conversion ratios for new leads to paying customers are at an all-time low. I am encouraging you to be aware of these new ratios. Sellers who ignore these new ratios fall into the Sales Trap easily because they are simply not working enough leads at once.

After studying our clients from a broad range of industries worldwide for the last 20 years, I've been able to simplify the new lead conversion ratios. (In other words, I can tell you how many contacts you'll need to reach your sales targets). Before we examine the conversion ratios, let's clearly define our lead generation categories:

> **Contacts.** Contacts are the prospective companies or individuals whose name you have in your database. You have not spoken to them, and you don't know if they have an active need for your product. You just know that they fit your target market. Contacts can include people who stop by your booth at a trade show, request more information from a website, or are passed to you from a marketing campaign. They can also include names from a purchased list. Many of our clients refer to their contacts as anyone who has "raised their hand" to ask for more information or any business that has been picked by sales and marketing as a target.

> **Leads.** A lead is a company or an individual who has a quantifiable need for your product and plans to buy within a specified period of time. To use a retail analogy, these are not people browsing in the mall because they have nothing better to do on a rainy Sunday! Instead they are people who have come into your store with a specific requirement and budget to buy.

> **Prequalified leads.** These are sales-ready leads. Real opportunities with *money, authority,* and *desire* to buy. Use the MAD acronym as a simple way to remember how to prequalify a lead in your attraction radar:

> > **M**oney: They have money set aside in a budget to spend. Budget has been allocated and you know how much that budget is.

> > **A**uthority: They have authority to spend this money. In other words, they are the decision maker.

> > **D**esire: They are in active pursuit of a solution like yours. There may or may not be a competitive process, but a time frame, criteria, and a decision-making process are in place.

In order to remember this easily, consider the following diagram (Figure 3–1):

Figure 3–1. Lead Prequalification

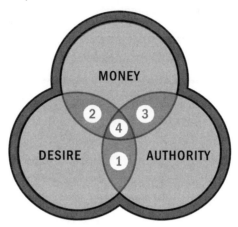

Look at the little circled numbers. Notice where in the overlapping circles of influence they fall.

1. If your contact has Desire and Authority *but no Money,* he is a dud.

2. If your contact has Desire and Money *but no Authority,* he is a window shopper.

3. If your contact has Money and Authority *but no Desire,* he is deflated.

4. If he has all three, then you can consider him a very viable *pre-prequalified buyer.*

Now, let's look at the average conversion metrics for these leads stages. I've been studying closing rates for a variety of markets for years, and based on this ongoing research the closing metrics in today's selling environments are:

➤ 38 percent of contacts become leads.

➤ 39 percent of leads become prequalified leads.

➤ 29 percent of prequalified leads eventually become sales.

Complicating these metrics are the current ratios of attempted calls to actual contacts made. Not even the best sellers have a one-to-one ratio! You might have to leave two to three voice mails and send an email to get one phone call in the current selling environment! As a result, it can take up to a total of seven events—calls, meetings, emails, and text messages— to move each prospect from initial contact to lead, and lead to prequalified lead. And it can take another seven events to convert a qualified lead to a sale.

Let's go back to our example in Step #2 on page 52. When we broke down your $500,000 sales target into individual sales averaging $50,000 each, we found that your client Attraction goal was 10 new clients. Figure 3–2 shows what the sales math looks like. (Remember, we are only talking about net new or "cold" contacts in this section, not sales to current customers.)

Before you put this book down in frustration let's look at what I am actually saying; it's only two things:

1. Only a portion of your total sales each year comes from net new clients in the Attraction state. The rest of your quota will be made up of warmer leads from existing customers. Balance is key. You can't ignore new sales or your business will stagnate. This is why Attraction is so important.

2. Here is a secret about this calculation. The results always show

Figure 3–2. From Contact to Sale

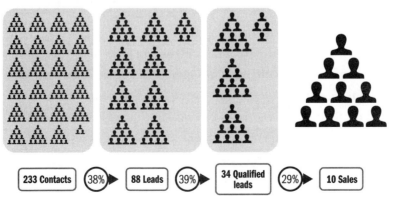

that you must make one attempt every day for every new sale you need. If you need 10 net new, then make 10 attempts a day. If you need 20, make 20. An attempt is a voice mail left, a contact made, or an email sent. To see this secret in action go to www.nonstopsalesboom.com and download the sales math calculator for yourself!

Be careful, there are a lot of sales experts out there who will try to convince you that selling is not about the numbers, and creating a Nonstop Sales Boom is about more than just crunching facts and figures. But that's not quite true. *You must know how the numbers work to be a success.* Otherwise, how can you possibly measure your progress along the way and replicate your success the next year?

The fact is that most people fall short when it comes to doing the sales math. They just focus on their revenue quota. Nonstop sellers take the time to break it down to say, "If I need 10 sales then I need 233 contacts." (And if you need 20, then double it to 466.) Go the extra mile. Do the math and figure out exactly what it is that you need to do to hit the sales targets that will make this year your best on record.

It may seem straightforward, calculating for 10 new customers, but if you're having difficulty calculating for 23, or 47—well, that's why we suggested you download the calculator from www.nonstopsalesboom.com.

PREQUALIFICATION: YOU DON'T HAVE TO SELL TO EVERYONE!

This is going to sound counterintuitive, especially after our discussion about the new sales math, but I am going to suggest that attracting *fewer* contacts is one secret to creating a Nonstop Sales Boom. Too many sellers believe that if a prospect comes calling they have to sell to her, as if buying were a right, not a privilege. Nothing could be further from the truth. Instead, creating a Nonstop Sales Boom requires you to be selective about the prospects you attract. Poor-quality prospects will always find their way to you. It's critical that you don't waste your precious hours nurturing them through client Attraction. Let them pass through your Sales Radar with little attention and instead focus your time on those best-quality prospects.

Recently we surveyed our 20,000-strong community at EngageSelling .com, and asked them what they would rank as this year's top sales challenges in their respective organizations. "How do I find the best customers?" came out on top. It's also one of the most common questions that I hear in my discussions with people during the sales training sessions I conduct. Indeed, there are steps you can take here, but first you really need to stop and ask yourself, "Who would I consider to be a great client?"

This is important. It's too easy to pin all the blame on your clients for not behaving the way you want them to, when really it ought to come down to matters of choice and expectations on your part. Rather than wasting your time complaining that too many of your clients are need-lessly cheap or are hard to sell to, ask yourself why you keep going back to these same people again and again, somehow expecting a different result than what you'd experienced before. When consistent patterns emerge, the constant is *you*!

When the temptation to go after everybody arises, remember this: It pays to be choosy. Participation is faster and easier when you're only trying to sell a round peg to a round hole. When your target market is well focused, you spend

ENGAGED SELLING:

There's no rule that says everybody has a right to buy from you equally.

far less time struggling. You're no longer devoting large chunks of your time talking to customers who don't want to listen. Instead, leapfrog over the competition by focusing on people you enjoy selling to. You'll reduce the number of objections you encounter, and you'll gain more repeat sales because you'll be dealing with people who want to have a long-term engagement with you. Preach to your own choir.

The bottom line: Once you have your quantity goals, the next step is to make sure those numbers include the right kind of prospects. This means that you should do two things:

1. Develop a profile of who or what *you* would consider an ideal client.

2. Focus your efforts on attracting the attention of that kind of customer.

After 20 years of selling, training sellers, and helping others to sell I have witnessed every type of prospect imaginable, from the very best to the very worst. Sellers who create a perpetual boom in their sales results are very good at identifying the good and bad prospects very quickly. In the Attraction state of engagement, they keep the good prospects in their sales pipelines and qualify the bad out of the pipelines based on three things:

1. Alignment with the ideal client profile

2. A quick but thorough prequalification questioning process

3. The observed behavior of the prospect during the prequalification

The ultimate goal of the prequalification process is to identify your MAD leads: those who truly have the money set aside, the authority to make decisions, and the desire to move quickly toward a purchase.

The Ideal Prospect Profile

To identify the most promising contacts and leads, you need to know what your ideal prospect looks like. There are three ways to develop the ideal profile for a prospect. The first way is to create the ideal target based on your most lucrative and sustainable clients.

Determine Your Ideal Target

Think about your current clients for a minute and consider these questions: How much are they worth to you, and how willing are they to buy?

Do a certain subset of customers rise to the top? Those who do are likely your most valuable clients as well as those who are the easiest to sell to. Your best prospects will have the same characteristics. Consider Figure 3–3.

First, plot your best customers in the top right quadrant and note what is similar about them:

> ➤ Are they all from specific industries?

> ➤ Are they similar in size?

> ➤ Are they in similar geographies?

> ➤ What is their organizational structure? (Public, private, family owned, nonprofit?)

> ➤ What is the title of the buyer?

> ➤ What is the average order size?

> ➤ How long did they take to close?

Once you have answered these questions you will have a clear picture of your ideal target.

Figure 3–3. Your Ideal Target

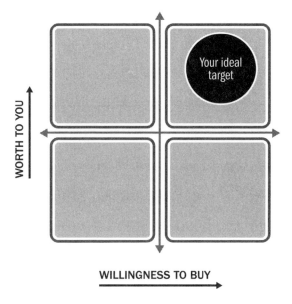

Determine the "Ideal Sales List"

Another more detailed way to set your targets is to ascertain what your ideal sale looks like. Instead of drawing up a profile of the ideal prospect, the goal here is to draw a profile of the ideal *market segment*. The idea is to target your approach and focus on only a single niche market. By focusing all your efforts on a particular group, you'll be able to build solid relationships and establish a proven reputation much more quickly.

Take a moment to fully grasp the power of this concept. There is always a small group of ideal contacts you want to attract who are cheaper and easier to sell to *and* who also bring greater rewards. You likely have some of these "ideal customers" right now, but if you're like most salespeople, they probably represent a relatively small portion of your client list and you have not identified them clearly yet!

Ask yourself: "Who are my best buyers?" If you sell in the consumer market, whether you're a dentist, accountant, chiropractor, real estate broker, or financial advisor, chances are your best buyers live in the best neighborhoods. They have the most money and the greatest sphere of influence. So take a look at your current customer list, identify where your best customers live, and target your marketing efforts to others in those neighborhoods. You will end up spending the same amount of time, money, and energy to nurture this best buyer as you would a general buyer, and I can guarantee that it will bring you higher profits.

If you sell in the business market your best buyers might be the biggest companies—Fortune 100 if your business sells internationally, or the biggest companies in your area if you sell locally. Have you identified this small but invaluable Ideal Sales List?

Once you have a profile of your ideal customer, look at your current client list and determine how many of them meet that profile. Ask yourself what they all have in common. Are they privately held businesses or are they publicly traded? Are they government organizations or are they consulting companies? Are they international or domestic? Are they all run by women? Once you've found the common thread that weaves together this "best of the best" client list, use the same criteria when reviewing those who are in your prospect database.

Let's look at an example. When Donald first started working with Engage Selling, his sales goal was to achieve a million dollars in sales from temporary staffing jobs. We took a look at his database to develop his target market, and discovered that all of his best customers fit into one specific niche market. Here's what we advised: "Go after that market and be the number one provider to all of the companies that have this particular need." Next, we recommended that he look at expanding that group. We said: "Okay, if all of these customers are food producers then could you also look at the beverage producers? Could you also look at dairy? How about the pet food industry?" Then we started branching off into those kinds of subniches based on that one target he was pursuing.

As a result, Donald achieved and *exceeded* his target by 90 percent. He wanted to reach a million in sales. *He achieved $1.9 million instead.* He did that by narrowing in on who he was selling to, and then selling more to that market because the sale became effortless. He was able to displace his competition because he was a specialist in that area. I'm particularly proud of Donald's accomplishment because he achieved this record-smashing growth at a time when the market in which he was operating (the HR market) was being upended by the recession.

Don't let the size of Donald's company fool you. Targeting isn't just effective for smaller companies. It will positively affect larger firms as well. Consumer credit giant Experian segments its most strategic sellers by target market. Antivirus giants Trend Micro and MacAfee also create sales teams by target market size, and The Royal Bank of Canada segments its sellers by product type and market size. All are great examples of companies in a Nonstop Sales Boom.

My favorite example is Harley Davidson. This is a company that knows exactly who its target customer is. What's stated in its unique selling proposition is this: "To hell with it all, let's ride." Harley doesn't care whether its value proposition appeals to people outside of that target range. It delivers something that matters to a well-defined demographic.

Find what works best for you. Whether it's focusing on a specific geographic area, product specialty, service offering—the possibilities are

ENGAGED SELLING:

Ready! Aim! Fire!

endless. The key is finding customers you enjoy working with and vice versa, determining their needs, and concentrating on selling to them in a manner that fulfills those needs.

Develop Your "Perfect Client" Profile

Some sellers require a more detailed view of their perfect prospects, one that helps them understand their business objectives and goals before spending time pursuing and qualifying the opportunity. In these cases I recommend using the Perfect Client Profile.

The Perfect Client Profile is a tool that you use in the early Attraction state conversations with a contact to help you with prequalification. A questionnaire that helps you identify your "perfect client" does two things: First, it enables you to understand the contact's business better so that should you choose to move forward you have a more thoroughly prequalified prospect. Second, it allows you to determine, at this early stage in the process, whether this contact is a fit for your Sales Radar and is worth pursuing.

Doreen Ashton Wagner, cofounder and managing director of Greenfield Services has developed a great process around the Perfect Client Profile. Greenfield provides lead generation services including list building, prospecting, lead nurturing, and content marketing for the hospitality and meetings industry. A few years ago she developed a "perfect client questionnaire" to help her clients better understand who they wanted Greenfield to attract during their lead generation projects. At the same time Doreen knew that her best clients had a very specific profile of the leads they were trying to generate. So, by understanding her prospects' lead generation requirements thoroughly up front, Doreen could learn whether a project was an ideal one for her. An example of this client questionnaire is shown in Figure 3–4.

Figure 3–4. Greenfield's Perfect Client Profile

WHO IS YOUR *PERFECT CUSTOMER?*

The idea behind this exercise is for you to answer key questions and provide as much information as you can. Your answers will help us to pinpoint the profile of the very best possible group clients for your property... your perfect customers.

Philosophy aside we realize that perfection is uncommon in this world, but we find that the better we can understand what your ideal is, the better we can craft our call approach to elicit the information and leads you want...! As famous American football coach Vince Lombardi once said: "Perfection is not attainable, but if we chase perfection we can catch excellence."

The questions below are designed for a hotel meeting/event/group customer. But it can easily be adapted to a CVB, AV company, speaker bureau, DMC or any other hospitality or meetings industry supplier.

So from your perspective what does your "Perfect Customer" look like? This may be in the form of ranges with regards to several key factors such as:

- What is the ideal group size? (may vary according to seasons/months)
- What is the ideal range/extent of meeting space requirements? (e.g. size of main meeting room, average number of breakouts or room-to-meeting space ratio)
- What are your ideal customer's food & beverage requirements?
- What are the ideal rates/fees paid? (ranges may be provided, allowing for variability according to seasons/months)
- To what extent does your ideal customer use other facilities such as audio-visual, staging, business centre, etc.?

What are your key geographic feeder markets (regions, cities)?

What are your prime market segments—corporate, association (local, state/provincial, national, international), government, SMERF (social/military/educational/religious/fraternal), third-party planners/site selection companies?

In the corporate segment, what industries or type of companies do you attract? Who are the largest employers or other sectors of interest in your area that might incite a group to meet in your vicinity? Are there certain companies/types of companies for whom you have executed particularly successful programs?

Is there anything else you'd like to share with us that would paint a more accurate picture of your perfect customer? What are the qualities, characteristics and attributes of your perfect customer?

Completing the Perfect Client Profile is central to Greenfield's attraction process. Doreen asks her client to complete the document before a lead generation project is defined contractually. This helps her assess how committed the client is to using her company's services. This also helps her initiate the conversation around expectations and deliverables. With a clear picture of the prospect's client profile, Doreen and her client can decide together whether the project is a fit for Greenfield Services. Prospects that are a perfect fit are moved to the next sales steps, and prospects that are not are moved off her radar. Since implementing her Perfect Client Profile, Doreen reports that closing ratios on net new opportunities have improved but more importantly she and her team are not getting bogged down trying to close prospects that are not ready to buy, or servicing customers that are a terrible fit! As Doreen states:

> The Perfect Customer Questionnaire is something that I was resisting at first because I thought it would scare people away. Instead, our meetings industry clients saw that we really cared about getting it right for them, so those who were serious about undertaking lead generation seemed even more committed to using our services. And a few times the answers to the questions made us realize that the client's expectations were completely unrealistic—they were seeing their facilities as attractive to markets that we didn't think had *any* potential for them. So it helped us to convince some they were on the wrong path, and others we simply released to our competition.

For Greenfield overall this has ensured that team morale, performance, and turnover have all improved—and of course company profits have increased as a result.

The Prequalification Questioning

The best sellers use a prequalification questioning process to qualify their prospects into the next step or out of the next step. They always remember that some contacts are not worth persuing; a comprehensive series of questions helps them quickly identify the best contacts to keep and the worst contacts to remove. This is like a sales bouncer who knows who should be let through the velvet rope.

Remember not all contacts will move forward. It's your job to identify those poor-quality contacts quickly so that you have more time to spend with the best-quality contacts. Do this by asking questions. Specifically, in the Attraction state you must find out:

1. **What is the prospect's requirement and why does that requirement exist?** This question lets you know if the need is real, and if you have a solution to meet it. Here are five alternative ways to ask this question:

   ➤ *What inspired you to talk to us today?*

   ➤ *What's happening now in your organization that makes our solution so attractive?*

   ➤ *How long have you been looking for a solution?* (Followed up with *Why?*)

   ➤ *What have you tried so far?* (Followed up with *How did that work out?*)

   ➤ *Why are you looking for this solution now?*

2. **What is the time frame for the decision?** This question helps you to determine how much of a priority this project is now, or if it will be a long-term project. Here are five more alternatives you can use:

   ➤ *When are you hoping to start using the new solution?*

   ➤ *When are you hoping to have a go-ahead?*

   ➤ *What's your expected start date?*

   ➤ *Are you hoping to get started this month/quarter/year?*

   ➤ *When's the latest you want to have this in place?*

3. **What is the prospect's decision-making process?** This question will help you understand his organizational structure and introduce you to other influencers or buyers early on in the process.

Here are five alternatives you can use:

> ➤ *The last time you made a decision like this how did you go about it?*

> ➤ *Is there someone besides you driving this initiative?*

> ➤ *How do your colleagues feel about this?*

> ➤ *How do you typically make decisions like this?*

> ➤ *Who else is affected by this?* (Followed up with *How do you suggest we get them involved?*)

4. **What criteria will the prospect be using to make a decision and what is their order of importance?** This question helps you to understand what is important to them and whether those criteria match up with what you are good it. The best five alternatives for you to use are:

> ➤ *How will you make a decision?*

> ➤ *Which of those criteria is the most important to you?*

> ➤ *What criteria are you using to evaluate your options?* (Followed up with *Why those particular ones?*)

> ➤ *How will you know what the right solution is for you?*

> ➤ *What are your objectives for this?* (Followed up with *Why those particular objectives?*)

5. **Is there money set aside for this?** This question will help you prioritize the buying time frame for the prospect. Five alternatives to ask this question are:

> ➤ *Has budget been set aside?*

> ➤ *Have you considered how much you want to invest in this project?*

> ➤ *Do you have quotes from others already?*

> ➤ *What are you hoping to spend?*

> ➤ *What investment have you set aside?*

The questions above will help you determine the trajectory of the prospects. Are they moving quickly or slowly toward a decision? Toward you or toward the competition? Based on the answers you may choose to keep them in your sights, or disqualify them completely and wipe them from your radar.

Clues from the Prospects' Behavior

Another way that top sellers prequalify contacts is based on the prospects' behavior during the prequalification. Are the prospects acting in a way that leads you to believe that they have serious intentions for moving forward? Or do you suspect they are stringing you along? Almost every seller I meet has a very strong and accurate gut feel about buyer behavior. But only the best act on that gut feel. In order to create a Nonstop Sales Boom you must learn to trust your gut feel about poor contact behavior and disqualify them based on what you see is happening. It's worth disqualifying prospects who behave in one of the following ways:

1. **They ask you about price before you have even started to understand their needs and they insist on knowing that price before answering your questions.** Prospects who ask about price early in the sales process generally have already found a solution that they like, and are now trying to justify the price. Unless you can move this prospect off the price discussion to have a proper qualification conversation, you won't win the business. Mediocre sellers make the mistake of thinking that prospects who ask about price are "hot prospects" who are ready to buy. True enough they are ready to buy, but not with you! Trust me. Prospects who ask about price early have already made up their mind to buy from someone else.

2. **Prospects who won't tell you what their budget is.** While not all prospects will have funds allocated at the start of the buying process, if they do and they are just not willing to share this information with you, trust has not been established. Prospects who make statements such as "Just give us your best price" or "It's not

fair for me to share this information with you" are either playing games, are not serious prospects, or do not have power to buy.

3. **Your contact won't allow you to speak to anyone else in the organization.** Decisions are not made in isolation. To make a sale you must have access to all decision makers and influencers. If your prospects will not make those introductions early on in the Attraction state this is another sign that trust is lacking. If the prospects do not trust you they will not buy from you. Push to meet the additional contacts, go around your prospect to contact the real buyer directly, or disqualify this prospect and move on.

4. **They don't return calls or emails after repeated attempts.** While it's common for the initial contact of a new prospect to take up to seven attempts, it should become easier to reach your prospect over time as your relationship develops. This is a sign of a trusting relationship. If you find that as your relationship builds your prospect is not getting more responsive, then you have not developed trust, she has been distracted with another project, or she has already made a decision to buy from someone else. Absence doesn't make the buyer grow fonder. Perpetually booming sellers have learned to trust their gut and disqualify silent buyers.

5. **They set up a buying process that requires you to fit into their schedule.** I once had a buyer tell me, "If you can't meet me next Monday at 2 P.M., then we can't move forward!" This is a clear sign that you are being used at the last minute to justify a purchase decision for another product. If you want to create a perpetual boom you must not waste your time with these buyers. Suggest an alternative approach, and if the buyer will not work with you as a partner, or if he is unwilling to consider alternative views, politely disqualify him and move on to a better prospect.

6. **The competition is the incumbent but the prospect wants a proposal from you anyway.** The best sellers are very wary of prospects who ask for proposals for solutions that their incumbent

supplier can provide. While it might seem like a great way to grow market share, it's very difficult to unseat a competitor with exactly the same solution. Ask tough questions and specifically find out why the buyer is not purchasing the solution from his supplier. In most cases, when buyers approach you for a quote of something they can get from a source they are familiar with, they are simply trying to scout the market for the best prices in order to apply pressure to their incumbent supplier.

7. **Buyers who repeatedly put you off and say, "Call me back next month," and, when you do call them back, ask for another delay.** These are buyers who feel terrible about rejecting you, and they can't say no directly. You know that "Call me back later" is really a camouflaged no. It's better for you to end the relationship now and spend your time focused on a real buyer who has a need and an interest in making a decision.

8. **Prospects who don't know answers to three critical questions.** When prospects answer three substantive questions with "I don't know," they need to be disqualified. Examples: "How will you know if the project we're discussing is successful?" "I don't know." "Tell me who will have a say in this consideration." "I don't know." "When do you need to be up and running?" "I don't know."

Discretion is a critical component of the Attraction state of your Sales Radar. Without discretion you run the risk of chasing too many of the poorest prospects. This detour takes you away from the Nonstop Sales Boom. Discretion has two components: First, understanding the quantity of prospects to allow onto your Attraction radar; and second, understanding the ideal quality of those prospects that merit further work and follow-through. Consider it breadth and depth.

Discretion is an easy and powerful tool that all top sellers use. Yet, talking about it is not profitable. Only using it is.

Before you turn the page to Chapter 4 and our discussion on where to find all these great new prospects, I want you to complete two preparatory tasks:

1. **Do the sales math.** Figure out exactly how many contacts and leads you need before you start planning the Attraction activities to find them.

2. **Identify your ideal customer.** Make sure your ideal client is clearly described to you and your team so that you only focus your efforts on attracting the best new prospects.

These two tasks will take you through the first critical steps in using the Sales Radar to create a Nonstop Sales Boom. Why not do them right now? The rest of the chapter will still be here when you finish.

ENGAGED SELLING:

If you don't know what you're looking for, how will you ever find it?

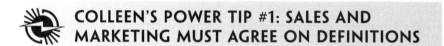

COLLEEN'S POWER TIP #1: SALES AND MARKETING MUST AGREE ON DEFINITIONS

Regardless of the method you choose for identifying your most promising contacts and leads, do not conduct this exercise in isolation. Perpetually booming organizations ensure that sales and marketing are aligned on which specific prospects or types of prospects to pursue, and that both sales and marketing have access to accurate data and insights on the target prospects. When sales and marketing are in agreement with the definition of a target, more contacts and leads will emerge, and more sales will close—and close more quickly.

Why is this so critical?

First, companies that achieve Nonstop Sales Booms have their sales and marketing teams working in harmony, not in disharmony. They work side by side to define contact and lead criteria, prequalification methodology, and Attraction activities. They also share responsibility for contact and lead counts. This runs counter to many organizations, which tend to *pit sales and marketing against each other,* isolating them in silos. The result is serious tunnel vision and boom–bust sales cycles. But when sales and marketing work as a team to calculate the quantity and identify the quality criteria of leads—and together pursue those leads—the resulting efficiency and effectiveness creates a Nonstop Sales Boom.

Either everyone plays in the same key delighting all those who hear it, or they play in various keys causing noise that drives people away.

The second reason that marketing and sales coordination is critical is that it prevents potential long-term prospects from being discarded by the short-term priorities of a sales force. When contacts are passed to the sales team for conversion to leads, questions around buying time frame must be prominent. In other words, "What is the time frame of the purchase decision?" For sales teams, a quick or timely time frame is key. But if sales and marketing are working together, the time frame will be considered in the context of other factors, which prevents losing future opportunities, or chasing poor leads in the present. For example, if the time frame is not right for an immediate sale but this contact is of an ideal profile, the contact can be nurtured by marketing until the time is ripe. If marketing and sales are not aligned with this process, there is a great risk that high-quality contacts not ready to buy yet will be eliminated from your radar completely, as sales is distracted by those leads moving quickly toward a sale on the radar.

This works the other way around, as well. Marketing may have developed a lead where the timing is excellent, but if the lead is less than ideal, the seller will disqualify it out of the Attraction radar completely because the likelihood of winning is too low.

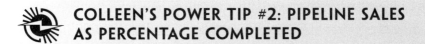 **COLLEEN'S POWER TIP #2: PIPELINE SALES AS PERCENTAGE COMPLETED**

It's common for sellers to measure opportunities in their sales pipelines by the probability of the deal closing. That's a common mistake. Probability of close is a subjective measurement that requires the sales rep to make a judgment about the chances of making a sale, often skewed by optimism or forecasts. It requires interpretation, is subject to bias, and is rife with abuse. Instead, you should be measuring the progress of a prospect through your sales pipeline, with each stage representing the percentage distance of the way through the pipeline that the opportunity has reached. A complete sale is defined as one that is either closed or lost.

When sellers think that merely moving an opportunity through the pipeline increases its probability of close, they're less likely to use that pipeline accurately. Emotion and ego get in the way. They hold back on moving deals into fully qualified stages until they are convinced that they will close. They limit opportunities entered into the initial pipeline stages so as to avoid scrutiny from their management. I once was told by a sales rep, "I only use the pipeline to track deals that I am going to win. I don't want my manager nagging me about the deals that I might lose." And they arbitrarily change the probability percentage to match how they "feel" about the opportunity.

The trouble with this behavior is that it limits your view of the true health of your pipeline; it does not provide an accurate assessment of where you are, nor does it provide what is necessary to create a Nonstop Sales Boom. If sellers are not entering prospects into the pipeline until the end of the pipeline, neither the seller nor the leadership can measure conversion rates or length of the sales cycle accurately. This prevents growth and holds sellers back because no one can tell where sales issues are, nor can they step in to help a sale that might be floundering.

The best sellers know that their pipeline is the science of sales. The numbers don't lie. They track each step with precision so that they know whether they are ahead, behind, or exactly on target, and can track and create the required activities to hit their goals.

However, when the measurement is changed from *probability of close* to *percentage complete*, sellers will use the pipeline to track all opportunities and you will have an accurate measure of how opportunities convert from inception to close. And this is why we include the right-hand column on Figure 3–5. It shows you the percentage complete for this opportunity.

This change requires a shift in thinking, of course. Saying that a negotiation is 90 percent complete no longer means that it's necessarily 90 percent likely to close. You may only close 60 percent or 70 percent of the deals you negotiate, which is something that you'll know based on past data and history. Accurate measurement of every step is critical.

In rethinking the sales process this way, every step of your pipeline represents a set of tasks or activities that have to be completed in order

Figure 3–5. Pipeline 3.0

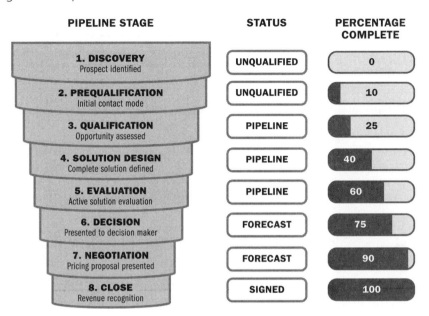

PIPELINE STAGE	STATUS	PERCENTAGE COMPLETE
1. DISCOVERY Prospect identified	UNQUALIFIED	0
2. PREQUALIFICATION Initial contact mode	UNQUALIFIED	10
3. QUALIFICATION Opportunity assessed	PIPELINE	25
4. SOLUTION DESIGN Complete solution defined	PIPELINE	40
5. EVALUATION Active solution evaluation	PIPELINE	60
6. DECISION Presented to decision maker	FORECAST	75
7. NEGOTIATION Pricing proposal presented	FORECAST	90
8. CLOSE Revenue recognition	SIGNED	100

to move the deal through the pipeline. The pipeline no longer tells us *the probability of close*—a subjective opinion—but *the percentage complete in the sales cycle*—an objective statistic based on facts.

When a pipeline is properly used everyone has a truly accurate view of the conversion ratios between one stage and the next. After watching these conversion ratios for a few quarters, you will be able to create an accurate forecast based on historical facts. From here, you can develop a forecast that is within 5 percent accuracy every time.

Kinnser Software changed its approach in 2011. Until this time it was managing its sales pipeline as a typical organization does—with probability of close. Revenue forecasting was about as accurate as an amateur game of darts, and while it was hitting targets most of the time, Sales VP Scott Hestor had no idea what the revenue number would actually be until the last day of each quarter. This created tension between sales and the CEO. By adopting a percentage complete approach Scott is now able to predict his forecast within 5 percent accuracy every month. This has led to a high level of confidence with investors and the CEO, as well as allowing for planning of marketing events and development investment because the leadership team knows how much revenue is coming in when.

By applying this fundamental change of measuring percentage complete as opposed to probability of close to your sales process, you'll not only gain accuracy in your forecast but also will encourage your sales team to utilize the sales pipeline in the way that it is supposed to be used and in the way that will allow you the most visibility into your opportunities.

. . . .

In this chapter, you learned how to calculate the quantity of contacts you need to make to achieve your sales targets, and learned how to identify the best prospects and weed out the worst. However, in today's world buyers find the sellers more than the other way around. This means that the key to successful prospecting is knowing how to be found by potential buyers. That's the subject of our next chapter.

CHAPTER 4

"Wow, I See You Everywhere!": Leveraging New Pathways to Reach the Prospect

NOW THAT YOU HAVE SELECTED your most lucrative targets for net new business, the next step in Attraction is to engage those contacts in selling conversations. Before you do that, it's critical that we take a step back to examine how the front end of the selling process has changed in the last few years. As you'll see, you can't just try to attract new buyers today in the same way you did a few years ago.

In recent years, buyers in the sales process have become increasingly educated, and with that, the sales process has undergone a transformation. The sales team has transitioned from leading the sales process to facilitating it, and understanding this change is essential to effectively fulfilling your role in the process.

THE OLD SALES PROCESS

Let's start by taking a look at what a standard sales process used to look like. In a standard selling process, the salesperson was typically in control, driving the sales process from finding the right prospect through to the close. Typically it would have looked like Figure 4–1.

Sellers began with prospecting and research. By going online, looking for information, and networking, a sales team would identify information about their target contacts in a process *completely driven and controlled by sellers.* You would then make calls, and build rapport with your targets through smart, well-researched and well-rehearsed, cold call conversations. In the past, sellers controlled 90 percent of these first steps, with buyers only engaging when the seller made a direct contact attempt.

The next step for sellers in the old process was qualifying the prospect. Through a variety of questions, sellers would determine whether the prospect was a good fit and, if so, would move forward with developing a solution and a proposal. Qualification was completed from a selling perspective, meaning, *"Is this buyer a good candidate for me?"* with little regard for how the buyer felt about the seller. Most sellers would aim for a 50/50 share of control for the qualification hoping that the prospect was at least as engaged as they were. The reality is the seller was doing 70 percent of the work, while the buyer was putting in only 30 percent of the effort. Time share sellers are great examples of how the old sales process worked because they do all the heavy lifting up front to make sure you are well qualified, fit the criteria, and are a good fit for their organization before they take you on a tour and present you with an offer. When I went through the process for my research on selling styles, I found that I hardly uttered one word during the first half of the presentation. The seller did most of the talking, asking me specific questions to make sure I was a good fit for him.

The sales process would end with a presentation and the closure of the business—a 50/50 give-and-take between the prospect and the salesperson.

Figure 4–1. Traditional Selling Process

For years, this was a standard sales process, but in today's selling market, things have changed dramatically—and as a result, sales teams must adapt in order to fit the buyers' expectations and needs.

Now don't get me wrong. As a seller, you don't want to waste time working with the wrong prospects. You must still prequalify your contacts and make sure that they are in a position and have the will to buy, and they fit the characteristics of the type of clients you want to acquire. What has changed is that in the past, prospects would audition for the seller, and wait to be accepted. Today, as I describe in the next section, sellers must find ways to audition for the prospects—and this audition is vital to the success of the sale.

THE NEW SALES PROCESS

The new sales process contains some subtle yet powerful changes. If you look at Figure 4–2 you might at first glance miss them, for it appears to be the same process as Figure 4–1.

But look closely at who is taking control of each step.

The new process still begins with research and prospecting, but an important transformation has taken place. Today, the research and prospecting process is *dominated by the prospects*. They go online, research who has solutions for the problems they're facing, read case studies, and talk to their colleagues. This shift is so dramatic that a recent DemandGen white paper, "Breaking Out of the Funnel: A Look Inside the Mind of the New Generation BtoB Buyer," shows that only 3 percent of all sales transacted are resulting from an outbound cold call from a seller to a buyer. In addition, the Hinge Institute recently discovered in a study

Figure 4–2. Modern Buying Process

titled "How Buyers Buy Professional Services" that 43.9 percent of buyers uncovered the opportunity themselves and then sought out potential provider(s) instead of waiting to be contacted by a seller. Today, contacts visit your website and determine whether or not you're qualified to do business with them, not the other way around! They request information, fill out "contact us forms," and download free materials. Contacts are taking action and reaching out to sellers proactively more than ever before! *Before, they didn't know you were there until you called. Today, you don't know they are there until they buy!*

As we move through the middle of the new sales process—qualification and solution development—we also see it is largely controlled by the prospect instead of the seller. Why? Because prospects understand better than ever what they're looking for and what's on the market.

Instead of leading this part of the process, it's now the seller's job to *guide* the prospect through the process. A smart sales team will simultaneously make sure the prospect is a good fit for their business, but the new sales process dictates much more give-and-take at this stage. While it's an often-used example, Apple sets the benchmark for this. While known for building great-looking, innovative products, it's no secret that they are perceived by some as being uncompromisingly pricey. This is a qualifying factor for Apple—and for Apple customers. Apple targets the well-heeled buyer and Apple buyers specifically seek out the best-looking but not the cheapest products. Despite the economy, despite an array of cheap alternatives in the marketplace, and even in spite of a campaign by a competitor that emphasizes that price difference, Apple sales always boom.

Presentation and closing phases still require a 50/50 effort from both prospect and sales team, but the tenor of closing now involves guiding the buying decision, not leading it, facilitating instead of selling.

By understanding the shift in the sales process and the increased control of the prospect, sellers can better leverage this new decision-making and buying process. This is especially important in your Sales Radar Attraction state: To attract the right prospects today you must develop proactive prospecting skills, direct *and* indirect, and use them in tandem.

Ask any perpetual boom seller and she'll likely admit to you that one of the cold, hard facts about this profession is that you can't sell to every legitimate prospect. There is always going to be somebody otherwise qualified who, for some reason at some time, either will not or cannot buy from you. That's why consistent and varied attention to client Attraction is absolutely vital. And let me emphasize again, just because prospects are taking more control of the beginning stages of engagement *does not mean* you can rest on your laurels and wait for contacts to come to you. You must continue to be proactive in your marketplace. In fact, it's the number one activity that you need to do daily—and do well—to achieve long-term success as a sales professional.

BE UBIQUITOUS

Let's shift gears now and talk about where you can find these prospects. Napoleon Hill once remarked that your ship cannot come in unless you first send it out. Nothing could be truer for sellers. Let me paraphrase: Your sales cannot close unless you first engage with some prospects. Sellers who actively prospect every day (send out their ships) will always outperform those who just sit and wait. In fact, if you are waiting at your desk for the phone to ring and sales to come in, you are simply an order taker. And you will wait a long, long time to be successful. I have never met a wealthy order taker. I have met plenty of wealthy sellers.

The best prospectors hedge their bets. They use multiple prospecting techniques to "send their ships out to sea." Some will return with a big bounty, some with a little one, some with nothing. You can never count on a "one-size-fits-all" approach to prospecting, or a 100 percent close rate in sales—even Columbus was smart enough to send three ships out to sea!

Given the new sales process we discussed at the beginning of this chapter, it's critical that you practice what I call *ubiquitous prospecting*.

Ubiquitous prospecting means that you are spreading your client attraction nets wide and far, using a multitude of approaches so that your target market finds you wherever they go. It involves using every tool available to you and not just relying on the telephone or email, as so many sellers do (who end up in a bust). You might imagine that it looks like Figure 4–3.

Take the Time for Both Direct and Indirect Attraction

Considering that Attraction is one-quarter of the Sales Radar, I'm going to suggest that you spend at least one-quarter of your time on net new prospecting activities. This time does not include calling existing customers, or doing project work. It needs to be focused only on activities that will attract new business from outside your current client communities—attracting net new business from net new clients.

The time you devote to prospecting should be spent on both direct (e.g., making calls) and indirect (e.g., attending association meetings) Attraction activities.

Some great examples of Attraction success in today's new buying markets are PetMeds, with 8.5 percent growth year after year, successfully moving pet owners from medications purchased from veterinarians to

Figure 4–3. Ubiquitous Prospecting

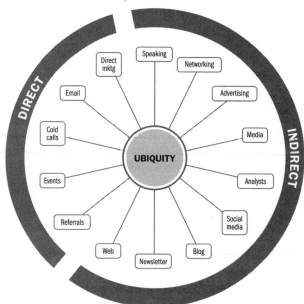

online purchases; and Audi, which is converting new clients to its cars in new markets such as Mexico, China, India, Japan, and South Korea (countries that in the past have not been associated with high sales for German cars) fast enough to be moving in on the number one automotive brand in the world based on size.

One-quarter of an "ordinary" workweek is approximately 10 hours per week. Of course, if you are brand-new in business and don't have any customers, you might spend more than a quarter of your time on new business Attraction, but most of you have prospects and clients in the other three stages of the Sales Radar so I am going to assume one-quarter of your time will be the most productive for you.

Assuming you have 10 hours per week to spend on net new client Attraction, here are some activities to consider. There are two lists below. One that you can use for direct prospecting activities and the other for indirect activities. Choose a selection from both lists to create ubiquity. The goal is to ensure when you do call prospects, the call is not cold. They are familiar with you and your company and have been warmed up from their own research, prospecting, and prequalification efforts. The list adds up to more than 10 hours. That's because you can pick and choose the activities that are best suited to your market.

DIRECT ATTRACTION ACTIVITIES	HOURS PER WEEK
Call 10 lost prospects per week to maintain communication and for potential reactivation	1
Call 10 leads prospects per day for prequalification	5
Call 10 contacts per day to fill the pipeline with potential leads	3
Attend a networking event or association meeting once per week	5
Plan "in the neighborhood" meetings for when you are traveling	1
Send special mailers—research papers, news articles, case studies—to your target list	2
Send emails with a value-added message—links to articles, referrals, new ideas—to contacts and leads for nurturing	2

INDIRECT ATTRACTION ACTIVITIES	HOURS PER WEEK
Network with one association once per day by phone	2
Attend a networking event or association meeting once per week	3
Write an article for your blog, newsletter, or association trade journal	2
Publish tips and ask questions on social media	1
Monitor group activity on LinkedIn or association forums	1
Research your target list to refine your Attraction approach	1
Develop alliance, referral, or reseller partners outside of your client network	2.5
Participate in online forums where your target market are members	1
Research trade shows to attend for promotion	1
Follow your target contacts and leads on Twitter to listen to their news and see if any issues arise you can leverage in a conversation	1

(You may be wondering about referrals, perhaps the strongest marketing position of all. We'll get to that in Chapter 13, once this foundation has been established.)

Go Viral

"How can I do a better job of gathering new business and new prospects in today's market?" That's a question that I get asked quite often as a sales consultant. Indeed, the simplest answer is that you need to build and sustain a high-potential, highly active network. In particular, you need one that can help you get the word out on the street about your products or services, help you build a name for yourself in your industry, and give you support when you need it.

You need to be highly viral, to put it in contemporary terms!

Over the last 20 years I have been studying the habits of the top sales professionals worldwide, and one common habit always emerges. Those who create a Nonstop Sales Boom are *ubiquitous marketers*. You have to seem to be everywhere, a continuous presence on the radar of the buyer.

It's important to keep in your mind as you are planning your ubiquitous Attraction plan that your buyers will range in sophistication. Some buyers will respond well to advanced Attraction offerings while others will respond better to simpler, more traditional approaches. You even might discover that multiple buyers inside the same company have different preferences. For example, a start-up healthcare software company I worked with this past year found that the best way to reach a hospital CEO was through a cold call—but its Community Outreach officers responded best to automated slide shows and video. For that reason I recommend a multifaceted approach that embraces a wide variety of Attraction activities. Here are lists of both traditional and sophisticated Attraction approaches that you can use to create your ubiquitous Attraction plan.

Traditional Attraction Techniques

1. Many software companies that we have worked with over the past 12 years have implemented live weekly product tours that prospects can attend to learn more about the product and ask questions in a nonthreatening sales environment.

2. Whether your market is saturated with hard-copy mail pieces or not, I suggest using it. Why? Hard-copy mailers stick around longer than electronic marketing pieces, are read more thoroughly, and can complement the work you are doing online. Most important, while two emails a week might cause the prospect to feel you are stalking her, one email combined with one mailer will not.

3. A sales manager from Wilhelmsen Ships Service once sent to me: "The more often our team visits the client the more inquiries and orders we receive!" Simply put, nothing beats a face-to-face meeting with a client or a prospect.

4. Live chat applications on your website such as www.liveperson .com allow prospects to speak directly with a sales or service per-

son anonymously, without feeling pressured to buy and without risk of being "stalked" for having expressed interest. These tools can be used effectively to warm up the prospect and either close the sale or convert the online conversation to an offline, in-person call. Best practice examples of how this can work to attract new business can be found on the websites of resort and spa company Sandals Resorts, the art and design website CanvasPop.com, and telecom provider Bell Canada.

5. A start-up genetics company I worked with a few years ago found that cold calling doctors via email yielded a 10 percent response rate. This is much higher than the typical 1 percent response rate seen by most email marketing. The secret was to personalize each email with information found on the Web regarding the research the doctor was doing, and the results that had been reported to date.

Advanced Attraction Techniques

1. A manufacturer of cutting-edge technology in chemicals created a series of video animations to show how its patent product was created and how it works to improve results. At first these videos were published in a unique video brochure for its clients to keep. Next they were posted to YouTube and finally to its own dedicated website.

2. A leading antivirus company sells through a reseller network. A few times a year its channel department invests time and money to "buy" an entire day of sales activity from a specified reseller. For that entire day the reseller devotes its entire outbound sales effort to the antivirus company's products.

3. A global office products company allows its sellers to use social media including LinkedIn and Facebook after, and only after, they have attended an internal training class on how to properly leverage those tools. As a result, those sellers who have access to social media are able to connect with prospects online, request introductions, and post comments and announcements on official compa-

ny social media platforms. In this environment it's common for sellers to request connections in LinkedIn to executives in their company and to encourage referrals internally both inside their prospects' accounts and their own. As a result, they have a healthy pipeline full of prospects and are in the midst of a Nonstop Sales Boom.

4. Kevin Poppel from Ag-Power Enterprises is in the process of releasing new services into a well-established market. While this might seem counterintuitive, he has had the most success in releasing these new services to new prospects and those who had stopped buying from his firm over 12 months ago.

When someone says, "Wow, I see you everywhere," it tells you you're doing a good job of staying on their radar. When you've achieved that, it's much easier to turn a prospect into a customer and move that person through your Sales Radar, because you're no longer a stranger.

HARNESS THE POWER OF SOCIAL MEDIA

While I believe that all media and all selling activities are inherently social, I can't ignore the power of Web-based networking tools in creating your ubiquitous prospecting plan. And, while this book is not a book on "social media selling" per se, some very profitable uses of social media in prospecting for new business have clearly emerged.

It's also important to check your assumptions about what these social media platforms and tools can and cannot do. Because social media choices and activities can be overwhelming, I often hear sellers moan, "The more I use social media the less social I become"—nor is it always clear what the return on your time is, especially for business-to-business sellers.

It's understandable that some leaders are still a little wary of social media—we do see some companies outright banning or blocking social media sites from work computers. While I don't think that extreme measure is the right approach, time is too valuable to waste on sites that have no value for you.

We just need *to learn how to use it correctly* in the Attraction state of your Sales Radar.

Top-ranked social media sites share some important characteristics that are invaluable to create your Nonstop Sales Boom:

1. They can filter content and connect you directly, one-on-one, with buyers who have problems that you can solve or who need the opportunities you can create.

2. They help keep you in the conversation loop on topics that matter to you and your prospects, including those that mention you or your company by name.

3. They provide you with an easy-to-access medium through which you can be as useful to others as that medium can be for you.

4. They provide you with a listening tool to discover what is on your prospects' minds, what they are working on, and what problems or successes they might be having.

The best social media sites have in common a key attribute that all top-ranked salespeople look for in networking: They are places that can help you showcase your value as a resource to a well-defined group of buyers. That's something to be valued well ahead of all other benefits associated with social networking, and yet it's the one that I find is still underused by professionals. The Web is the ideal repository of high-quality, targeted, and directed content that can meet specific needs.

If you are becoming less social while using more social media, you are not using it correctly. Social media is not meant to replace direct prospecting efforts or direct contact with a buyer. It's meant to complement those activities, providing an additional outlet to listen to and engage with your clients. In this marketplace you need as many customer contact outlets as possible to become ubiquitous and stay in that coveted top-of-mind position.

Your challenge, therefore, is to find ways to make social media part of your client-Attraction system without it becoming the only tool you use.

Here are eight ways you can build on the *social* in your social networking activities:

1. **Add value by sharing useful tips, articles, and announcements on Twitter.** This includes retweeting good news about your customers. Don't simply tweet what you are eating and drinking that day! For example, tweeting a tip on how you can use your product better, a real picture of a client using your product, a client success story, a link to a client or your company in the news, or a quick training tip can all add value to your clients' experience and attract new buyers into your radar. The more valuable information you give away for free the more new prospects you will attract who want to pay for products and services from you. While this might sound counterintuitive at first, what the client is really thinking when she reads your great content is, "If I get this much value for free, imagine what I will get when I pay them!" Companies such as IBM, Air Canada, Royal Bank, and Hilton create ubiquity by using multiple Twitter accounts for different marketing purposes. One account might be for sharing product updates, another for news stories, and yet another for a question-and-answer forum.

2. **Ask and answer questions.** Sellers who create a Nonstop Sales Boom are active members of multiple groups on LinkedIn and they use these groups to engage in meaningful dialogue with their prospects. For example, I coach a number of professional speakers, trainers, and consultants. These professionals have reported to me that asking and answering questions on LinkedIn in the groups they belong to routinely produces high-quality leads. In one case, Michelle was able to secure a $30,000 training contract by providing a detailed answer to one prospect's question about how to improve workplace productivity.

   By participating in the networks of your prospects, you increase the chances they will want to engage with you offline more often. One Engage Selling client answered a question from a prospect looking for consulting services on LinkedIn. Specifically the prospect wanted to know if anyone had experience working with start-up firms to help them optimize production schedules. As a result of the value he offered in his answer, he was granted a meeting and that meeting led to his securing a $40,000 consulting sale.

3. **Encourage the free flow of comments on your blog.** While some marketers worry that negative comments will dominate, the opposite is true. The more open your communication, the more of the best prospects you attract and communicate with. Prospects crave authenticity and they want sellers who are not afraid to deliver real information and engage with people who agree or disagree. Two leading consultants and authors, Seth Godin and Alan Weiss, have very informative blogs. But Alan encourages commentary and responds to others, while Seth doesn't allow commentary at all. Guess who is seen as more accessible and easier to contact?

    And this illustrates the discussion at the beginning of the chapter, about how the sales process has changed. Alan is engaging with the 80 percent of prospects from the first two steps of today's sale process, as seen earlier in Figure 4–2—prospects who are actively doing research and engaging in conversations with companies and sellers before the qualification begins. Seth? Not so much. If you don't allow prospects to engage with you early in their research you lose the ability to connect with them when they are ready to buy. If you block communication it appears you have something to hide (whether you do or not). If you do have something to hide, perhaps it's time to move on. Stop being afraid!

4. **Create special offers for followers who are prospects.** Encourage participation on your social media sites by giving away products and offering special discounts. This can also include inviting readers to request online newsletters and other promotional material. While this practice is common in retail operations or consumer products it's also very effective in a business-to-business environment. Wolf Steel, a maker of commercial and residential fireplaces, patio heaters, and grills uses its Facebook

page to post photos of successful installations, share design ideas, and hold contests. Installers, architects, and building managers are encouraged to stay in touch for the latest product announcements and incentives.

5. **Use your "on-hold message" for testimonials.** Remember Tim Welch from TalkSwitch in Chapter 1? The addition of testimonials to TalkSwitch's on-hold phone message proved to be a very successful lead generation tool. While prospects were waiting for the seller to pick up they heard clients sharing their successes and tips for the product. This warmed up the call and made it easy for the seller to ask questions and move the opportunity forward.

6. **Elevate awareness by promoting live events and hosting virtual product or service launch parties and special event pages.** Invite customers to participate online and reward them for inviting others. It's a great way to attract new clients and reward existing ones. Think about this as another way to speak at events. Makers of personal faxing software Protus created new leads each month by hosting virtual "lunch and learns" for their prospects. They would invite all the buyers in a target association or office, and host a private one-hour tour of the product set with a question-and-answer session, and sometimes a visit from a happy customer providing quick tips and success stories. Rather than flying across the country to present at an association lunch, they presented virtually and received high-quality leads at a fraction of the cost.

7. **Make yourself available using a live chat application.** Some prospects like to remain anonymous while they are researching new potential solutions. They know that if they request information from a website the sales calls will start within an hour of the information being received. Why not appeal to both the buyers who are ready for the contact as well as those who are not? While not all might be ready to pick up the phone and call you, they may be receptive to chatting with you online. It's less formal and helps build trust because the dialogue was established on their terms. In my office at Engage Selling we see an annual ROI of 100 times on our live chat application, and our best sellers in a business-

to-business environment find they can convert more of the best targets to opportunities using a balance of email, telephone, and live chat applications.

8. **Follow your prospects on Twitter and LinkedIn.** Even if you don't post anything yourself, listen to what your prospects are saying and doing and use what you learn to warm up cold calls or introductory emails. One Engage client recently identified on his Twitter feed that a competitor's customer was experiencing a service problem. Using this as a leverage point in a conversation with the buyer inside that less-than-satisfied company, he successfully secured a meeting and won $125,000 in new business on a project to help solve the problem.

Social media and social networking sites are worth the effort as long as you follow the number one rule: Go where your clients are. There is no point in setting up social media channels to find new prospects if your best prospects are not on social media. And remember: Using social media in the Attraction state does not replace the legwork you have to do as a salesperson in seeking out prospects, determining what they want, and finding ways to meet those needs. Rather, it is an extension of those efforts; one more element in your arsenal to help you hit those sales targets month after month, year after year.

As you can see in Figure 4–4, *you* are the conduit between the prospect and the pipeline. Whether you will be an enticement or a barrier is up to you.

STEP AWAY FROM THE COMPUTER

The fastest way to build your network is to figure out where your prospects and existing customers are gathering and go there. Jeremy Reese from Trupointe, an agriculture products retailer cooperative in Ohio, struggled with how to use social media in his sales environment for months before deciding to investigate his prospects further. After a quick

Figure 4–4. Prospecting with Social Media

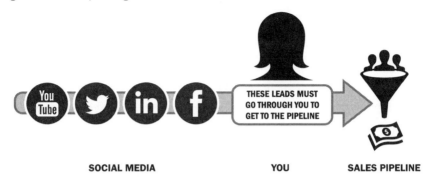

SOCIAL MEDIA   YOU   SALES PIPELINE

conversation with his key prospects he discovered that most of them didn't know what social media was! Jeremy switched gears quickly, invested his energy and money into other prospecting methods, and grew his business 25 percent past goal in 2012. On the other hand, I recently had a conversation with a business owner who spent over $10,000 setting up her Facebook page and Twitter account only to find out that her buyers don't have access to social media at work nor are they users personally of the technology. What a waste of time—and profits!

By all means use social media to do your research but then step away from your computer and make calls and start meeting prospects face-to-face. Recently I worked with a staffing agency that was continually producing between $38 and $45 million annually. They were up and down in that range for five years, never able to grow, and they called me to conduct an audit of their sales team. What I found was an excellent group of top sellers who were spending too much time online, using technology, and trying to connect with prospects on social media, rather than talking to customers.

When we limited their use of social media, email, and Web surfing, and required them to make calls to customers every day between 9–11 A.M. and 1:30–3:30 P.M., their sales rose to $60 million in one year without adding any new staff or resources. Why? Because they stopped using social media as *the* prospecting tool and went back to using social media as *one* prospecting tool.

MAKE SURE SALES AND MARKETING ARE IN SYNC

Some of the indirect Attraction activities could be best completed by a marketing department. Maybe they already are. If that's the case at your firm, fine. Regardless, it's important to note that companies often create busts by *not aligning their corporate structure to work together to attract the best leads.* In the Attraction state of your Sales Radar, this most often means that sales and marketing are not working together to fill the Attraction pipeline. Regardless of whether you have people or a department to carry out some of the prospecting activities, those companies that create Nonstop Sales Booms ensure that their sales teams are part of the discussions and decisions made by others on who to approach and how to approach the target market. While it may have been a badge of honor for sellers and marketers to "not get along" in the past, today nothing could be further from the truth. And if you want to create a Nonstop Sales Boom, nothing could be more detrimental.

In order to create a perpetual sales boom sellers and marketers must work together and be in alignment on the following Attraction activities.

1. **Target market definition.** Both sellers and marketers must have the same target market definition and buyer profiles in mind when they are embarking on client Attraction activities. I suggest that this definition be reviewed once per quarter to ensure everyone is on the same page. At this time results should also be measured to ensure lead quantity and quality metrics are being achieved.

2. **Lead definition.** A major issue arises when sellers and marketers are not on the same page regarding the definition of a lead. Specifically make sure you both understand what criteria must be established before sellers start the prequalification process. Define:

   ➤ What contact information must be confirmed?

   ➤ Does a buying time frame need to be established?

   ➤ What level of buyer must be passed on to sales?

   ➤ What size must the target be before it's considered a lead?

3. **New client attraction tasks.** Specifically who will do what, and when?

   > Is sales expected to be at trade shows?

   > Who will be the speaker at the event?

   > Is social media a sales or marketing (or both) responsibility?

   > How many activities are required to hit the leads' targets?

   > If there is a gap between the leads received and the leads required, how will this gap be closed?

4. **New client attraction results.** Too often sellers and marketers don't measure the results of specific Attraction activities. Instead they only measure the end results—sales at the end of the year. Companies that create Nonstop Sales Booms measure the specific results of each Attraction activity and then decide together which activities should be continued and which should be canceled.

5. **Incentives.** If marketers and sellers are to work together to create a Nonstop Sales Boom, then their performance pay should be aligned to the same metrics. For example, companies that incent marketers a small bonus or commission on new sales made on the leads they generate ensure that marketing engages in the highest-quality activities to produce the best result. At the same time, when those companies incent the sellers for closing those new opportunities, sellers work better with marketers to ensure that lead quality and quantity targets are being met.

The best companies, those producing Nonstop Sales Booms, review marketing and sales operations together on a quarterly basis. Of course, nothing stops them from getting together informally to discuss progress more often.

Trend Micro's U.S. midmarket sales group does something innovative—and wildly successful. Field marketing sits (literally) within the sales department and communicates tactically on a daily basis with the sales directors in the group. Planning occurs monthly, and quarterly communication time is set aside to monitor results and make strategic decisions about new client Attraction activities for the following month. At the same time, this is only one of five marketing resources assigned to the group. The channel marketing team works to raise awareness of the products with channel partners; the evangelist team leverages experts, blogs, and social media platforms; the product marketing team bridges the technology and business issues solved by the products; and the integrated marketing specialists ensure everything ties together seamlessly. Regardless of whether you have the resources to assign individuals or unique teams to each of these functions, the roles can be played in all organizations of any size. This structural alignment and intense communication are two of the reasons why the sales team has produced a Nonstop Sales Boom.

COLLEEN'S POWER TIP #3: NINE KEYS FOR PROSPECTING PERFECTION

Attracting new leads, the skill of prospecting for net new business, outranks every other skill and every other business habit simply because, frankly, you can't really be active in any of the other states of engagement in the Sales Radar until you have created new opportunities for sales. That's a fact that remains true no matter how successful you become and no matter how many sales records you break. When you stop attracting new contacts, you create a sales bust. It's as simple as that. And yet prospecting remains one of the most misunderstood aspects of selling. That's why I have prepared a list of nine key points that you need to know about this absolute must-have business habit.

1. **It's more than a part-time job; it's your livelihood.** One of the biggest mistakes that we make about new client Attraction is they think it's only something you do aggressively when your business is in a bust. If you're in sales, prospecting is not something you do on a part-time basis. Client Attraction is your business. Just as new sales targets are a certainty in your organization, you need to continuously find more people to sell to. That's simply not something you can do on an occasional basis. You have to treat prospecting as an activity that is as vital to

you as getting paid. Because without it (and in less time than you think) there might not be any more pay! It's that simple. The stakes are that high.

2. **Prospecting is not about short-term goals.** Another common mistake is to treat Attraction as something that's really only needed to be done aggressively when you need to give an extra boost to your sales performance figures in a particular quarter. The real truth about prospecting for new business in the client Attraction state is right there in the word "prospecting" itself—it's borrowed from the Latin word *prospectus*, or "distant view." Prospecting is an activity that serves far more than short-term goals. Think of it as an investment that helps you shape your future and pays dividends not just in the next sales quarter but in years ahead as well. By constantly finding and developing new leads, you ensure that you always have an audience for your product or service—no matter what kind of market you're faced with. Consistent prospecting equals a Nonstop Sales Boom. For example, the inside sales team at a Seattle office does a weekly analysis of their prospect lists for new business that can close in the current quarter, the next quarter, and two quarters in the future. They know that, based on the time it takes a new deal to close, they must look at least six months into the future to ensure that the pipeline is building. While in January they might expect their teams to have three times the prospects they need to close for the first quarter, they would also expect that they have just the right number of prospects they need for the second quarter, and only half of what they need for the third quarter. By tracking lead generation three quarters into the future they ensure the team never falls behind.

3. **It's a discipline.** There are plenty of skilled sales professionals out there who know how to close, who can navigate past objections, and who are adept negotiators and great at networking. And sadly, all of those skills will never really be applied fully unless those same salespeople each possess the discipline to get to their desk every single day and make those prospecting calls. It's not enough to just be good at prospecting; you have to be good at being persistent about it. Upon an analysis of his teams' time management, Mark Volk from Corel software

discovered that his inside sales team was spending less than two hours on average per day on the phone. Once we increased that to be on average over three hours, sales increased by 50 percent.

4. **It takes more than you think to get it right.** During the sales training and coaching sessions that I conduct, I'm often asked how much prospecting people need to be doing to maintain a healthy pace that meets sales targets. A lot of people are surprised by my answer: Take your sales target *and triple it*. You read that right. Your prospecting activities need to produce three times as many qualified leads as the sales you are expected to produce. This is the number that the new sales math gives us from Chapter 3. If that sounds like it entails a lot of work, well, that's because it does. And there's no getting around it. Any prospecting sum smaller than that and you're more likely than not to be the victim of a very sobering statistic: the rate of missed sales quotas. Consider this: A recent study by CSO Insights found that while just over 50 percent of salespeople hit or exceed their quotas every year, the remaining 49 percent don't (csoinsights.com). The best way to avoid winding up on the wrong end of that statistic is to make sure that your sales funnel is big enough. Size matters. In this case, most definitely.

> **ENGAGED SELLING:**
> Triple your targets. If that sounds difficult, think about how difficult zero prospects would be.

5. **Never lose sight of what needs to be done.** For sellers who have enjoyed a string of successfully met sales quotas, it can be really tempting to forget about prospecting—to see it as nothing but business development or to start looking disdainfully at cold calling. But the need for prospecting never goes away. In fact, that need grows just as your sales targets do. So it's important to never lose sight of what you must do to ensure that your success rate remains constant.

6. **Get a handle on the daily time commitment.** Prospecting is a daily commitment. But how much of your time each day should you devote to this activity? It's a point of contention among a lot of sales experts. It depends on whether you track your closing ratio on your phone calls. If you don't measure this, plan to be on the phone prospect-

ing every day for at least two hours. That will yield between 25 and 40 calls, out of which you ought to be able to secure three qualified appointments per day. If, on the other hand, you do measure your closing ratio, make as many calls as you need to so that you will hit your sales targets. Keep in mind that the new sales math tells us that three qualified leads will yield you one sale.

7. **Urgency: If you don't do it now, it won't get done.** Much like the discipline that's behind exercising, if you don't do your prospecting first thing every day, chances are good that it won't get done at all. Sure, you can make excuses about how you're going to get it done at lunchtime or late in the day instead, but really—and be honest with yourself—all you're doing is procrastinating. But it's something you *must* do, so get it done first, and then move on with your day.

8. **Be choosy.** Prospecting is vital and it requires a daily commitment from you to get it right. It's also important that you know where to look. As you develop your list of target prospects, be sure you zero in on those who have the money, the decision-making authority, and the desire for your product or service. Use the MAD analogy we discussed in Chapter 3: *m*oney, *a*uthority, and *d*esire. It's not enough to choose two out of three—all three must be there for a qualified lead to turn into a sale.

9. **Take control of your fate.** The more you engage in prospecting, the more new leads you have to turn into net new sales. Through hard work and discipline, you essentially give yourself more opportunities to create a Nonstop Sales Boom. It means that you're in charge of how successful you want to be. That's a much better place to be than just leaving things to chance and hoping that business will pick up or that a great sale will wander in off the street and help you make your quota. Be successful on purpose rather than by accident. Take charge. Commit to prospecting as much and as often as your sales targets demand.

Investing in the skill of prospecting reaps dividends. It's the easiest of sales skills to master. If you're disciplined and persistent at prospecting—engaging with prospects every day at a rate that is three times that of your sales quota—odds are very good that you'll master this skill. The key requirement here is the time you invest in getting the job done.

COLLEEN'S POWER TIP #4: BE CONSISTENT

Whether you're publishing a newsletter, cold calling, attending trade shows, finding leads on Twitter, walking around your territory, calling channel partners, or any number of other prospecting activities, the key is to be diverse and consistent. Commit to ubiquity. Decide on a schedule that works for you and that is convenient for your new and prospective customers. The key is to find a schedule that helps you attract and engage with as many of your best-targeted prospects as you can, and then stick to it. Vince Kearns, director of small and medium business at Trend Micro, sums it up nicely by saying: "We need to have conversations the way customers and prospects prefer—not the other way around. And the different ways different buyers want to have those conversations need to be reflected in our marketing. A one-size-fits-all approach means missed sales opportunities."

You can create your own weekly prospecting schedule based on the templates we provide at www.nonstopsalesboom.com. Before you move on to the next chapter of this book, go back to those direct and indirect Attraction activities lists and create your own Attraction plan. Your Nonstop Sales Boom depends on it.

. . . .

In Chapter 4, I introduced you to the power of ubiquitous prospecting. The goal is to be everywhere, because in today's selling environment, the buyers, not the sellers, are the hunters in the equation. They are the ones taking the initiative to research and find the sellers who will have what they, the buyers, are looking for. Today, selling is as much about being visible as it is about making contact. Chapter 4 covered some of the ways—from direct and indirect Attraction activities to use of social media—that will increase your visibility to prospects. In Chapter 5, we plunge deeper into the concept of visibility. The goal is to create a presence not just as a supplier of product, but as an expert who provides solutions. Chapter 4 was about being in the right place; Chapter 5 is about knowing the right things.

CHAPTER 5

The Expert Salesperson: Publish What You Know—In Every Way Possible

IN CHAPTER 4, we covered some of the key direct and indirect activities and sales channels that can be used to attract the best prospects. In this chapter, we focus on the type of content to deliver through the various channels, content that will get the attention of prospects, and make them trust you.

The key to successful content creation is not to push your products, but to push your knowledge. Ahead of all other traits, the best salespeople are experts *and they know it*. They're available to help people with expert advice in a specific field of knowledge. To get a buyer's attention you must offer her something of value. If you start the conversation based on what you need, you are a salesperson, and a mediocre one. And today, no one buys from salespeople; they only buy from experts. So you must begin the conversation with *what the buyer needs*.

How do you make yourself available and get noticed as an expert? By building or promoting a platform where you can share what you and your company know better than anyone else.

The platform can be varied, and include book publishing, blog posts, regular emails, podcasts, market- or association-specific websites, social media groups, newsletter articles, and public speaking—all with content fine-tuned to address topics that are relevant to your target audience. This is not a place for product pitches or demonstrations. OpenView Venture Partners is an example of a venture capital firm that does this exceptionally well. Its OpenView Labs website is a perfect example of a platform that was created by experts and promoted by their team to attract and retain the best prospects. What they do exceptionally well is provide access for their clients and prospects (all start-up and expansion-stage technology companies) to the best information on starting, growing, and maintaining a thriving business. They provide expertise from their own partners, as well as experts (including me) in a variety of formats such as articles, audio, and video.

The more opportunities you create to be seen as a familiar, trusted expert who helps people solve their business problems, the more likely it is for you to get meetings with new buyers. The outcome is that the opportunities in your Sales Radar start growing like never before.

BECOME A PUBLISHER

In the past, salespeople were completely focused on selling their products. Because establishing credibility as an expert is so important today, salespeople must not only be salespeople, but also publishers: creating content and publishing it so that the prospects looking for the right seller will notice.

Publishing as a client Attraction tactic is a very easy process that is a highly effective way for salespeople to attract the new leads that are required for a Nonstop Sales Boom. Figure 5–1 shows you the steps:

Figure 5–1. Becoming a Publisher

Most sellers overthink this process and as a result never showcase their expertise. They are not the ones creating a Nonstop Sales Boom. Things that used to require an entire industry to do over a period of months, sellers can now create on their own over a period of days. This is a huge shift and a major opportunity for anyone in the selling business. It also means that there are no excuses. Sellers who want to create a Nonstop Sales Boom can start creating and publishing expert content now. Let's look at all three steps now.

Step 1: Create Interesting and Surprising Content

CREATE CONTENT

- Create new content
- Take content from existing corporate sources
- Take content from industry experts

The best way to capitalize on the new sales process and maximize your Sales Radar isn't by pitching more of that impersonal marketing collateral that everyone has seen and read before. *The real solution is to share your ideas, in your own voice, as a subject authority.* This is what customers crave. Feed that appetite. Whether you're a small company or part of a large organization, creating or sourcing great content needs to be one of your top goals.

What do I mean by content? Taking your ideas and insights and sharing with a mass audience of target buyers.

Creating Your Own Unique Content

If you work for a company that will permit it, you can create your own content from scratch. Content can be created on topics such as:

> **How-to lists for using your service more effectively.** This could be a best practices guide for implementation, secret tips for effectiveness, or even step-by-step instructions on getting the most out of a product.

> **Frequently asked questions.** Most companies have these on their website. I suggest being more proactive. For example, when Aeroplan, a customer loyalty program company based

in Montreal, announced a new program this year it sent emails to all of its customers to help them better understand the new service.

> **Case studies of successful clients.** Interview some of your best clients and share their success in print and video. Use these as lead Attraction tools on your website as well as in email or direct mail and during your sales presentations. Prospects respond best to the success of others.

> **Industry trends and analysis.** If you have a research or analysis department (most banks do, for example) use its published and approved research to start conversations with your prospects.

The possibilities are endless. For example, Shopify.com offers a variety of best practices at www.shopify.ca/blog. While the company is an e-commerce and website software provider for small business, its blog is full of articles on how to improve your small business. Only rarely does the company publish a piece that would be considered a sales article for its software. Instead, it works hard at creating compelling content that its prospects can use and profit from. In doing so it builds strong trust with its buyers before they become clients.

Use your experience to provide expert opinions on what you see happening in your marketplace, trends that should be capitalized on or ignored. Here is an exercise to get you started:

1. Open the newspaper (or go to your preferred online news source) and pick a headline from the business section.

2. Ask yourself, "How does this positively or negatively affect my target market or my business?"

3. Write four sentences explaining your position.

4. Secure any approvals or permissions that are required before you publish it!

Now that was easy, wasn't it!

Back What You Say with Facts and Research

Sharing what you know is about a lot more than just stating your opinion on something. Once you get into the habit of creating content or sourcing content from others, start backing up what you have to say with facts and research. Whether that comes from your own research in your company white paper, or sharing the results of an industry-leading think tank, insight and knowledge thrive best when it's shared. You can do this by commissioning your own studies, creating surveys, and interviewing industry experts. You can also back up your opinions with primary research completed by others (and be sure to give them credit). As Google CEO Eric Schmidt reminds us, we live in a world now where every two days we create as much information as from the dawn of civilization up to 2003. Use that to your advantage.

If you are a seller at a large organization or a sales VP for a multinational Fortune 100 company, use your company's resources as content for publishing. A Fortune 500 third-party logistics company we work with has a corporate newsletter that is created by the expert marketing team at their headquarters. All the sellers have to do—regardless of their location internationally—is to add their prospects to the list, and the previously created content gets shared with prospects and clients worldwide.

ENGAGED SELLING:

Just because your company won't let you create content is no excuse for you not to publish expertise that others create for you.

Show How the Content Applies to Real Life

Engaging content sticks with people. Use examples, tell stories, and provide real-life scenarios. Explain how the content will affect their business and provide examples of other clients who have used it to their benefit. Make the content real to them and their business. This makes your content even more memorable because it's not about you: It offers something of value that your prospects recognize as similar to them. The most client-attractive content is that content where the prospect can say, *"Hey! That's just like me!"*

A simple and powerful example of this is again at Shopify.com. When you visit their websites they personalize the first headline you see to the country your IP address is associated with. So, when I visit their website from my Canadian office I see "Canada's ecommerce leader," but when I log in from our Miami office I see "America's ecommerce leader." This small change ensures that Shopify's prospects feel the content is perfect just for them.

Now . . . what to do with all this great content you have created?

Step 2: Choose the Platform That Fits Your Prospects and Customers

You are the sum of what you create and share.

Where is the first place people go today to find out more about you, your company, and your products or services? Who knows these days! It

could still be the phone directory or your company brochure, though highly unlikely. (You don't see ads for the Yellow Pages anymore.) Google and other online search engines are key, but if you only appear on your website, you have little chance of "showing up." This is why the ubiquity that we discussed in Chapter 4 is critical. And ubiquity depends on the platforms that you have for your content.

What do these platforms look like?

Advertising legend Lee Clow, chairman and global director of TBWA\Worldwide, says that today "everything is media." Here are some examples:

You can shoot how-to videos and post them to a special YouTube page for prospects as BlendTec did. Using $100 in supplies it created over 100 videos (some fun, some informational how-to), posted them to YouTube, and saw sales rise 700 times (www.socialens.com/wp-content/uploads/2009/04/20090127_case_blendtec11.pdf).

You can create a personal magazine or presentation on your smartphone or tablet and share product demonstrations of your favorite success stories. The specialty products division of an international fertilizer manufacturer did this with the launch of a new product line. Now all sellers are equipped with iPads to show videos of successful customers as well as demonstrations of how the product helps with increasing farm production. As a result product sales are higher than expected and product is sold out.

Another platform is to collect your blog posts from your company and self-publish your own booklet or e-booklet. An internationally based staffing agency we work with recently did this to create *The Little Book of Everything HR*. In it was a collection of tips human resources managers could use worldwide to hire and retain the best staff. While the content was created by the firm (as would be the case with most Fortune 500 companies), sellers would be responsible for promoting this platform by mailing this booklet to 10 new prospects per month and follow up the mailing with an email and a phone call. In doing so they were able to secure conversations with all 10 prospects each month. Of course, not all of those conversations converted to sales but, at the very least, the seller was able to gather information on how the buyer was using the booklet in order to create more content for the next version.

Online newsletters are another profitable platform to attract new clients. Here are two options. While a territory manager at Rosen's Diversified Inc., Chris Wooley developed his own newsletter for prospective resellers of his product. This newsletter contained three items. The first was a personal introduction and a photo of a relevant event in his area. The second was a tip or success story about the product and the third was a list of dates and prices or specials to be aware of. Chris was successful in not only growing sales each year for the four years we worked with him, he also grew his margins and profits. In this case Rosen's gave Chris leeway to create his own content and platform for promotion.

But what if you work in a highly regulated industry for a company that is concerned about compliance? Or one that has an army of marketers, evangelists, and experts already creating content?

Good news, you get off the hook of having to create the content and only have to promote it through the platforms best suited for your environment. Here is an example from finance:

First American Equipment Finance's approach to its newsletter is different from Chris Wooley's. Here, the corporate marketing team creates all the content and passes it to the sellers for personalization. Each seller sends the newsletter to his or her prospects with a "from the desk of . . ." banner and adds a few opening lines specific to his or her territory and prospects. This entire exercise takes their sellers less than 30 minutes a month and ensures that high-value information is delivered in a varied platform to their prospects. This attracts a perpetual boom of new leads onto their Sales Radar.

With every article you post, every personal video you create, every free e-book you publish, every product review you share, and every comment you make via social media, you are building your profile, sharing what you know, and adding value to your relationships with others online.

Active and Passive Platforms

When considering platforms it's easy to be overwhelmed by the variety of choices. I break them down into active and passive platforms. *Active platforms* are those where you actively send your content directly to specified buyers. You are in control of who is sent what content and when. Active platforms include email, newsletters, mail, and phone calls.

Passive platforms are those where you can't control who views what content, nor when they view it. These include all the social media sites, forums, your own websites, blogs, and YouTube, where people can come and view your content at their leisure. While you can actively market these passive platforms to draw people to them, you can't direct what or when they will watch, read, or listen to specifically.

Active platforms are the most effective. For example, sellers in the oil and gas markets use a three-pronged approach to help secure the attention of executives quickly. First, they send an industry analysis report directly to the executive's office by courier. Next they follow up with a phone call referencing the report's contents. Finally, if they reached the executive or the phone call is returned within 48 hours, they send an email requesting a meeting, with the original report attached. All three contacts are made within six business days for maximum impact, and in the rare cases where no response is received, the seller waits two to three weeks and starts the process over again, sending a new report. The key to their success is the variety of platforms (telephone, email, mail) used. Because buyers interpret different platforms in different ways, they view each message differently and don't feel you are overwhelming them with information *as long as you mix your platforms.*

There is a fine line between persistence and stalking. Three emails in a week to one buyer might be considered stalking. But a call, followed up by an email, and finalized with a mailing is only persistent! To create a Nonstop Sales Boom you must embrace all approaches to increase the number of times you can reach out to your prospects.

Your choices are much broader with passive platforms. The best way to narrow it down to the best ones for you is to ask: *Where are my best prospects congregating?* Followed up with, *Which of those are the best platforms for my content?*

Here are some examples of both active and passive platforms:

A hospital system we work with produces excellent answers to frequently asked questions. The doctors it is recruiting tend to congregate at dinner events and meetings. Email is not a great option for them as they often only use their email address at the office. So, the hospital system president decided to publish their content in paper copy and take it to live events.

On the other hand, David Jewell from HelmsBriscoe works with meeting planners who are heavy users of Facebook. His content is perfect for online publishing because it is picture-heavy and text-light. Therefore, he uses his business Facebook page to highlight hotels and share meetings industry research with his prospects.

Air Canada discovered that its frequent fliers and members of the Altitude Frequent Flier Program were heavy Twitter users. It now has a dedicated Twitter account just for frequent fliers, @ACAltitude, which handles questions about the program, makes announcements, and fixes customer service issues.

Shopify.com prospects are all online small businesses. They chose to publish not only on their own platforms but also on platforms such as techcrunch.com and those of other small business gurus such as Tim Ferris (author of *The 4-Hour Workweek*).

Once you have chosen the active and passive platforms that are right for your business you are set to start the final step.

Step 3: Publish on a Tight and Regular Schedule

You have created engaging content using your expertise or leveraging the

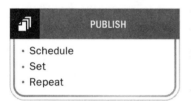

expertise of others and you have chosen two or three active and passive platforms for your content. Now it's time to publish.

If you look closely at perpetually booming sales teams you will notice that they publish on a rigorously regular schedule:

> - Chris Wooley's newsletter goes out on the first of the month every month.
> - Shopify.com publishes on its blog three or four times per week.
> - Kinnser Software posts weekly on its blog.
> - A seller with a third-party logistics provider sends a quarterly newsletter produced by corporate headquarters.
> - Large multinational fertilizer companies broadcast monthly market updates based on commodity process and current crop yield results.
> - Agricultural products seller Bob Lucia sends a monthly case study about a farmer using his products to successfully improve his farming operation.
> - Peak Sales Recruiting blogs every three days, posts on its Facebook page daily, and sends at least one tweet a day.

> ➤ Adecco publishes and mails a quarterly HR magazine.

> ➤ Trend Micro sends a different newsletter each month to each of its consumer, small business, and enterprise clients with content targeted to their specific needs.

> ➤ FundRaiser Software offers two educational webinars a month.

When the Engage Selling newsletter started going out on a regular schedule, every two weeks without fail, *open rates improved by 20 percent, the response rate from new prospects increased 25 percent, and new subscribers increased 50 percent.*

Developing a wealth of content and publishing it on a consistent schedule helps you tackle two important dynamics in your selling marketplaces.

The first dynamic is that not only has the sales process changed (as noted in Chapter 4), but also the decision-making cycle is longer than ever before. Therefore, you need to be more persistent at being persuasive.

One of the key ways you do that is by publishing your expertise on a regular schedule and contributing something of value to your prospects on a regular basis. By regular, I suggest the following schedule for some of the most popular platforms:

> ➤ **Newsletter,** once per month. Either write your own or create one using the content written and approved by your company.

> ➤ **Facebook corporate page,** once per day. Add updated links to new stories and client successes.

> ➤ **Twitter,** three to four times per day. Retweet what your company is tweeting or what your clients are sharing. Create your own unique content if you can.

> ➤ **LinkedIn,** once per day.

The second important dynamic is in how quickly information spreads. As Google CEO Eric Schmidt noted to *The McKinsey Quarterly* in an interview in its November 2008 issue entitled "Google's View on the Future of Business—An Interview with CEO Eric Schmidt":

The harsh message is that everything will happen much faster. Every product cycle, every information cycle, every bubble, will happen faster, because of network effects, where everybody is connected and talking to each other.

When you create and share thoughtfully developed content, you help your readers gain knowledge faster . . . and that positions you as a trusted resource.

Selling is far more relationship-based than it used to be. Adapting to the new normal isn't an option anymore; it's *essential*. You are your own media channel, if you want to be. Make it happen by making content creation a top goal for yourself and your organization!

PROVE IT! CASE STUDIES REINFORCE YOUR EXPERTISE

Let's examine that statement "Selling is far more relationship-based than it used to be." Relationships are based on rapport and credibility, and for many years, developing trust and rapport was considered the hallmark of a great sales process. Attracting prospects required exposing your sales team to a maximum number of buyers and developing trust and rapport with those prospects. As such, the primary objective for most salespeople has always been to find as many qualified prospects as possible to speak with and to spend their time developing a relationship and trust with that prospect network.

The theory has always been that, all things being equal, if prospects trust you more than another potential supplier, when the time comes for them to make a purchase, you've won their business. Knowing, liking, and trusting potential suppliers is still important, of course, but today it is not enough. It's important that prospects also see *proof* that you are an expert in their business—one whom they can trust not only personally but professionally to guide them through their purchase and future business problems.

If this weren't the case, Willy Loman would still be alive and prospering, using a shoeshine and a smile to lose business. But trust and even likability take a backseat to pragmatic expertise.

We've discussed how buyers now consider expertise an essential element in any purchasing decision. Once you have developed and published content around your expertise, it's essential that you demonstrate it and prove it to your clients. Buyers seek proof of your expertise in order to mitigate the risk they take on in making a purchase with you. That proof goes beyond just your word that you are experienced and well-versed in the issues your clients face. The best sellers undertake activities that demonstrate their expertise and help to build their network at the same time. *Case studies* and *testimonials* in the Attraction state of your Sales Radar provide the best proof of your expertise. That's why these should be constantly created, improved, and publicized.

A Formula for Case Studies

Develop case studies around client success stories that demonstrate your company's understanding of common and specific client problems and how your solutions address them. FundRaiser Software does this for each specific type of nonprofit that it sells to: religious organizations, Habitat for Humanity, animal-focused charities, and disease-specific nonprofits. Each type of organization and a specific case study shows the original concern, the product and service from FundRaiser that solved the issue, and the result. A quote from the client is included for each case study. This formula, as shown in Figure 5–2, can be repeated for any of the case studies you need to create.

Figure 5–2. Elements of a Case Study

Here is an abridged example (with the name of the real client removed for protection!) from its website, www.fundraisersoftware.com:

Performing Arts nonprofit groups are special to us. Making your fundraising easier is one of our priorities.

We know that it can be tough to keep track of all the details related to running your theatre efficiently. From your performances to your donors and volunteers, there are a lot of pieces that must be attended to in order for things to run smoothly. FundRaiser Software is designed to make it all streamlined.

FundRaiser's powerful database management systems are ideal for tracking all of your patrons, donors, volunteers and contacts. Our integration with Wintix box office software by Centerstage also allows you to track your ticket sales and identify patterns among your ticket buyers from inside of FundRaiser.

Use FundRaiser with Wintix integration to turn your patrons into donors, to manage your volunteers and tasks, to keep track of your projects, and, of course, to manage your donors with ease. Let FundRaiser take the weight of donor management off your shoulders so you can focus on your performances!

"We used FundRaiser with TREMENDOUS success right from the beginning; raising $7000 needed to buy new chairs for our community theater." —*Troy R*

Make Case Studies Part of Your Strategy for Client Attraction Calls

You can also use case studies to begin conversations with prospects. This tactic is most compelling when the case study is one that the person you are calling can relate to specifically in her line of work.

If I share with a prospect a sample of the great feedback I received recently from a client who works in that same industry, I'm making it clear that I understand the challenges she has to deal with in her work. There's also a deeper message being processed by the person I'm calling: *"If Colleen has worked with them, then she understands what we need and if she understands what we need, then she understands me."*

COLLEEN'S POWER TIP #5: MARKETING IS NOT JUST FOR MARKETERS

Salespeople who create Nonstop Sales Booms are, beyond all else, entrepreneurial. They think and act like they're running their own business, which means they market personally and continually. How specifically salespeople involve themselves in marketing depends on the size of the firm.

In smaller businesses, salespeople control all sales and marketing communications. To use a theatrical metaphor, they produce the show. They create their own expert message and schedule, marrying the right impact with the best opportunity. They follow up assiduously and relentlessly.

In the midmarket companies, salespeople work seamlessly with marketing teams in place to define and refine the message, choreograph the approach, and establish the cadence (repetition) needed. They serve as directors of the performance.

Finally, in larger firms, sellers are informed in advance of the marketing material and are given the opportunity to offer feedback. Even in large firms, they are involved as collaborators as opposed to being presented with a fait accompli. Here they are the actors.

The commonality among the three is involvement in an influential way in the creation, distribution, and leverage of all relevant material, no matter who generated it. Nonstop Sales Booms require the abandonment of turf and employee status, and the pursuit of an entrepreneurial and personal accountability.

For today's best sellers to have new client Attraction, an overlap of skills between sales and marketing is required. Specifically, sellers have to think more like marketers (*How can I attract people to me?*) and less like salespeople (*What can I sell that person today?*). To be a top seller, you must *behave* this way consistently as well. The best sellers actively participate in what were traditionally considered marketing activities to attract prospects in addition to the normal sales activities they undertake to convert those leads to customers.

For example, a top-performing sales team in corporate banking had to attract very specific customers onto their Sales Radar. These were privately held businesses with over $500 million in revenue. Cold calling the CEO, CFO, or president was not working, often despite a long, frustrating crawl of two years trying to make contact! In this large international bank, the sales team did not have the option of writing its own articles, blog posts, or participating on social media. However, the sales team did have a group of analysts, marketers, and underwriters who were approved to create the content. All the sales team needed to do was promote those platforms and content. For example, they could send letters out via email, or hand out research at networking events. As a new client Attraction activity, each seller emailed or mailed a new analysis or report to the top 10 prospects in their network on a regular 30-day schedule.

By the end of the year they had secured meetings with each prospect.

ENGAGED SELLING:

Erase the boundaries you've created between sales and marketing. Blow up a few walls.

· ·

In Chapter 5, I have asked you to transition from seller to expert in order to attract the best prospects. Your purpose is to show clearly that you can add value to your prospects' operations, and then to back that value up with proof of your past performance. When prospects see that you are an expert in your field and that you can prove it, they will be naturally more attracted to you.

From reading and implementing Part 2 of *Nonstop Sales Boom*, you now have all the tools you need to successfully attract new leads onto your Sales Radar and prequalify them so they are ready for full qualification and (if appropriate) conversion to a client. In Part 3, Participation, we will show you how to qualify, close, and deliver an ROI quickly and profitably with the leads you have attracted so far. Part 2 was about attracting prospects onto your Sales Radar; Part 3 is about converting them to paying customers.

PART III

PARTICIPATION

OUR NEXT FOCUS IS PARTICIPATION, which we discuss here in Part 3. It begins with your highest-quality leads and includes all the steps for sealing the deal: proposal, negotiation, closing. In other words,

PIPELINE STAGE	STATUS	PERCENTAGE COMPLETE
1. DISCOVERY Prospect identified	UNQUALIFIED	0
2. PREQUALIFICATION Initial contact mode	UNQUALIFIED	10
3. QUALIFICATION Opportunity assessed	PIPELINE	25
4. SOLUTION DESIGN Complete solution defined	PIPELINE	40
5. EVALUATION Active solution evaluation	PIPELINE	60
6. DECISION Presented to decision maker	FORECAST	75
7. NEGOTIATION Pricing proposal presented	FORECAST	90
8. CLOSE Revenue recognition	SIGNED	100

Participation will cover all of the remaining pipeline stages, from qualification to closing. As you will learn in Chapter 8, the Participation state of client engagement goes *beyond the pipeline*, as salespeople must stay involved during the post-signing onboarding and implementation phases. This is of vital importance. Your job does not end with the close of business, despite what other advice you might encounter. A client signing on the bottom line doesn't signal the time for a handoff or a lateral; instead it will be the time to help your new client run with the ball.

The Sales Radar approach ensures that you engage in what I call the "new closing." But before we get to that step, there is some business to take care of. Chapter 6 covers the qualification, solution design, and evaluation stages, while Chapter 7 will lead you from decision making through the negotiations that lead to the traditional contract-signing close. We then go on to discuss the last phase of Participation, a phase that doesn't show up on the sales pipeline: implementation.

CHAPTER 6

Before the Negotiations: Collaborate with Qualified Prospects on Proposed Solutions

IN CHAPTER 3 WE DISCUSSED ATTRACTING LEADS up to and including the prequalification stage. I encouraged you to prequalify all leads to ensure they were your perfect prospects and that they met the MAD criteria: *money, authority, desire.* Now we take a look at what to do with those prequalified leads in your sales pipeline to quickly and profitably convert them into clients.

The first step is the full and final qualification. Once you're sure that a prospect has the potential to be a lucrative customer, you then collaborate on the design of the proposal to anticipate any objections and problems.

QUALIFICATION REQUIRES INTIMATE KNOWLEDGE OF YOUR PROSPECT

To qualify effectively you must develop an understanding of the prospect's detailed budget including constraints and ownership, the prospect's decision process and criteria including the priority of those criteria, and your competitors (internal and external) within the opportunity.

Make sure you pay attention to all competitors, not just those inside the opportunity but also for those opportunities that might take your buyer's time, attention, and money away from your focus. Recently, a client of mine selling desktop computers to a large insurance company lost the sale because the executive board decided to reallocate the project's budget to video conferencing instead. These days your competition can come from both inside your opportunity as well as from outside!

You'll also meet with all decision makers and quantify the ROI they are expecting, the required outcomes, as well as the effort you will have to make to win the deal. Finally, you'll identify the internal team at your own company that will work on the sale and the influencers inside your prospect's company that can act as advocates and support. One of our top sellers in Taiwan likes to call these advocates "spies," as they help her gather inside information on company politics critical to her winning the deal, but not openly available to her as an outsider!

Probably most important, you must remember to slow down the qualification process in order to speed up the closing process. I know this sounds counterintuitive, but it is one of the most valuable pieces of advice I can give.

For some sellers with tangible products serving a well-documented need (such as meeting space at a hotel, commodity agriculture products, small-business accounting software, computer hardware, and temporary staffing services), the qualification process can take one or two meetings over a relatively short period of time. For example, sellers of temporary staffing services can often qualify an account in one 60- to 90-minute meeting.

For other, more complex sales (such as customized software, research studies, premium agriculture products, consulting services, and new products or service entrants into any market), the qualification process can take months. For example, the qualification process for large-business or government sales at Open Text, an enterprise information

management software company, could take as long as six months. Specifically, when I was selling new database and email management software to the Information Systems departments in the U.S. Air Force, my completed qualification process included meeting with six major commands (from Honolulu, Hawaii, to O'Fallon, Illinois) as well as the Pentagon officials over a 12-month period. But, in month 13 we finally got our $5 million win! It was at this time that I learned that if you take your time with the qualification and do it right you will more quickly win the sale. Rush to qualification and you will lose the sale.

ENGAGED SELLING:

Slowing down the qualification stage will speed up the sale.

VITAL QUESTIONS: WHAT YOU NEED TO KNOW

In order to complete the qualification and exit the qualification stage in your pipeline, you must have a full understanding of the items on the following list. I have included a few of the best questions to ask in each category to get you started:

1. Know the prospect's current situation.
   - ➤ *How are you doing this today?*
   - ➤ *What's the current process for handling this?*
   - ➤ *What have you tried? And how has that been working?*

2. Know the prospect's size by revenue as well as the number of users who will be active with your product.
   - ➤ *Who else will be affected by this project?*
   - ➤ *What scale of implementation are you expecting?*

3. Know the prospect's fiscal year end.
   - ➤ *When is your fiscal year?*
   - ➤ *Is there a time frame you need to be implemented by?*
   - ➤ *Is there a budget cycle we need to work around?*

4. Know what the prospect is looking for.

> *What does an ideal solution look like today?*

> *Have you seen this ideal solution in the market?*

> *What would you like it to do?*

> *How would you like this handled?*

5. Know all the buyers and their role in the process.

> *Who else is involved in this?*

> *How do you suggest we include them in this discussion?*

> *How will a decision be made?*

6. Know the influencers and their level of influence: who has a say in this decision and how valuable their advice is to the buyer.

> *Whose advice will you lean on for this?*

> *Do you need to get input from others? Who?*

> *What is your role in this project?*

> *What is most critical to you?*

7. Know the decision criteria and the order of priority—the relative importance—of each of those criteria.

> *How will you make a final decision about the best solution for your firm?*

> *Which of those criteria is the most important for each of the decision makers?*

8. Know what stage of the buying process the prospect is in and know his or her timeline.

> *When is the latest you would like to start using X?*

> *In order to start by that date, we will need to have a go, no-go decision by X. Is that workable for you?*

9. Know the prospect's business drivers and buying triggers. What is driving this decision? Why now?

> *What inspired you to look for a solution now?*

> *What's going on that is making this project critical to you now?*

10. Know your competitors. Who are you competing with internally or externally? Have they worked with that company or group before?

> ➤ *Who else are you considering?*

> ➤ *Why them?*

> ➤ *What other projects are priorities for you right now?*

11. Know the estimated price on your opportunity.

> ➤ *How much are you budgeting for this investment?*

> ➤ *Is that money allocated for this year?*

For a complete list of qualification questions please visit www. nonstopsalesboom.com.

SHOULD THEY STAY OR SHOULD THEY GO?

Qualifying the prospect is a huge step toward completion of the sales pipeline; and, at this stage in our example, you're 25 percent through the work required to convert an opportunity to a sale. At this point you will have to make a critical decision: *Is the information received in the qualification good enough to continue the relationship or is it time to disqualify the prospect?*

There are only three outcomes of a completed qualification. One, the prospect is qualified fully and can move to the next pipeline step. Two, the prospect needs work to qualify, but the opportunity is worth monitoring over the long term. Three, the prospect is not worth keeping around at all. This is shown in the decision tree in Figure 6–1.

Figure 6–1. Qualification Outcomes

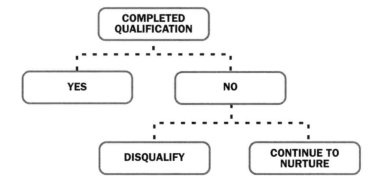

In thinking back over 20 years of my sales career I've met only five kinds of people whose behaviors lead me to believe I should disqualify them as prospects forever. You may have run across them in your work as well. They are:

1. **The Shopper.** You learn that the prospect is considering two well-known competitors with whom she has a long, successful buying history. You are the last one into the process and the prospect cannot tell you clearly why she would consider an alternative, nor is she willing to allow direct communication with the decision maker. This is a sign she is using you to compare pricing and features.

2. **The Snail.** A time frame and a budget cannot be established. The prospect is telling you that *someday* in the future there *might* be a reason to go forward but nothing can ever be set in stone. Deadlines come and go. This is a sign that while he might be interested there is no urgency. After six months of following up with a prospect, I once had a sales VP say to me, "*You know, Colleen, I'm retiring this year and don't want the expense to hit my budget and reduce my bonus. This project can be my successor's project!*" Some projects are just not ready to be pushed forward. We will discuss how to create urgency on page 130.

3. **The Hide-and-Seeker.** You can't meet with the decision maker. If you are being prevented from meeting the buyer, this is unequivocal proof that you cannot win the business. A software executive I work with is assertive in this qualification step and states to his prospect: "*In order for us to move forward I will need to meet with (name of the buyer).*" If the prospect says no, or stalls, he continues, "*I'm sorry then, we can't go forward.*" This is a nonnegotiable item for the seller. Notice that his position is a statement, not a question, which positions him as a peer, not a subordinate. Subordinates beg to speak to the decision maker; peers tell gatekeepers how the process works. In this example, our seller is successful in getting to the buyer 75 percent of the time. The other 25 percent he drops the buyer and focuses his time on the buyers who are serious about

doing business with him. Not surprisingly his Nonstop Sales Boom has lasted over five years already.

4. **The Stacked Deck.** The decision criteria are obviously set up for the competition. A number of years ago, an American-based prospect of mine listed as his number one and nonnegotiable criteria that the software had to be made in the United States. This was a deal breaker for us because the company I was selling for at the time was based in Canada. Buying something locally made in the United States was more important to the prospect than the best fit. At this point it was better to disqualify the prospect and move on. Why waste time with a prospect who will never buy?

5. **The Criminal.** You see signs of unethical, illegal, or subversive behavior! A client of ours was recently asked if her daughter was single during the sales process. She took this as a sign that she should move on! Another business services client (and a Fortune 100 company!) recently took a call from a client who had no website, no listing in the phone book, no credit history, and asked if he could pay cash on delivery. Yet another was asked for courtside tickets to a Los Angeles Lakers game before the decision was to be made. Best to walk away.

Your decision tree *after* the qualification should look like the one shown in Figure 6–2.

Figure 6–2. Qualification Outcomes and Next Steps

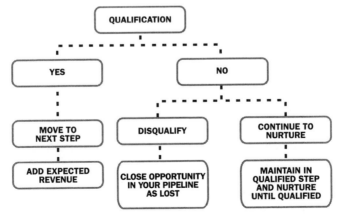

COLLABORATE WITH QUALIFIED PROSPECTS ON SOLUTION DESIGN

If you have decided to pursue an opportunity, it's now time to work with the prospect to design the right solution. You must do this before you complete a formal proposal and presentation. By doing so you will reduce objections and speed up closing times because you will be presenting a solution the client had a hand in creating.

In the solution design stage, it's important that all concerns, objections, and impediments are aired, and that the team understands any budget constraints so that the solution you are proposing in subsequent steps is precisely what the customer wants.

In order to complete the solution design step, you must:

> ➤ Define and approve the criteria for success.
> ➤ Develop a draft proposal based on this criteria.
> ➤ Establish that the proposed solution meets the prospect's needs.
> ➤ Receive internal approval on the draft.
> ➤ Confirm the pricing model is accurate and agreed to.
> ➤ Validate the decision and the implementation timeline.

Completing solution design brings you to *40 percent completion in the sales pipeline*. To collaboratively design the solution, you must begin by first asking the clients what they want in the solution, and then creating a draft proposal that you present to them before preparing the final proposal.

Ask Design Questions

Most sellers are scared to ask prospects what they want in a solution because they worry that the prospect will ask for something they don't have, something they will have to *design into a preexisting solution*. This is wrong thinking: First, it is very rare that at this point in the dialogue prospects will be looking for something vastly different than what you can offer. They would not have gotten through the qualification if they were not considering solutions that you can provide.

Second, if, in the rare case they are looking for outcomes that are out of your scope, it is still more profitable for you to walk away now than waste your time and company energy putting a proposal together that you can't win. One thing that Nonstop Sales Boom sellers do is manage their time ruthlessly. If they can't win, they abandon the lead quickly to focus on something they can win. Abandoned leads move back into the Attraction quadrant of your Sales Radar for longer-term nurturing.

Listen, and Repeat

A third reason—and perhaps most important—reason for asking design questions and listening carefully to the answers is that when you hear what prospects want, in their own language, you can tailor your proposal to reflect the conversation. Presenting solutions in the prospects' own language dramatically increases your chances of winning the opportunity because clients feel like they are buying their own designs.

Jim Cummings from Skyline Ottawa once noted that when they changed the language of their proposal from the technical language of their specifications to the specific language their prospect had used during the design phase, their closing ratios increased by 20 percent.

Here are some questions you should ask at this stage:

> - *How would you like to see this resolved?*
> - *What have you done so far?*
> - *How is that working?*
> - *What's the ideal for you?*
> - *Have you seen anything like that in the market?*
> - *What do you want it to look like?*
> - *What's the most critical outcome? Why that one?*
> - *Where do you see the most value? Why there?*
> - *How are you hoping this will work?*

For a complete list of qualification questions, go to www.nonstopsalesboom.com.

Once you have noted the client's design preferences for the solution *in his or her own language*, you have completed the solution design stage and are ready to start the second part of the collaborative design process: the draft proposal. It is during this process that the prospect has the opportunity to evaluate you, your team, your company, and the solution. Now you can move the prospect's position in the pipeline to "evaluation" and *note that you are 60 percent completed with the process.*

EVALUATING A PROPOSAL THAT'S HARD TO REJECT

The most important part of the evaluation process takes place during the draft proposal. That's because during this process you are working as a team with the client, discussing options, finalizing details, and agreeing on objectives together. As a result of your teamwork a perfect proposal for the client is created.

Always Start with a Draft

The real mastery behind creating a Nonstop Sales Boom has far less to do with closing skills than it does with having great command of everything that leads up to the point where you and your customer are ready to seal a deal. For that reason, never let the final proposal be the first proposal he sees.

To increase your win rate on proposals, you need to present each one as a draft to every customer first. By that, I don't just mean you should just *think* of it as a draft: You should literally stamp the word "DRAFT" in big, bold letters on every proposal. You can present this draft in a telephone conversation, in person, and in the shortest of sales it can even be done verbally without writing a draft. But it must be done before the final proposal goes out if you want to close opportunities more consistently.

Yes, this means more work for you. But more work now will increase your chances of closing later. Let's face facts: It's a mistake to assume that closing more business hinges on simply persuading people to make the commitment to buy from you *at the very end of a sales process.* They must be committed by the time you get to the end of the process. Draft proposals help secure that commitment.

Keep the Conversation Going

Even a draft proposal can be ineffective if there's not an ongoing conversation between you and the prospect. Before I send any proposal in hard copy or email, there are two questions that I always ask to ensure that my relationship with the prospect and the design process in which we're engaged is based on an open conversation.

Question 1: May I make a suggestion?

A great way to start the closing dialogue during the solution design step and before a proposal is completed is by asking: "May I make a suggestion?" And then say you'd like to present them with a *draft* of the proposal. You can then explain that you want to make sure that you don't miss anything in the proposal and that you want to make sure to get it right, the first time. That's a request that's pretty hard to turn down. In fact, I have never met a prospect in 20 years of selling who has said "no" to that simple yet highly effective question.

Question 2: How about we agree to review a draft of this proposal on . . . ?

You must secure a *specific date and time* to review the draft proposal with your customer. This gives you the opportunity to gauge her reaction, and respond to it while she is still engaged. In doing so, you will gain a golden opportunity to review the investment options with your prospect and handle any pricing or terms objections in a live selling environment—and then make changes to your proposal where necessary. Donald Leblanc at The Placement Office does it this way:

DONALD: May I make a suggestion?

PROSPECT: Of course.

DONALD: I want to make sure we captured your requirements perfectly the first time out and I know you want a final proposal from me on next Monday.

PROSPECT: Good idea.

DONALD: So with that in mind, how about we agree to sit down this Thursday at 10 A.M. to review a draft first. That way I can make any changes you need, incorporate them in the final proposal, and get it to you by our deadline.

Compare that approach with the common approach of sending a proposal to a client without reviewing it with him first. The most common result is that *if the client doesn't like what he sees, he tosses the proposal aside and ignores your calls.* Sounds harsh, I know, but it's true. Be honest with yourself. How many proposals have you sent in the last five years that have met a disappearing prospect?

The reality is that if prospects don't like what they see it's easier for them to ignore you than it is for them to have a conversation. In their minds, they received your proposal, didn't like it, and are now set to move on. *You are the only one who can prevent this from happening,* and that's by engaging in that much-needed conversation first.

When you are able to talk to the client directly about her concerns and present the proposal in draft first, your chase for answers stops, and the number of closings you accomplish every month grows.

Your draft proposal review gives you a front-row seat into the mindset of your customer. For example, if you sell software and you know that your customer is comparing your draft proposal to those of two competitors, the extra time you've spent in drafting mode gives you the opportunity to ask questions. For instance: "What do you think of our approach?" or "Does this structure provide you the outcomes you need?" Listen carefully to the answer you're given. It will give you a clear indication of whether you need to make changes to your proposal and how close you are to a win. You will also get a chance to judge the sensitivities to pricing, value, and terms.

If the prospect engages with you, answers questions, asks for changes, and marks up the proposal with you, you are closer to a win. Clients are then taking ownership of your approach and the document becomes theirs. In the end, it's more difficult to say no to something they built!

If, however, during your draft proposal meeting the prospect is silent, nods but doesn't ask questions, requests nothing of you, then you are in trouble. This prospect is moving farther away from the sale. Chances are the client may favor a competitive offer. Of course, it goes without saying that if the prospect stands you up for the draft meeting, you have likely lost the sale.

The top sellers at Allied Van Lines originally resisted this approach as too much work. So we insisted that they try it with their most profitable corporate clients. Those who did *doubled their closing ratios* on their most important opportunities.

Once your draft meeting is over and feedback is in your pocket, you can now customize the proposal based on the feedback, and present the prospect with a final proposal. Your win rate goes up dramatically at this point because prospects rarely throw out the solutions that they helped design.

Investing time on these elements means less risk of unwanted surprises at closing time. Spending the extra time on opening up a dialogue with prospects during the qualification and solution design steps demonstrates that their input is valued. As a result, prospects are more open to share with you what's important in their decision-making criteria. You can also be sure that investing time in the draft approach helps because this extra step is something that a lot of your competitors simply aren't bothering to do.

ENGAGED SELLING:

Slowing down the solution design stage will speed up the sale.

So plan ahead. Take the time to adopt the draft approach in building a great business proposal. You'll be amazed by how much easier it gets to close more business while building a great rapport with your customers and sharpening your winning edge against competitors.

KEEP THE PROCESS MOVING: HOW TO CO-CREATE THE URGENCY TO PARTICIPATE

Urgency is crucial in Nonstop Sales Booms, especially in the Participation state of client engagement. You are trying to move prospects through a number of pipeline stages and take them to closing. Ironically, you have to take your time to create urgency! That's because there are three types of urgency, all of which are important:

1. **Customer-sensitive urgency.** The customer recognizes that urgency is required. The leak in the roof requires repair. The dip in new business requires a remedy. The toothache requires a dentist.

2. **Customer/seller discovery.** Here, the two of you agree on urgency as you recognize that a window of opportunity may close. The new product is needed before buying decisions are made in the fall. The capital improvement should be made during the current, more favorable tax time.

3. **Seller-mined urgency.** The salesperson uncovers urgency that the buyer was unaware of. A new technology will allow for faster customer responses. The decline in business travel requires a substitute allure for frequent flyer points.

Rather than only thinking of how you can create urgency on your own, think about urgency as something you and the buyer discover together. Working together to create urgency ensures you ask questions to uncover issues, pressure points, deadlines, start dates, and, most critically, project end dates that are important to the client. In doing so, you ensure that the urgency is based on something on which you and the client have agreed in advance or that the client has expressed as important.

Fire Sales Don't Work

Before I show you how to co-create urgency with your client, let's address how you can prevent a *lack* of urgency getting in the way of a Nonstop Sales Boom. Sellers who are frantically trying to create urgency are also those sellers with scant opportunities in their pipeline. They need the sale more than their prospect needs to buy and so they furiously try to manufacture reasons that the client should buy now—only because they have not done a good job in the Attraction state of engagement.

If you always have a full pipeline of three to four times what you need to close, then urgency will not be an issue for you. Some leads take longer to close, and some opportunities are not ready yet. Sellers who are frantic to close opportunities because they are desperate to make sales end up attempting to force urgency with tricks such as "limited time discounts," manipulation such as "this is the last red car on the lot," or aggressive follow-up (stalking). This creates a sales bust as prospects are turned off and buy from others. To prevent this behavior, and create a Nonstop Sales Boom, pay attention to client Attraction and always be prospecting.

ENGAGED SELLING:

No one believes the old "fire sale" or "going out of business" tricks; these will influence customers to wait for an even better deal.

Let Questions Drive the Urgency

How do you and the buyer create urgency together? Once you are in the sales process there is a magical question you can use to develop the urgency for a prospect to participate quickly: *When is the latest you need to be using this product?* You are asking a question about when the project needs to be completed. Here are some real examples of how my clients use this. Choose the one that is most applicable to your sales situation. You can ask:

> ➤ *When is the latest you want your teachers teaching this math program in the classroom?*
>
> ➤ *What is your ideal go-live date?*

> ➤ *When do you want this project wrapped up?*
> ➤ *When is the latest date you want this seed applied?*
> ➤ *When do you need to have this system up and running on the desktops?*
> ➤ *When are you planning to roll out the results of this study to the team?*
> ➤ *When do you need to have this new executive in place and up to speed?*
> ➤ *When does the design have to be submitted to the manufacturer?*
> ➤ *When does this load need to arrive at the port?*

After the prospect provides a date, confirm your understanding with a follow-up question. Start with either "*Is that because...*" or ask simply "*Why?*" These secondary questions will identify how important that completion date is to the client. For example:

YOU: When do you want the teachers using this material in the classroom?

PROSPECT: September 4th.

YOU: Is that because the 4th is the first day of classes next year?

Or

YOU: When's the latest this load has to arrive on the dock?

PROSPECT: August 17th.

YOU: Why the 17th?

Nonstop Sales Boom sellers always differentiate between the date the customer wants to make a decision and the date he needs to be using the product. You find urgency when you know clearly what date the project needs to be completed and why that date is important.

Top sellers go one step further and never even ask the buyers when they are going to make a decision. Instead, they always *work backward from the project completion date* to tell the buyers when they need to buy in order to hit their own goals. In doing so, urgency is found.

Figure 6–3 illustrates the steps to take. The conversation between you and the buyer goes like this:

> Okay, so if you need the shipment to arrive by September 5th, it will need to leave your loading dock no later than August 20th. In order to ensure we have the trucks required for the pickup you will need to make a yes/no decision about whether to contract the load to us by August 15th. That gives us five days to find the specific trucks and drivers you need to meet your deadline. If I have a quote to you by August 10th can you make a decision before the 15th?

Or,

> Okay, in order for you to be using the software by October 1st we will have to start the data transfer and training on September 1st. That gives us the three weeks plus a week's grace to get you trained and your data converted. Our trainers and developers book up quickly, so in order to get your preferred dates we would have to lock them in by August 1st. This would mean you would need to make a yes/no decision on our system no later than July 31st. If I have a proposal to you this week is that decision date possible?

Customers do not understand the lead time it takes between signing an agreement and completing the project or receiving the product. Most believe the turnaround or completion time is quicker than it really is! As a result, they think they can make a decision today, and be using the product tomor-

Figure 6–3. Leading the Customer to the Close

row, often delaying the decision to the very last minute to everyone's detriment. If you want to speed up the Participation state of engagement, you must educate clients on the decision and project timelines, show them the lead times, and tell them when they need to buy in order to hit their own urgent deadlines.

COLLEEN'S POWER TIP #6: 4M MEETINGS GET THE JOB DONE

Success in the Participation state of client engagement depends to a great extent on successful meetings with the prospects—meetings in which you will be qualifying prospects, co-creating designs, negotiating proposals, and agreeing on final terms and solutions. My 4M meeting methodology is designed to make sure that you are completely prepared for the meeting, and that you leave the meeting with an accomplishment in hand.

While I first discovered this approach on my own in the 1990s, I have come to learn that the original technique was developed by Alan Weiss nearly 20 years earlier! This 4M approach (see Figure 6–4) has always served me and our Engage Selling clients well and in the last few years I have modified it to meet the needs of the modern buying market.

So, what do those four *M*s stand for?

The first *M* is for *maximum*. What is your Plan A for this meeting?

Figure 6–4. The 4M Approach

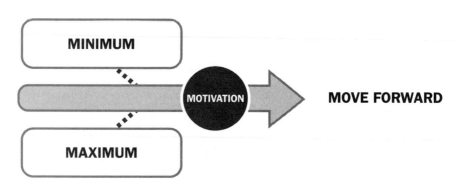

What is the best-case scenario? What are you hoping to accomplish? Examples include:

> Closing the sale

> Completing a qualification conversation

> Building rapport

> Meeting the team of influencers or buyers

> Being referred to a different department

There is no right or wrong maximum (as long as it's a legal, moral, and ethical goal), but it needs to be tied to the specific customer and meeting you are attending.

For example, the inside sales team in a Detroit shipping services office is charged with making introduction calls and follow-up calls. The maximum they often set for an introduction call is to finish the call with permission to set up a meeting or otherwise follow up. Their best-case scenario is to establish the next call in all cases. On their follow-up calls, however, the maximum can vary widely depending on the size of the account. For a large account, the maximum for a follow-up call might be to secure an inside meeting; for a small account it might be to achieve verbal approval for the first shipment (their sale) in the future or to provide a quote in real time and get a yes/no on the call.

The second M is for *minimum*. As Mick Jagger is fond of telling us, *"You can't always get what you want."* The best sellers always have a contingency plan, or a Plan B, should the meeting not go as planned. What is the minimum you need to get out of this meeting to ensure it was a good enough meeting for you to decide whether the prospect is worth pursuing?

Minimums can include:

> Asking questions to see if the prospect is worth your time

> Finding out whether the prospect is considering options

> Understanding who is in charge of the decision

> Setting up a next meeting

> ➤ Getting permission to provide a proposal

> ➤ Securing the date and a time for a demo

> ➤ Closing the sale

Some of those minimums the same as the maximums? Smart catch, for many of you. And that's because your 4M is situation-dependent. Here are some examples:

Going back to our Detroit shipper's office for a minute, on a follow-up call they may make their maximum on a small opportunity to quote the shipment and secure the sale. If they can't get that far, sellers are prepared with their minimum: to find out when the next shipment is that is available for quoting.

David Jewell from the global meeting procurement company Helms Briscoe reports that he might set his maximum goal at a first meeting to qualify a client and find out if the client has any meetings he can secure space for. His minimum might be to understand what types of meetings the client plans for each year.

Software executive Genie Collins says she might have a maximum objective during a presentation to achieve consensus on the budget and timing and to get a verbal approval to move forward with a proposal. Her minimum might be to better understand everyone's role in the buying process.

Minimums and maximums depend on where you are in the buying process, the complexity of the sale, and what you already know about the client. They are never standard and are always tailored to the customer. When you take the time to set your goals for the meeting you will increase your chance of moving the sale forward each time. As Doreen Ashton Wagner, managing director of Greenfield Solutions, puts it, *"Setting my minimum and maximum before the meeting guarantees I will always close the sale or move forward to the next steps the client and I decide on together."*

The third *M* is for *move forward*. Your move forward is your next step. Specifically, what next action are you going to agree to with the client? In setting your next steps, I do have one rule for you to follow: Your move forward must be decisive and measurable. Next steps must include date and time for the follow-up. Stating that you will "call the prospect in a few days" or that you will "wait for the prospect to call you back" is not a decisive move forward action. It leaves you helpless.

Your move forward actions can include:

> A date and a time for a next meeting. Get your calendars out and schedule it before you leave.

> A date for you to provide references to a client and a time frame for the client to follow up.

> A promised date for a proposal and agreement to meet to discuss the terms.

> A date by which you will get back to the prospect the answers to questions he or she had.

The smartest sellers always plan for two move-forward requests: one if they achieve their maximum and another for if they achieve their minimum. For example, back to our Detroit office, a seller who achieves his or her maximum—for example, gaining agreement from the client to allow him or her to quote on the next shipment—will set as the move forward a date and time to call the client prior to that next shipment to secure the details. In the same office, a seller who achieves his or her minimum—for example, understanding who the decision maker is—will set as a next step the date and time he or she will call that decision maker and attempt to arrange a meeting.

Top seller Lori, in corporate airline sales, sets her next steps as a date and a time for a corporate presentation to all frequent fliers in her prospect's headquarters once she receives verbal approval from the buyer that the airline she represents is approved by the buyer's travel desk.

Sellers for the meetings and events market set as their next step establishing a date and a time for a venue visit once they achieve their maximum: confirmation that the prospect is planning a meeting and their venue is under consideration for its location.

The fourth and final step in your 4M planning is knowing the *motivation* of the prospect. Specifically what is motivating her to want to continue to conversation? What would motivate her to take action? Why is she motivated to meet with you? Knowing the motivation helps you to frame the meeting, ask the right questions, and suggest the correct alternatives. For example, a seller in the shipping business would benefit from knowing that his prospect's motivation is the recent theft of $100,000 worth of merchandise during transit. Therefore, the prospect is motivated to find more reliable drivers. A seller at a live music venue might learn that the motivation of his buyer is to find a fun location for her next corporate event because the last corporate event received poor reviews.

Lori in airline sales might have discovered through a press release that her new prospects have opened an office convenient to a newly expanded air route her firm just announced. The motivation for this prospect could be easy and reliable access to that new office. Motivations drive how you prepare for meeting because they help you frame your conversation.

The big lesson with motivation is that motivations are the *customers'* motivations—not *your* motivations. Before you meet with the prospect you must be able to answer the question, "Why is this particular prospect motivated to have this conversation with me?"

By setting your 4M before you start each sales meeting, you create the opportunity to close at each meeting. You are either closing the sale or closing on the next steps. No more chasing the prospect, no more unreturned calls or emails, no more unresponded-to proposals. This is because 4M ensures that all sales meetings are driven from the buyer's motivation, that your objectives have been met, and that you and the prospect have agreed to a fixed set of next steps. Additionally, you are always prepared at the meeting with the right questions and tools because you have set a purpose for the meeting.

This is simple and commonsense advice yet many sellers choose to ignore it. Which is why so many fail to create a Nonstop Sales Boom. Sadly, 80 percent of the sellers I meet for the first time are unprepared for their sales calls. Here is a typical scenario I experience as I am sitting at a desk with a seller about to make a call, or sitting in a car with a seller outside a prospect's office:

ME: What's your objective for the meeting?

SELLER: To close the sale.

ME: Great! Let's see your proposal (*or* pricing, *or* contracts).

SELLER: Oh, I didn't think to bring that with me today.

Opportunity lost. This particular *M* stands for *mindless*.

One last note before we move on. Planning your 4Ms should be a five-minute exercise. This should not take all morning! Far too many sellers overthink the process and strive to find the perfect 4M when one does not exist. Pick a maximum, minimum, and your move forward, and know the prospect's motivation. Gather the tools you need to execute on your plan and make the call. Overanalyzing this process will only contribute to a sales bust. Remember that your goal during this stage of your Sales Radar is Participation. That means engaging with the prospect quickly, and moving him through the sales pipeline. Find motivations and propose solutions that make sense and are effective, not perfect, or you'll never leave the office.

. . . .

Accelerating Participation requires accelerating a series of yeses to move the prospect from prequalified to closed. We have just covered how to do this during the qualification, solution design, and evaluation phase of your sales process. At the end of these three steps *you are now roughly 75 percent complete with your sales process* (remember, we are no longer tracking probability of closing) and ready for the final negotiation and closing steps. In Chapter 7 we will address the closing cycle, from decision to win—specifically, how to present your solutions so more are accepted more quickly and with fewer objections.

Fearless Negotiating: How Candor and Rigorous Follow-Up Clear the Path to Closing

IN THIS CHAPTER, you will move from decision to closing, the last three stages of the pipeline. You are now in the heart of the Participation state of engagement on your Sales Radar. There is ongoing communication between you and the prospect as you hammer out a final proposal and deal with any objections that come up. In this stage, sellers often get tripped up because they are afraid to ask about or preempt objections and concerns, or because they take a passive wait-to-hear approach that can allow the sale to sink from neglect. As we move in this chapter through decision, and negotiating to a close, you will see that fearless candor and rigorous follow-up are the keys to a successful sale. The last three stages of your pipeline process are shown in Figure 7–1.

DECISION: THE BUYER COGITATES ON WHETHER TO ACCEPT A PROPOSAL

After an opportunity has been qualified, you have worked with the prospect to design a solution, and you have run through a draft proposal for the

Figure 7–1. Final Pipeline Stages

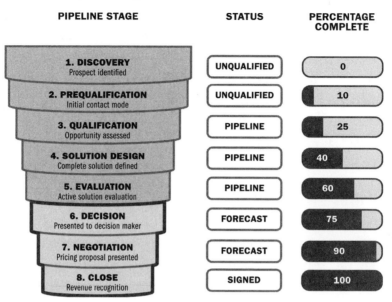

PIPELINE STAGE	STATUS	PERCENTAGE COMPLETE
1. DISCOVERY Prospect identified	UNQUALIFIED	0
2. PREQUALIFICATION Initial contact mode	UNQUALIFIED	10
3. QUALIFICATION Opportunity assessed	PIPELINE	25
4. SOLUTION DESIGN Complete solution defined	PIPELINE	40
5. EVALUATION Active solution evaluation	PIPELINE	60
6. DECISION Presented to decision maker	FORECAST	75
7. NEGOTIATION Pricing proposal presented	FORECAST	90
8. CLOSE Revenue recognition	SIGNED	100

buyer to evaluate, most buyers enter the decision phase. At this point the buyer is deciding whether she should move forward. This might take days or weeks but it always happens before the buyer asks for the final proposal.

For example, after presenting a verbal draft proposal, the sellers at Kinnser are often asked for a five-day trial of the software to evaluate before a contract is sent for final consideration. A fertilizer sales team finds that the buyers will often ask for two or three days to think about it while they "run the numbers" before accepting (or rejecting) a proposal for the newest fertilizers. After a written draft proposal from FundRaiser Software is reviewed, the client will often simply say, "Sounds good, can I see a final contract?"

During this decision step, the prospect may still be comparing your solution to the competition's, though that probability diminishes as you proceed through this process. Sometimes, the prospect is also comparing your solution to the cost of doing nothing at all. Remember, as we discussed in Chapter 4, the buying process has changed dramatically. Qualification no longer depends only on your decision about whether you are ready to move forward; it equally depends on the buyer being ready to move forward. If the buyer is not ready to move forward you cannot send a final proposal. *A premature final proposal always leads to increased objections, stalled opportunities, and losses.* Always make sure your client is ready to see the final offering before you commit it to writing.

The decision to do nothing is also a distinct possibility and a valid alternative for many prospects.

Is An Internal Option Still Alive?

Before a final proposal is sent always make sure that buyers are only deciding on external solutions. If they are still considering an internal solution (build versus buy), then move *backward* in the pipeline and re-visit the evaluation phase, solution design phase, or even the qualification phase to better understand what they feel their internal capabilities are. You will not be able to build an effective proposal if you don't understand why an internal solution is being considered and what costs are associated with that solution.

Never listen to sales experts who say you can't move backward in the process. Sometimes new information, people, or criteria are discovered, forcing sellers to take a step back and requalify and reassess the process. It's okay. Movement—forward *or* backward—is always better than stagnation.

By the time the buyer has reached the decision phase (and probably well before), you will undoubtedly know who your competitors are, and have an understanding of their strengths and weaknesses relative to your solution. Providing references, case studies, and testimonials is common at this stage as the prospect seeks proof of concept or demonstration of capabilities, but at its heart, this stage is full of engagement with the client as he is making his decision.

In order to exit the decision phase, your opportunity must meet the following criteria:

➤ The evaluation and decision are complete. Your buyers have agreed verbally that they want to move to the next step.

➤ A business case (ROI) for moving forward has been confirmed.

➤ The client has agreed to pursue an external solution.

➤ You have received verbal confirmation of being short-listed. (Sellers in Nonstop Sales Booms never submit proposals if there are more than three competitors still in the race.)

Completion of the decision stage moves you to at least a 90 percent complete pipeline. Once this is done you can move on to start negotiating final terms.

Proposal: Don't Just Send the Paper

Once the client has agreed to accept a proposal from you or has verbally confirmed that you've been short-listed to one of three external providers, it's time to create the final proposal or contract. At this point you can *officially forecast revenue.* If you have your own historical data about the percentage of closed deals after this point, use that to create your forecast. If you're looking for a baseline, typically one-third of proposed revenue is realized.

While every business has its own unique way of presenting contracts, here are four universal best practices from the Nonstop Sales Boom community. Once a client is ready for the final contract use these best practices to increase your chances of winning.

Schedule a Follow-Up Meeting First

Commit to a contract follow-up meeting before the proposal is submitted. Before you try to schedule that meeting, however, you need to know when they need the contract, when they will be reviewing it, and when you can expect them to sign it (your three crucial *whens*).

Once you have this information, say: "I can have that agreement to you by (*requested date*). How about we agree to meet/talk again on (*one day after review date*) so that you have a chance to ask any final questions before your decision on (*decision date*)?"

This question serves two important objectives. Its first objective is to help you continue the dialogue after the proposal is submitted. Far too often, the prospect disappears once final pricing appears. When this happens, sellers are reduced to chasing buyers, trying to find out what happened and never knowing what the final decision was. Nonstop Sales Booms are created when you stop chasing buyers and instead start following up as planned with scheduled appointments.

The second objective of asking for a follow-up meeting is that the request serves as a trial close. If the prospect agrees to your meeting request, you have received a solid indication she is serious about you and thinks of you as a business equal. If she declines the meeting request, this is a sure indication that you are not the preferred choice. If the buyer won't commit in advance to a post-proposal conversation, use this as an opportunity to push back. Ask questions such as:

> ➤ *I sense that you have some reservations about moving forward. Should we address those now?*
>
> ➤ *It seems like you are not sure whether my proposal is going to meet your needs. Do you have questions that should be answered now?*
>
> ➤ *Is this the right time for a proposal, or do you need to have some additional internal discussions before we can finalize our approach?*

Bringing buyer hesitation to the forefront is not something to shy away from. By bringing it up now, you will often uncover hidden roadblocks that can be addressed before it's too late.

Present Options

Most sellers make the mistake of presenting only one solution to meet the buyer's needs. It's a take-it-or-leave-it proposal. In doing so you ensure the client has a 50/50 chance of saying no. The best sellers are always looking for opportunities to improve those odds. If you offer two or three options, you increase your odds of the prospect doing business with you. Alan

Weiss says it best in his book *Value-Based Fees* (Pfeiffer, 2008): "When you offer options you change the conversation in the buyer's head from should we do business with you to how should we do business with you." I can tell you honestly that this advice has served the Engage community well, routinely increasing closing rates from 30 percent to 50 percent or higher in our own company as well as for The Privacy Information Agency (a privacy consulting company), Greenfield Solutions (a lead generation specialist), and MHPM Project Management (a project management company for large construction and building projects).

Those sellers who create a perpetual boom always offer a selection. In today's buying market, there's a fine line between the two or three options we mention above and a complicated pick list of components and variables. While the buying climate has changed, the old adage still applies: A confused buyer never buys. To create a Nonstop Sales Boom today you must keep it simple. Offer two or three ways the buyer can achieve his outcomes in packaged solutions. For example:

➤ In a software solution sale Carnegie Learning, a math
   curriculum software company, offers one option with onsite
   personal training, a second option with one-on-one coaching and
   training, and a third with remote training only. All three options
   satisfy the customer requirements but at different price points.

➤ In a product sales environment Trend Micro offers options for
   a one-year, two-year, or three-year licensing agreement. All will
   meet the client's requirements of antivirus protection but at
   different discount and commitment levels.

➤ In a service sales environment UBM, a research, patent
   protection, and publishing company, can offer off-the-shelf
   or customized research—both satisfying the client's need for
   research in a specific market area.

Present in Person

You will always increase your chances of winning the deal when you present your proposal in person. When at all possible, and at a minimum for your most important opportunities, get in the buyers' office to present your solution! You want a three-dimensional interaction, not the two dimensions of telephone or single dimension of email.

For some of you reading this book, personal meetings are easy because you live and sell in the same community. If this is your case, ensure you are presenting to buyers in person as often as possible. Doing so will ensure you are able to handle objections in real time, make adjustments, and get a sense of what is happening in the buyer's office.

For the rest of us, we have to adapt.

A leasing company I will call Francis Finance is a great example of the adaptation I am suggesting. Based in a small city in upstate New York and selling complicated leasing programs to premier universities and hospitals in major U.S. centers against national players such as GE Capital, Francis Finance faced an uphill battle. The national players had offices throughout the United States and could easily meet buyers in person at a moment's notice. This always provided a selling advantage. In an attempt to level the playing field, Francis Finance adapted a sophisticated use of webinar and web camera technology to place its sellers in the buyer's office. These virtual "in-person" presentations increased Francis Finance's closing ratio because they were able to build stronger rapport and trust by having the buyer see them. Even in cases where the buyer was only able to see the video but not broadcast video back (in other words, where the Francis Finance seller could not see the client to read the buyer's body and facial responses), *more proposals were won than with no video at all.*

Always Discuss Pricing

The easiest way to handle a pricing question is when you are face-to-face with the buyer. Yet, most sellers are scared to talk about money. Stop it!

When you are face-to-face with buyers (literally or virtually), look them squarely in the eyes and mention the price in the proposal with confidence. Of course, you should be doing this as part of the draft proposal meeting, as we discussed in Chapter 6, but repeat it when presenting the final proposal. *It's important that you see, and not just hear, their reaction.* Do they look relaxed and happy? Do their brows furrow? Do they fall off their chair? (That one's hard to miss.) Do they nod and look pleased?

Their response to your statement of the price will give you a strong indication as to what is required in the next pipeline stage, negotiation.

If you are sensing that they are happy with the price, ask candidly: "Does this fit with expectations?" or "Can we shake hands now and proceed?" or "So, is there anything stopping us from going forward?"

If you are sensing that they are uncomfortable with the pricing, deal with it now. Ask, "I sense there are some issues we need to resolve. What's on your mind?" or "Seems as though you are not a hundred percent happy with this proposal. What did I miss?" or "Have I made the ROI clear enough?"

Don't hide behind the proposal and refuse to talk about price. You must talk about money in order to secure a commitment quickly. Being uncomfortable at this stage will create more negotiation because you show the buyer that you lack confidence.

In order to exit the proposal stage, the following should occur:

> ➤ Discuss pricing and terms and know what the outstanding issues are.

> ➤ You must be told you are the winner (proceed to negotiation) or loser (proceed to closed/lost).

> ➤ The implementation phase is being discussed.

> ➤ Partner agreements are complete.

> ➤ An action plan with firm timelines is agreed to.

> ➤ Target close date is refined.

> ➤ You are guaranteed there are no other approvals or filters.

All these mean that a decision has been made. You are now ready to begin negotiating your final terms.

NEGOTIATION: BE INVOLVED AND HOLD FIRM

Submission of a final proposal is generally the penultimate step in the sales process, followed by degrees of negotiation, from a handshake to an arm wrestle. Legal departments on both sides will often be involved in the terms and conditions, and all individuals involved in the approval and signing stages are identified at this point. Note that all negotiations are not about pricing, nor do they all involve legal teams. And remember that while a negotiation indicates your deal is moving along, many deals fall apart during the negotiation if they sit too long without action. I once lost a deal due to the inaction of two legal teams. While they did nothing to move a deal to final conclusion a tornado ripped through Fort Worth and destroyed the headquarters building of my client. Six hundred thousand dollars gone in five minutes.

It is essential to manage this stage ruthlessly. Avoid abdicating responsibility for negotiation to the legal team, HR, or your manager. Of course, those teams may have to be consulted and apprised, but remember the longer the negotiation takes, the more at risk the opportunity is. Only you have the sense of urgency required to ensure the deal is moving along.

Towards the end of negotiation, you present the contract to the client, confirming the transaction path and required paperwork. The discussion of contract terms is the final piece of the negotiation stage. Let's take a look at the most common objections you will face and a model to apply that will help you handle them successfully.

My husband, Chris, loves to negotiate. So much so that whenever I need to buy new running shoes, he always buys a pair, too, with the hopes that he can swing a "deal" with the store by buying two pairs at once. Of course, he never gets a discount, but what I find fascinating is the number of times he asks for a discount, doesn't get it, and still buys the item at full price anyway.

I started thinking about this from the seller's perspective, by analyzing my own negotiation techniques and those of my clients. The questions I wanted to answer were: Exactly what makes a successful negotiator? And what do they do differently from the rest of us to get the price they want, while still leaving their customers feeling that they're getting a good deal? Thinking this way led me to the Engage Four-Step Negotiation Plan.

THE ENGAGE FOUR-STEP NEGOTIATION PLAN

This four-step process can help maximize your results each time you negotiate. Even better, I find it works wonders at every stage of the sales process, from negotiating price to discussing delivery, added product features, or any other terms your prospect is looking for a break on. These steps aren't necessarily easy, and in fact may take some discipline to implement. But for those of you who are willing to put in the effort, I promise that they will help make negotiation easier, and more natural. But prior to taking any actions in a negotiation you must get into the right frame of mind! Do you really believe that your products or services are worth the price you're charging? If the answer is no, then you won't be able to negotiate successfully. Period.

If you implement the four steps of this plan, shown in Figure 7–2, I can guarantee that those who truly believe that their products are worth the price they charge will walk away with more deals at full price. Those of you who think your products are too expensive, on the other hand, will continue to sell at a discount.

Figure 7–2. Profitable Negotiation

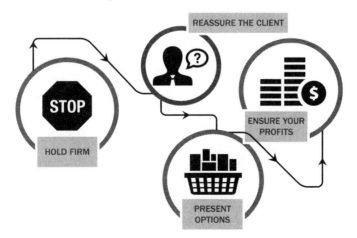

Step 1: Stop and Hold Firm

I notice that the top 20 percent in their fields never cave in on the first round. Don't give in to what your prospect is asking for right away. Remember, to those who love it, negotiation is a game. It's the "art of the deal." And to make those people happy, you must be willing to play.

ENGAGED SELLING:

The first sale is to yourself.

Nothing frustrates negotiators more than a salesperson who caves in and drops the price on the first round. If a client asks for a 20 percent discount and you immediately say yes, the prospect walks away feeling two things:

1. The price must have been inflated to start with.
2. I should have asked for a bigger discount. Next time, I will!

Neither of these outcomes is good for you. So the next time your prospect asks for a reduction in price, instead of just giving in, try responding with one of the following instead:

> ➤ *I can appreciate that you're looking for the best deal, but I can tell you that we've already given you our best price.*

> ➤ *You're smart to be looking for the best deal, but our pricing is always competitive, and I just can't go any lower.*

> ➤ *A discount? (in a surprised tone) What if your customers ask for a discount? If you don't give one, why ask me? If you do give one, you need me more than you think!*

This is the stage of negotiation during which your belief system is challenged. In order to be successful, you need to believe that you are already giving your prospect a great price. Early in her career Autumn Shirley from FundRaiser Software was once approached by a client who wanted a 10 percent discount on his software package. She was so shocked by his request—nobody had ever asked for a discount before, and she knew that she had the least expensive plan he was considering—that all she could say was, "What?" Not very professional, she admits. But he responded with "Well, I just had to ask anyway . . . ," and then paid full price for the software!

In my experience, typically 40 percent of buyers will respond the same way, with either "I had to ask" or "I just thought I'd try." Unfortunately, over 50 percent of sellers cave in on the first try and give the client the discount she's asking for. This is lose-lose for everyone. Your company reduces its profit. You reduce your commission. And your customer walks away dissatisfied because you refused to play the game.

Learn how to hold firm, and practice your responses in advance.

Step 2: Reassure the Client

Some buyers press ahead with their request for a discount even after you've given them one of the responses outlined above. The vast majority of them, however, are just looking for assurance that you really are giving them the best possible price, and there is no room to move. In other words, they want to make it a little uncomfortable for you, making sure that you sweat just a bit.

Don't buckle. Work to reassure your buyers that they're getting the best price, and remind them of all the hard work you've both put into the deal. Try something like: "We've been six months putting this project together. I would hate to see it not go ahead because we can't settle on price" or "I knew you'd be tough, so we provided aggressive pricing up front. I would hate to see this not go ahead because we haven't been able to meet your budget."

Engage clients find that an additional 20 percent of all business is closed at this stage—that's 60 percent of all business closed without ever having to reduce your price. Unfortunately, by this point, 80 percent of all salespeople have also already caved.

You do the math.

Step 3: Present Options

If after all this your prospects are still pushing for a discount (and 40 percent of them will be), take their minds off the cost. Find something else to give them that doesn't reduce your price: Free shipping. Extra manuals or training. A client profile on your website. What you choose will be specific to your business, your markets, and your client base. The key is to have the list of things you're willing to offer prepared in advance, so you can draw on it during the negotiation.

It's hard to think creatively in the heat of a negotiation, so planning ahead could give you a ready-made solution that leaves both you and the client feeling satisfied with the transaction. For a copy of the worksheet we developed to help you plan your "no money" concessions, go to www.nonstopsalesboom.com.

Step 4: Ensure Your Profit

Finally, if your buyers are still asking for a discount, you may have to give it to them in order to close the sale. But before you do, always ask them the following question: "What is important to you about an X percent discount?" or "Why is an X percent discount important to you?"

This question will flush out any last details that could help you find a different way to structure the terms and pricing and could allow you to retain your price while letting the customer walk away with needs met as well. If, however, you ultimately do have to reduce your price, make sure to follow these two rules:

1. **Never reduce your price without getting something in return.** Getting something in exchange for a pricing concession is key to managing customer expectations, i.e. communicating that future discounts will not be easily dished out. As with the "no money" concessions above, what you get in return for a price reduction will be unique to your business and markets, but could include references or case studies, a bigger order, introductions to senior-level executives, or partial payment up front. Again, prepare the list of concessions you will ask for in advance so you can respond quickly and smoothly.

Here are some examples:

➤ Project management software seller Lori asks for testimonials and referrals to other clients when providing a discount in a new market she is trying to open.

➤ Software seller Ryan offers a discount only if he can pick up the signed agreement on the same day that the offer is made.

➤ Sellers in the fertilizer business reduce their price only when the buyer doubles the order size.

➤ Consultants who follow Alan Weiss's approaches (in more than 50 books covering value and fees) will routinely offer a discount of 5 to 10 percent for full payment in advance, which concurrently allows them quick use of their money and guarantees that the client's project can't be cancelled internally.

2. **Get a firm verbal agreement from the buyers that this discount is all they will need to get the deal done.** Try asking them something like "I'm not sure if I can get you this price, but if I can, is it fair to say that we can go ahead?" or "I'm not sure I can get this discount for you. If I can, though, are you willing to sign the agreement this week?"

Nothing is worse than coming to an agreement on price (especially a reduced price!) only to find out that your prospects are still looking for other concessions. By asking them this last question, you can ensure you get all the issues on the table first, giving you the chance to deal with them fairly once and for all.

In order to exit the negotiation phase:

➤ The prospect must accept the presented proposal and negotiated terms.

➤ An outline of the implementation model is presented to the client.

➤ Roadblocks to implementation have been identified.

➤ All prospect approvals are in place and anyone with the power to block the project has given it a blessing.

➤ Negotiation is complete.

➤ Pricing in the opportunity is reviewed.

Once you exit the negotiation stage, 90 percent of the sales pipeline is complete. At this point, you've won or you've lost, and your sale is about to close!

COLLEEN'S POWER TIP #7: TURN CONFRONTATIONS INTO CONVERSATIONS

During the Participation state of engagement on your Sales Radar, you will be engaged in important, meaningful conversations with your buyers. Note the word "conversation" and not "pitch." You will ask questions and answer theirs and you can expect that they might even object to some of the points you make, including the price you offer. If you want to get to the close, then you need to do yourself a favor and stop thinking about these as stumbling blocks or objections; consider them as dialogue starters instead. My first rule of eliminating roadblocks is that it's always better that clients are still talking to you—no matter what they are saying—because once they stop talking the sale is over!

ENGAGED SELLING:

An objection, complaint, or question is a sign of interest. This is a *good* thing!

Think about it this way: Anyone, yourself included, who is about to make a large investment thinks twice about that decision before they commit. When a prospect is seriously considering buying, it's natural to reevaluate the criteria to make sure that the decision is the right one. Prospects are examining their own internal justifications and knocking the idea around vigorously to be sure it's not defective. They do this because they are seriously thinking about engaging!

If you continue to think of objections as confrontations you will always be in a defensive position with your buyer. When you are defensive you become argumentative. And when you are arguing, you are not creating an environment in which the buyer wants to buy. Do you want to buy from people who argue with you?

To help you maximize the conversation and minimize the confrontations, try the following.

Preempt the questions by bringing them up first. If you are the highest price, tell the buyer. If you can't get delivery on time, tell the buyer. Use these potential roadblocks as dialogue starters early in the Participation stage so the buyer cannot bring them up at the end of the sales process. If price always seems to become an issue for you, one of the most effective strategies is to preempt the question by dealing with it up front. Don't be afraid to talk about price. Train yourself to bring it up first and get it on the table as early as possible while qualifying your buyer. Try telling your buyer: *"You need to know that ours is not the cheapest product available. You'll always find someone who is less expensive than we are, and you'll always find someone who is more expensive than we are. We are always competitive, and always top quality. Knowing that we are not the cheapest, does it make sense for us to go ahead?"*

Prioritize the buying criteria. Ask tough questions about the criteria a buyer is going to use to make a decision and the importance of those criteria. For example, when sellers ask customers about buying criteria for fertilizer products, the response is usually "price, availability, and proof that it works." The best sellers on the team then respond with "Which of those is the most critical?" In less than half of the cases the answer is price. What are you assuming is the most important criterion for your buyer?

Don't be afraid to lose the sale. If you follow the prescription to a full sales pipeline that we detailed in Chapter 3, you will always have an overabundance of leads. This will give you the confidence to walk away from a buyer who is insisting that the most important criterion is something you can't or won't do. When you are free to walk away from a buyer, because you don't need the opportunity to succeed, your conversations will not take a desperate turn. You will stay relaxed and confident. My business partner and husband, Chris Voice, has a saying, "When you don't need the business, whatever the client decides is a win for you. You either win the sale or you win the time to work on another serious prospect."

Always act like you don't need the business. And, if you do, go back and work on your pipeline!

COLLEEN'S POWER TIP #8: USE THE ENGAGE SALE METHODOLOGY TO ANSWER QUESTIONS

If you reframe all objections as simple conversation starters you will reduce your anxiety about discussing them and will be able to work through them more effectively.

Use the Engage Selling SALE methodology, shown in Figure 7–3.

S = Stop and listen. That's right. I am saying that the best first step in answering questions or objections is to stop. Do nothing. Say nothing. Just for three seconds. Three seconds is long enough to create some space, some thinking time between the question and your answer, but not long enough to be awkward. Try it now just to see what I mean.

Now I know that some of you will have a hard time with absolute silence and so, if that's you, you can get away with a "hmm," "huh," "oh," or a shrug. And that's okay, as long as you are not committing to anything. Silence is best. In doing so you create some space between you and the question, you give your buyer a chance to fill in the gaps, and, most important, you ensure you do not interrupt the buyer.

A = Acknowledge the question. When you are selling you want your buyers to be talking and asking questions. That is a sign they are engaged. Silence or apathy is deadly. In order to keep the conversation going, thank them for making the statement. I am not advocating that you agree with them. Just that you acknowledge. A simple statement such as the ones below will do the trick:

> ➤ Thanks for sharing that.

> ➤ You raise an important point.

> ➤ I've never thought about it that way.

> ➤ You are smart to be concerned about that.

Figure 7–3. Engage SALE Methodology

- ➤ Thanks for bringing that up.

- ➤ I appreciate you being honest with me.

Showing appreciation will show clients that you care about the conversation. When you show that you care about the conversation, and value what buyers have said, they will say more. Remember, the more the buyers are talking the better chance you have to make the sale. The minute they shut up is the minute the sales start slipping away.

L = Ask a question and **listen** to the answer. Before you answer the question you must truly understand what the client is stating or asking. Use one of the following questions to clarify what the buyer is asking for and to help you better form an answer:

- ➤ What do you mean by that?

- ➤ How much of a discount are you looking for?

- ➤ Why is that important to you?

- ➤ Have you seen something else that includes that?

- ➤ What do you like about that approach?

- ➤ Is that a deal breaker for you?

- ➤ How much too high are we?

Continue asking questions until you truly understand the issue your buyer has raised. Only then will you be in a good position to answer it properly. Keep your questions conversational and always listen to the answer fully. Kevin Poppel from Ag-Power Enterprises always likes to advise his team: "Once the client has stopped talking wait at least two seconds before you say something. That's the best way to ensure you not only don't interrupt but you let the buyer completely finish his thought."

E = Provide an **example**.

The best way to answer questions from buyers is to use the words of your clients. Let's face it, your buyers will believe your clients more than they will believe you. You are, after all the "salesperson," trying to earn a living. While most sellers spend their time developing case studies and testimonials to provide outcomes data on their solutions for their website, the *best* sellers use this data to answer questions and deal with objections posed by clients. Let this become your million-dollar strategy—your killer app, the secret weapon that allows you to exceed your revenue goal year after year.

To create a Nonstop Sales Boom you must have buyers trust what you tell them and trust that they can obtain the results you indicate. And if they have an objection, they must trust your explanation on why it shouldn't be a roadblock. The September 2013 report from Nielsen (www.nielsen.com), "Global Trust in Advertising and Brand Messages," reports that testimonials are the single most trusted source of information for buyers, so using them for objections is the most important thing you can do for effective objection handling.

So here is what you need to do:

1. Sit down and write down your top three sales objections and questions.

2. For each objection and question, review your testimonial pool to find one that specifically addresses that objection. If you don't have one, go get one by identifying the customers who best demonstrate overcoming that objection and asking them for a testimonial (you can help them by drafting it for them).

3. Use those testimonials on your website and in your marketing materials.

Testimonials become the **E**—the **example** or **evidence**— in our SALE approach to handling questions. Chapter 12 shows you how to find, get, and *use* client testimonials to help overcome objections. In the meantime here are two examples.

A professional services seller gives this response—after having stopped, acknowledged, and listened—to a price objection: "At ABC Company they were also initially concerned about the price. What they found is that with the reduction in contractors required for data entry from three to one, they were able to save over $100,000 in labor costs in one year. This more than paid for the $24,000 project purchase and provided a four times return on investment in 12 months."

Lee Harbin at Dolphin Professional Services also stops, acknowledges, and listens effectively when addressing a question about the timing of delivery. He then states, "The implementation team at our largest client was originally concerned about our ability to deliver a project of this magnitude as well. What they discovered is that our structure allows us to ramp up quickly with the right resources, ensuring that we have never missed a deadline with them in over four years."

. . . .

The sale is closed and your job in Participation is done. Right? Not so fast.

In today's buying process, and to maintain a Nonstop Sales Boom, one more step is required before you can move on to Growth. While great sellers know how to close a sale effectively using the techniques described in this chapter, the best sellers know that in today's market a closed sale is only closed when the new client starts using your products. Client activation—implementing the product—is the final phase of Participation and the focus of Chapter 8.

CHAPTER 8

Participation Continues: Stay Engaged After the Close

TO CREATE A NONSTOP SALES BOOM, sellers must stay engaged in the last step of the Participation state on their Sales Radar. This is your product or service customer onboarding and project implementation step.

Traditionally implementation has been left to other departments—shipping, consulting, professional services, customer service, etc.—but it's exactly this disengagement from sales during delivery that can help to create sales busts. I'm not suggesting that sellers be in charge of the delivery. I am saying that they need to be *involved, present,* and *informed* of how the project is going at all stages of the work.

There are three critical reasons for why sales needs to be engaged during the delivery steps:

1. To reduce buyer's remorse with a quick start and early wins
2. To help customers take full advantage of the product or service
3. To communicate tangible and intangible value

Continued sales engagement in Participation will lead to success in the third and fourth states of client engagement on your Sales Radar, the Growth and Leverage states. Let's focus on the three benefits of continued Participation, beginning with reducing buyer's remorse.

HIT THE GROUND RUNNING: QUICK START, EARLY WINS, AND A THANK-YOU

The longer the gap between when a contract is signed and when the new customer receives and starts using your product, the more chance of buyer's remorse. Figure 8–1 shows this correlation.

As a seller, it's incumbent on you to ensure a quick delivery of your product. You can prevent buyer's remorse from happening by ensuring that the new customer quickly engages with the implementation/delivery team and sees quick results. Here in more detail are five activities that will set the stage for a productive and positive relationship between the selling company and the buyer. It all begins with a surprisingly simple but effective gesture.

Send a Thank-You Card

A handwritten thank-you note directly from you to the buyer the day after an agreement is signed is a good way to cement the deal and make sure your buyer feels good about the purchase. The bigger the deal, the faster it needs to arrive. Engage Selling clients who routinely close six- and

Figure 8–1. Buyer's Remorse

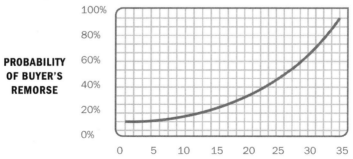

seven-figure deals are in the habit of sending a thank-you by courier the day after the contracts are signed.

Peter, a salesman with a Fortune 100 third-party logistics provider resisted my advice for a year, claiming I was being too soft and accusing me of trying to make him "sell like a girl." He finally capitulated, started sending thank-you notes, and achieved his entire annual sales targets in five months. A key reason for this was that each executive who received a thank-you card from Peter reached out to him personally during the implementation to thank him for the thank-you and to deepen the conversation about new opportunities.

In short, they liked buying from Peter more and so they trusted him more.

Even companies that have a no-gifts policy, and government departments, are allowed to accept a handwritten thank-you card.

Start Quickly

Even before the contract is signed you should introduce the client to your implementation process and delivery team. Even if that is only a team of one! Start this introduction process while you are still in the negotiation stage so that the buyer has a clear picture of what doing business with you will look like after the agreements are signed. During the final negotiations, lay out the implementation roadmap, set dates for the kickoff meeting, and introduce the team members or departments who will be involved in fulfilling their order. Show the customer how the delivery process will work.

This will have two positive effects:

1. When the clients are introduced to the post-sale service team and processes before the sale is closed, they start to imagine themselves using the product. This reduces last-minute cancellations and increases the speed with which the contract is closed.

2. When you start implementation planning before the contract is signed, you launch the actual implementation more quickly. This

ensures the client gets started quickly, which increases customer satisfaction, trust, and new opportunity potential. The trick is to *parallel the process during the negotiation steps.* You need to be thinking simultaneously, "How can I get this sale closed?" and "How can we get started on the implementation?"

Kent Blackburn is a top seller at the multinational professional consulting firm Modis. He implements this parallel process, introducing the team that will be recruiting and servicing the project before the contract is signed. He does this in a meeting during the final negotiations when he says, "I want to make sure you are comfortable with the team that will be supporting this project. Their names are Anna and Ron and they will be supporting you in the following way. Clients love working with them. Should I set up an introduction call now?"

Hilton Hotels is also excellent at this. It routinely involves its catering and events team on sales calls with the directors of sales as the sale is progressing. As the catering teams will be the ones with primary contact with the client after the meeting contract is signed, the earlier the relationship is formed, the better the client experience during the planning and the execution of the meetings. This helps to ensure fewer glitches in the planning process and during the event itself—and also increases the number of repeat corporate meetings.

> **ENGAGED SELLING:**
> Start the delivery before the client even realizes it's happening!

Rally the Troops

Once the contracts are signed your client wants results now! The best way to ensure these results is to kick the project off quickly and correctly. Within five days of the contract being signed, host a kickoff meeting or introduction call. Again, make arrangements for this call before the contract is signed so you can ensure everyone is able to fit the date on their calendars. Based on the size of your sale this meeting could be:

> ➤ A quick phone call to confirm your order on a product sale

> ➤ An introduction to the service team who will be fulfilling the order

> ➤ A one-hour teleconference with the participants to set goals and objectives

> ➤ An on-site kickoff meeting with the entire project team

If your sale requires a meeting with multiple people, make sure to include everyone who will be involved in the project; include those who were dissenters as well as your supporters. You will need them all on your side in order for this project to be a success.

A software company I work with that specializes in electronic patient records hosts an all-day, multidepartmental kickoff meeting. It knows that for a project to be successful, the clinician, doctors, technical staff, hospital administration, and community outreach teams have to be on board and supportive. As it can take up to a month to try to coordinate all these departments, the sales team works to put this meeting on the schedule at the same time that they are presenting the final proposal to the client. While the lawyers are busy negotiating the terms of the contract, the sellers and the buyers are busy negotiating a time for the kickoff meeting. Knowing that implementation meetings are being set up has the added bonus of keeping the lawyers on track for signing the final contracts!

Highlight Early Wins

Help the prospect realize value quickly by highlighting early wins, no matter how small. Right from the first week of implementation, look for signs of success. If deadlines are met by both sides, highlight them. If the product is implemented fully, congratulate them. If you receive notice that a delivery is received, call the customer and share the excitement. The more successes you highlight, the more successes the customers will find on their own. When they do this, it's hard to have time for buyer's remorse. At the same time they will start to want to do more business with you because they associate you with success.

Collect Internal Testimonials

Most sellers make the mistake of thinking that if there is good news inside a company it will be shared. Only bad news goes viral. In order to ensure good news is shared on your project, you must be the conduit of that information. In the same way you collect testimonials to share outside this project to attract net new opportunities, you need to collect testimonials inside the client to highlight the value you are bringing to the buyer.

During the quarterly review process on-site at Wilhelmsen Ship services in Taiwan, the sales and technical teams started sharing internal project success stories between departments and based on the KPIs—those key performance indicators we spoke of in Chapter 1— that had been established for the contracts. Within 12 months of sharing these cross-departmental successes, client defections ceased, complaints were decreased, and per-client year-over-year growth increased to record amounts.

HELP CUSTOMERS TAKE FULL ADVANTAGE

You'd be surprised at how often customers are only using a small fraction of the potential of the product or service they just bought. Tammy Marge, a sales executive from a consumer credit company, shared with me that the CMO of a large client who provided her with $45 million in revenue each year said to her, "Tammy, I can't do anything else until I have fully leveraged everything I already own. I feel like I've bought a DVR but all I know how to do is record. Can you help me understand all the other functionality?" Once Tammy and her team showed the CMO and his team the full power of the solution, which brought them immediate and lasting new results, the CMO was willing to refer her to other opportunities. Now, as part of each client's rollout, Tammy and her team ensure the product is fully utilized as quickly as possible so that the client receives the highest value the most quickly.

The faster your clients implement fully, the faster they will accomplish dramatic results. If they start by only using 10 percent of what's available, and then slowly go to 20 percent, and at the end of the year 30 percent, they're only getting a small amount of the full value. It might take them three years at this rate to realize full value and that's not fast enough. By then, your competition has already started a replacement campaign.

But if they're engaging fully right from the start, they are getting full value right from the start. And with it, massive results. For example:

1. When implementing new software from companies such as Infusion CRM, FundRaiser Software, and Attivio, clients who don't engage in training take longer to implement and use software packages than those who do. These untrained clients also miss implementing key features that can speed results and improve efficiencies. As one of *Inc. Magazine*'s fastest-growing companies, Shopify.com has resolved this issue by adding a team of inside implementation specialists called "gurus" who work with every new buyer to help him or her get started quickly.

2. An agricultural products retailer phones all farmers after delivery of products to the farm to make sure they arrived as expected and are being applied correctly. Spot checks are completed throughout the planting and fertilizing seasons to make sure protocols are being applied correctly.

3. Kim King, owner of LimeLight Communications Group Inc., ensures a quick turnaround between the time that the contracts are signed with entertainers and the time the client meets them for the first time. Having a kickoff meeting or a pre-event call before the start of the project ensures that clients can fully leverage the speakers and entertainers they have booked. This increases the experience of the audience and the profitability of the client.

4. The faster a retailer client of a national crop nutrition manufacturer sells the product to a farmer, the faster the retailer makes money

and can reorder. To help with this process, the manufacturer recently added an inside sales team to handle the post-sale service and delivery process. Doing so ensures that the product is received and stored properly and that the retailer has a resource to answer questions about how to sell and apply it. The result is faster sales to farmers.

5. Protus IP (formerly the makers of a personal faxing company until it was bought) discovered that those clients who were fully utilizing the products within the first five days were those who also stayed the longest, bought the most, and referred generously. As a result Protus implemented a sales plan for its teams to make post-sales check-in calls to every new client to ensure all the user licenses were installed and being used within five business days of an order being placed.

6. Mary Story of Optimus Staffing drives all her new employees to work on their first day on the job to ensure they are accepted, trained, and onboarded correctly. Ensuring the client does not delay getting the new employees up to speed quickly ensures they are productive before noon on the first day!

Of course, the examples above are all from clients who create Nonstop Sales Booms. They understand that if the client does not participate fully during the Participation state on the Sales Radar, the client's entrance into the Growth quadrant will be slowed.

Conduct a Three-Month Health Check

One way to showcase clients' success and also catch any problems early is to run a "health check" with them within three months of your product or service delivery. The health check is designed to do two things:

1. Uncover any usage problems or client concerns.

2. Identify any gaps in utilization that could be filled to ensure your client is using as much of your service as possible.

Complete a health check by asking the following questions:

> ➤ *How has your experience been so far?*

> ➤ *What results have you seen?*

> ➤ *How are you utilizing/enjoying _____ ?* (Ask this question for each major functional area.)

> ➤ *What changes do we need to make to _____?*

The inside sales team in the U.S. offices of Trend Micro has employed a customer service team to call all new clients at the three-month and six-month mark of their new purchase to ensure that the products have been installed and are working properly. In doing so, they improved their renewal rates—already well above industry average—by 5 percent in just six months, and have maintained higher than expected revenue growth year over year.

During a health check, your job is threefold. First, you must find out if there have been any challenges in using the product so that you can resolve them immediately. When problems exist, escalate the call to a manager, service, or help desk. Ideally, you can identify and solve the problem on this call. Second, discover any facets of the product that are not being currently used so that you can introduce them. Offer a quick overview on the sections not being implemented and showcase the results others have received from using them. Offer to schedule a more detailed training session if required and ask if other users should be included as well. And third, capture any early success stories and share them internally with their colleagues as well as within your own company.

Customers don't care about features and benefits. They only care about value and achieving their objectives. They're no longer asking the question, "How can this help me?" They're asking, "How can this make me the best?" Think about that change. It's profound.

ENGAGED SELLING:

Remember that *you* need to be the bearer of good news. Don't expect it to travel through your client's business on its own.

"How can this make me the best?" means that the client expects results and wants them quickly. As a seller, using your Sales Radar as a guide, in the Participation state you must deliver high value quickly by ensuring the customer is fully using your products and services.

COMMUNICATE THE TANGIBLE AND INTANGIBLE VALUE

To create immediate and lasting results for your clients, you must be acutely aware of all the value that you deliver and not be afraid to communicate this value regularly. Regardless of the industry you focus on, there is *always* both tangible and intangible value achieved.

Measure the Tangible

Tangible value is *objective and measurable* value. For example, it would include data such as the following:

> ➤ You help a buyer reduce costs by 10 percent by offering to streamline a process.

> ➤ Your system reduces employee turnover from 25 percent to 15 percent with a better hiring strategy.

> ➤ Your automated system reduces the time it takes to complete a task by 50 percent by eliminating redundancy.

> ➤ Your training increases sales by 20 percent by implementing an online ordering system.

Tangible value is always objective and readily identifiable. It's focused on quantifiable results and based on agreed-on KPIs. For example, a client emailed me last week to report that since working with Engage his closing ratio had improved from 1:12 to 1:6. Now that's a tangible value!

To find out what tangible value your clients are benefitting from, ask the following questions:

1. How are my clients saving money as a result of doing business with us?

➤ How much are they saving?

➤ What are they doing with this savings?

2. How are my clients making more money as a result of doing business with us?

➤ How much are they making?

➤ What are they doing with this extra revenue?

3. How are my clients saving time as a result of doing business with us?

➤ How much time are they saving?

➤ What are they doing with this time?

Once you have these results documented, you can communicate them to your client during annual business reviews, project meetings, and other conversations with buyers and influencers within your client. Don't be afraid to share the results internally. Many buyers don't share good news internally with their own peers, not because they are not proud of their results but because they are too busy, often putting out fires, to be remembering the great value they are receiving. Be the bearer of good news for your clients *and make sure they all know how they are benefitting from you.*

Intangible Value Is Just as Important

Communicating tangible value is not enough. To create a Nonstop Sales Boom you must document and communicate *intangible* value as well. Intangible and tangible value are not mutually exclusive. They are complementary. Consider intangible value as value-added, or value that is received that is not directly related to what your product or service does. You might consider intangible value as indirect or peripheral.

For example, while you are helping clients reduce their costs by 10 percent, you can also be providing them expert information at roundtable discussions, helping them benchmark their success against the success of others in their industry, and introducing them to a network of others in your community who can help with additional best practices. Intangible value can be delivered because you have become a "one-stop shop" for all research in your field, or because you provide industry information in areas to which they didn't have access before you, or even because you can make introductions to peers that they were unable to meet. In one case, a client of mine provided intangible value by introducing her buyer to a network of future clients not considered before.

I'm a member of Alan Weiss's global community of experts, and as I write this, many such members are interacting on AlansForums.com, whether he is present or not. That's a huge indirect benefit to his clients, and intangible value accrues to him for providing the opportunity, whether they use it frequently or infrequently.

An intangible value could also be that you provide networking introductions or opportunities. For example, one of my coaching clients, a huge global bank, offers an opportunity for its network of CEO buyers to attend luncheons and meet each other in small, intimate, and noncompetitive settings. They are able to have discussions about their business, ask questions, and share ideas in a way not often granted to them in their day-to-day lives. CEOs at these events routinely state that this "added benefit" of doing business with the bank is a key reason for them to stay a client. It's this strong intangible value that helps our sellers be successful maintaining their current clients as well as attracting new clients.

Obviously, tangible value is key. But in the best situation, you want to highlight both. Kinnser Software's competitors speak only of tangible value to clients—cost savings, efficiencies, labor reductions—while Kinnser speaks about these tangible benefits as well as the intangible value. The intangible benefits a buyer receives when doing business with Kinnser include:

1. Being part of the fastest-growing home health care community
2. Using a software developed with input from the client industry
3. A help desk based in Texas
4. A team of salespeople located across the country
5. Access to trainers who are insiders to the community such as registered nurses, former billing specialists, and agency owners

6. Invitations to user conferences and access to other agencies for best practice sharing and seminars

Kinnser founders Scott and Chris Hester understand that their buyers in home health tend to default toward a nurturing, caring, and nonconfrontational business approach—and away from business decisions solely based on cost savings, labor reductions, and profits. By showcasing and delivering both tangible and intangible value to their clients, the Kinnser sales team ensures that results are achieved quickly.

ENGAGED SELLING:

You need to add both tangible and intangible value, by delivering direct and indirect benefits, and you need to inform the prospect specifically about them!

TWO-LISTED SELLER: HOW GLEN KEEPS HIS CLIENTS INFORMED AND HAPPY

I assume that all of you reading *Nonstop Sales Boom* are focused on building long-term relationships with your clients. As such, I encourage you to sit down with your clients (or perhaps just those clients you want to keep!) twice per year to understand, document, and communicate the tangible and intangible value the client is experiencing.

Ask specifically:

➤ How are we helping you accomplish your goals?

➤ What other benefits are you receiving from us?

➤ Who else in the company needs to be aware of this value?

One of our clients in the financial services sector does this very well. He sits down every year with his biggest customers with two lists. The first list compares the client-furnished key performance indicators and whether they have been accomplished or not. If the KPIs were not met, Glen is transparent with his buyers in stating why results were not as expected and presenting ideas to improve the result for the next reporting period. He and the client then discuss what each of them can do to improve and create the implementation plan to ensure that these improvements take place.

The second list Glen provides is the intangible value the client has received across all departments. While Glen may be having this discussion with a bank vice president in Credit Services he will list intangible value received from IT departments, human resources, marketing, and others in order for the buyer to understand the full range of benefits Glen's solutions are providing the organization. These intangible values often include improved employee satisfaction, reduced turnover, higher levels of employee engagement, and improved client satisfaction. (There's a reason my company is called Engage Selling *Solutions*!)

In delivering this list, Glen associates testimonials and real-life evidence for each intangible value to showcase both the client's department as well as his own influence on the buyer's overall success. In doing so, Glen has been able to nurture a $45 million client for a number of years despite the economy, not only maintaining it but growing it year by year; this relationship, according to the executive team of Glen's bank, is "invaluable to the success of every department at our bank."

COLLEEN'S POWER TIP #9: ELEVEN TANGIBLE WAYS TO CREATE INTANGIBLE VALUE

There are many ways to create intangible value for your clients. Choose the ones that are best suited to your business and be sure to remind your clients regularly how they have benefitted from your relationship.

1. Offer user group meetings where your clients can get together as peers for discussions.

2. Make introductions to other professionals who can offer advice complementary to yours.

3. Refer new clients or new employees to your clients.

4. Invite your clients to social events, community events, or fundraisers to help them raise their profile.

5. Nominate your buyers for local or national business awards.

6. Send your clients interesting and relevant information on their business, industry, and markets.

7. Place buyers on client advisory panels to showcase them as leaders in their industry and be part of the development of leading-edge products and services.

8. Provide awards inside your community for "best of" clients.

9. Offer VIP plant or site tours of your facility to show them a behind-the-scenes look at how you are serving them best.

10. Invite buyers to be your guest at important industry trade shows and conferences. Offer to submit papers or be a reference on their behalf to speak at these shows, thereby raising their profile.

11. Provide content for them to publish in their own newsletters, blogs, and media sites.

. . . .

The best sellers, those who use the Sales Radar every day to create their Nonstop Sales Booms, know that closing only really takes place when the client is fully enabled. They have redefined the closing stage in their pipelines from simply meaning "The contract is signed" to meaning "The client is participating in our solutions fully." Only clients who are getting the full use of your product and service, and who are clearly informed of all the tangible and intangible value that results from the purchase, will be in a position to *grow* even more profitably for you. Not only will they give you more business, but they will also become your fans and advocates. You will thus be able to take them to the final state of engagement, *leveraging* their support into more sales from new customers. You will then have swept the full circle of the Sales Radar.

In the remaining chapters of this book, we cover the last two states of client engagement in our Sales Radar: Growth and Leverage.

PART IV

GROWTH

WELCOME TO PART 4. While you now have all the tools you need to begin your Nonstop Sales Boom, we're now ready for the excitement of the Growth state of engagement on your Sales Radar. In the Attraction state of engagement, clients were just prospects—unknown to you at the beginning but then, having come into contact with your company through one of your many Attraction tools and resources, interested in learning more. In the Participation state of engagement, clients became steadily more engaged as they moved through the qualification, evaluation, decision-making, and final negotiation stages of the sales pipeline, eventually signing a deal with you. In the final phase of the Participation state of engagement, the purchase is implemented, the first wins are logged, and clients are generally informed and satisfied.

In the Growth state, we're going to take a closer look at the clients we are currently serving to determine which ones have the greatest potential for new and bigger sales: what I call "incremental sales opportunities." We'll then focus our efforts on growing our sales to those current clients.

The finest salespeople balance attracting new clients with growing the revenue from their current clients. Remember from Chapter 3 that the percentage of sales from new clients and current clients depends on the circumstances of your firm. A young company might require as much as 80 percent of sales to come from new clients, and 20 percent from current clients, while a company with limited production capacity and little room for growth might get 90 percent of its revenue from current clients. Whatever the figures, the next two chapters will show you how to get the most from the clients showing up in the Growth sector of your Sales Radar.

CHAPTER 9

Who Wants More? Discovering the Best and the Worst of Your Current Customers

NOT ALL CURRENT CLIENTS are created equal nor should they be treated as equal. Your ability to create a Nonstop Sales Boom relies on your ability to classify your clients correctly so you can manage your ROI profitably. Far too often I see sellers spending their valuable time with clients who are not profitable or who are not in the Growth quadrant.

This is a shame because it's so easy to fix.

You must play favorites! While for some of you that feels like heresy, for perpetual sales boomers it's the norm. Let's be honest, some clients are never going to grow and some clients are vacuuming up the profits from your business faster than a Dyson! Yet, other current clients have huge potential or at least provide a steady stream of healthy profits. You only have eight hours a day. Don't you want to spend the majority of them with people who can add to your personal and corporate profits?

Before you enter the Growth state on the Sales Radar, the questions to ask are: "How do I identify which clients are the most lucrative for me to be spending my time with?" and "Who should I minimize my time with or eliminate completely?" The answers to

ENGAGED SELLING:

As a seller you must allocate your time based on the profit potential for each client.

these vital questions are revealed through a segmentation technique I call the Sales Leader Classification Model (SLCM).

SIZE AND *POTENTIAL* SIZE BOTH MATTER

Some of you reading this book have worked with me over the years. And as a result, you have seen the power of incremental sales opportunities (ISOs). One of my favorite examples of this is Donald Leblanc at The Placement Office, who added a million dollars in sales in one year to his business simply by focusing on selling incremental services to his best clients.

Most companies make a critical mistake when classifying accounts. They consider their best clients as those that currently spend the most. The SLCM fixes that mistake because it forces you to classify accounts based on a combination of *present levels of engagement* and the *future sales potential.* Classifying accounts is not a linear exercise to decide which is the biggest. It must also be about which has the most potential.

For example, a client that is currently giving you 10 percent of its available business might seem small, but it can also be a client that has great ISOs for you. Think of all the potential sales just waiting for you to take! This client should be carefully nurtured. On the other hand, you have a client who is currently giving you 100 percent of its business. There's no ISO, but this is still a profitable client you want to keep. In fact, both clients are valuable, but offer different potential for growth of sales. Through the SLCM shown in Figure 9–1, you will identify the clients that are unprofitable, profitable but with little room for growth in sales, and profitable with a high potential of more sales.

Figure 9–1. Sales Leader Classification Model

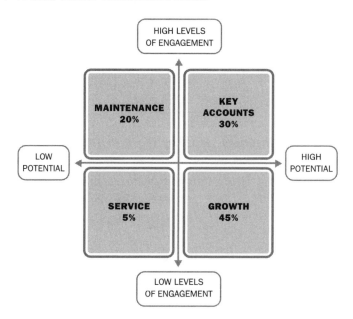

NOT ALL CLIENTS HAVE THE GROWTH GENE

If we examine the SLCM, we notice that there are two considerations. The first consideration, on the vertical axis of our model, is the level of engagement. High levels of engagement occur when both you and the client have developed multiple relationships between your organizations. When you are deeply engaged, you are entwined in the company account and move from being a partner to being an insider. When you are an insider the most profitable ISOs appear.

A highly engaged client might have the following relationships in place:

1. The seller has a key relationship with the buyer, the second and third in command, and the project manager.

2. The seller's manager has a relationship with the buyer's CEO.

3. The seller's project manager has a relationship with the implementation manager at the client's site.

4. The seller's accounts receivable department has an open (and friendly) dialogue with the buyer's accounts payable department.

5. The users of the product have a relationship with the customer support team and trainers.

Contrast this to low levels of engagement where you are considered a "vendor." In a low-engagement environment a seller might be the single point of contact with a single buyer inside the client.

On the horizontal axis of the model we have potential. Potential is simply defined as the future revenue potential this client possesses. Ask yourself:

➤ Is there a high potential for ISO?

➤ How many other competitors are selling to the buyer?

➤ How many other buyers exist in this client?

➤ What percentage of the total available business am I getting?

The answers to these questions will determine the scale of the potential for ISOs at your new client.

When you segment your current clients based on the combination of these two criteria, all your clients will end up in one of four quadrants of the SLCM.

Service Accounts: Low Engagement, Low Potential

Clients with low engagement and low potential are defined as *service accounts*. These are clients who call you sporadically for small orders but who are not interested in working with you on a larger or customized solution. They buy the same products on each order and price-check every quote. Work with them quickly and professionally but reactively when they call. Check in with them only on an annual basis and be sure to put them on any regular company correspondence, but don't be proactive about presenting new solutions with them. These are clients who treat you as a vendor, shop around for every purchase, and are not interested in a long-term relationship.

Maintenance Accounts: High Engagement, Low Potential

Clients with high engagement and low potential are *maintenance accounts*. Typically, these are large clients that are profitable but they are already maximized on your solutions and cannot grow. In some situations, they come to you because you have the only solution in the marketplace and it's the only thing they require from you. In other cases, your maintenance clients might be your most loyal, oldest clients who give you 100 percent of their available budgets. Whatever the case, you do not want to lose these clients since they represent a significant and consistent base of your income. For our agronomy sellers, the maintenance client is the retailer whose farmers buy all seeds, chemicals, and fertilizers from the retailer and sell back all their grain to the retailer's grain elevator. There is simply no more business a farmer can do with that retailer. Maintenance clients must be maintained profitably but they will never provide the growth you need to maintain your Nonstop Sales Boom.

Growth Accounts: Low Engagement, High Potential

Clients with high levels of growth potential and low levels of engagement are your *growth accounts*. These are excellent clients that are new in your community. While they represent excellent growth potential, you have not yet created the required relationships to ensure the potential can be converted into ISOs.

Nurturing and relationship building are required.

Carnegie Learning is a leading authority on math curricula in American schools. If it sells a middle school math program to a school district with only middle schools in the district, this client would have low potential because there is no ability to grow past the current schools already using the program. Therefore, this would be a maintenance account.

However, if Carnegie sells the same middle school math program to a district that has an elementary and high school system, this client would initially be a growth account because there are two additional ISOs for the seller, even though the initial level of engagement is low. This account would remain a growth account until Carnegie builds multiple relationships to include administrators and curriculum directors in the elementary and high school systems, and a few teachers within all three systems. At this point you could consider transitioning this growth account to a key account because the level of engagement has increased from low to high.

Key Accounts: High Engagement, High Potential

Clients with high levels of engagement and high potential for growth are your *key accounts*. These are clients that have welcomed relationship development with your teams and consider you more than a trusted partner—they consider you an insider. The people with whom you have high-trust relationships in key accounts are actively working with you and your teams to grow the involvement. In one case you might be working in partnership for a new release of your product or version of your solution, and in another you might have service staff embedded on-site helping them with implementation. A top seller at Helms Briscoe in New York manages the travel and events for a large American television network. He has three staffers working for him who are located physically on-site at the client, to ensure a high level of service—and to maintain his company's insider status. New opportunities for growth are more readily created when you are an insider and *have access to unique information and insights afforded only to those in high-trust positions.*

Another example comes from my own experience selling to the U.S. Air Force. While I only had small amounts of business with a few major commands, I knew that the potential for the account was $13 million (extremely high potential!). Because my sales team had relationships with the commanders of eight major commands, my implementation team had relationships with the civilian decision influencers, my development team had relationships with the technologists doing the required testing, and I had a relationship with the general in charge (extremely high engagement!), we classified this as a key account. I was able to grow the account over time to the largest account in our company's history because I was discriminating about how the team used their time and resources on this key account relative to other maintenance, growth, and service accounts. Had I only classified this account based on the amount of the initial sale, I might not have spotted the huge ISO—nor built the relationships required to close it.

In Chapter 10, we're going to explore ways to grow the sales of our clients with high potential. But first, there is some unpleasant business to take care of: firing the current customers who not only have no potential for future growth, but are actually costing you money every day.

FINDING THOSE YOU SHOULD FIRE: SEGMENTING THE SERVICE ACCOUNTS

The SLCM is valuable not only because it describes the four types of clients you have, but also because it tells you what to do with them. You continue to sell to your maintenance accounts, with whom you're fully engaged, but don't expect the figures per sale to rise. You're also fully engaged with your key accounts, and here there is great potential for growth in sales to these clients, so you'll want to focus on them. Your growth accounts also represent great potential for growth in future sales, but you first have to deepen your relationship with them.

And then you have the service accounts. This is not a homogeneous category, as are the others. If you segment your service accounts carefully, you will actually find three groups emerging, reflecting clients with a high potential for growth, low potential for growth, or no potential for growth (or, to paraphrase a classic film: the good, the not-so-good, and the ugly). Let's explore these three segments in more detail and see why the no-potential service accounts should be fired.

The Good: High Potential for Growth

Twenty percent of service accounts will become growth accounts over time. Unlike all other service accounts, these accounts are worth nurturing proactively. These are service accounts that spend the most and have the highest levels of engagement compared to other service accounts. In

Figure 9–2, these high-potential accounts are those accounts that sit in the right-hand corner of the Service quadrant, above the dashed arrow.

Some examples include:

> ➤ A first-time passenger on an airline pays for a seat in first class. While this passenger has engaged for the first time with this airline transactionally, he or she represents a good future potential for the airline based on the fare class paid. This passenger should be nurtured differently than a first-time passenger in the lowest-fare class.

> ➤ A customer places an order for a single product from your website; after the product is delivered, you discover that the customer is a leader in an organization of thousands of employees.

> ➤ A client buys one product from you annually and one year the client's company is acquired by a much larger organization representing growth opportunities for you.

> ➤ A retail banking customer starts a business that requires new corporate banking opportunities.

Figure 9–2. The Sales Leader Classification Model and Changing Levels of Engagement

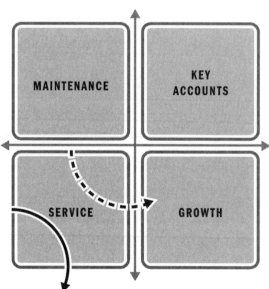

The Not-So-Good: Poor Potential for Growth

In the middle of the Service quadrant are those profitable transactional accounts that you want to keep but service reactively and passively. Sixty percent of your service accounts fall into this category and on the model they sit between the dashed and solid arrows in Figure 9–2. They have average revenue and average levels of engagement with you. Most important, they are easy to deal with, rarely negotiate, and make decisions quickly.

Some examples include:

> ➤ You're a staffing agency and a hotel in your territory hires three of your temporary workers to help out during the holiday season in banquets. It has limited capacity for growth because the holiday season is defined and it cannot handle any more banquets because of space and date restrictions.
>
> ➤ You're a research company and you sell a report to a business each year. It buys the annual updates but it has no requirements for other reports.
>
> ➤ You're a software company and a small business buys software from you and renews the licenses each year but it is not growing to expand its licensing requirements.

The Ugly: No Potential for Growth

At the bottom left of the Service quadrant you'll find accounts with the poorest value. They spend the least, have the lowest levels of engagement, and consider you only as a vendor. They are often difficult to work with and are demanding. These clients are serial shoppers, negotiate heavily for concessions, and take a long time to make decisions. They are clients that you knew you should not have engaged with at all, and are now regretting it. These are the clients that should be fired.

If you're not sure who should go, here's a hint: Fire any service account that consistently exhibits the following behaviors:

- ➤ Insists on "negotiating" every price and term in your agreement
- ➤ Consistently asks for concessions that make doing business risky, such as extended payment terms, payment on delivery or at the end of a project, or money-back guarantees
- ➤ Doesn't respond in a timely manner
- ➤ Is overly demanding or rude
- ➤ Won't answer business-related questions to help you qualify the business
- ➤ Is not profitable

HOW TO FIRE A CLIENT

If you are miserable working with a client and you know that they are not profitable for you or your company, they are not going to be well served by you. And, if they are not being well served by you, they will not achieve their desired results and you have created a lose/lose situation. You're not helping them reach their objectives and they're not helping you reach yours.

The easiest, most respectful way to fire a client is:

1. **Call them. Do *not* use email.** Thank them for their business to date and *explain that you're not the best fit for them moving forward.* Try, "Thanks for working with us. At this point I don't think we are the right fit for helping you meet your goals." Always keep the focus on their interests.

2. **Be professional.** Don't use this call as an excuse to tell the client all the things that are wrong with them and their approach. Simply tell them that *they will be more successful working with another company.*

3. **Recommend another option for them, even a direct competitor, so that they can find a new home quickly.** For example, I always have a list of other sales consultants that would be a better fit for prospects that call Engage if I don't want to work with them.

Of course, it's not just poor-quality service accounts—those "ugly" accounts you regret ever having engaged with—that you should fire. Clients in any category of the SLCM can also be candidates for firing. There are other issues besides profitability!

Here are other clients you should consider firing, no matter where they place on the model:

1. **The "no one else matters" client.** These are the clients that expect you to work only for them and all the time. They drag quick calls into 90-minute meetings and 90-minute meetings into all-day events. They call you on the weekends on your cell phone. I've learned over the years that these relationships almost never work and, indeed, often turn ugly when their inappropriate expectations aren't met or when you are not available to them when they expect it. I fired one of these "I expect you to be in my office at 8 A.M. tomorrow" clients after only one month. Life's too short.

2. **The "sword of Damocles" client.** Walk away from any client who constantly peppers you with threats. Perhaps they threaten to withhold payment, leave for the competition, or shop your solution around. Whatever the threat, you can't do your best work for them if you are constantly under negative pressure. Recently a staffing agency I work with fired a customer who used at least one "or else I will . . ." in every meeting. Morale in the office improved immediately and the client was replaced within the month.

3. **The "check is in the mail" client.** You are not a bank, even if you work for a bank! Cash flow is the lifeblood of any business. When clients start abusing the financial aspect of the relationship, talk to them immediately. If they will not rectify the situation, stop work until they do, or fire them immediately. If a client stands to decimate your cash flow and profitability, fire him right away, no matter how prestigious. Recently a software client of mine cut off software support and turned off the online database for a client

who was 90 days late with payment. The check was couriered overnight that day.

4. **The "four letter" client.** Some language is not acceptable when directed at people. Everyone has his or her limits. And, while it's one thing to swear like a longshoreman as your golf ball slices into the woods, it's another for you or your team to be sworn at, insulted, or berated. After taking a beating from the purchasing agent at a Fortune 100 company twice, I told him the abuse of my team and me had to stop. He apologized both in our conversation and in an email. But the very next time we met, the abuse resurfaced with language that would put Al Pacino's Scarface to shame. I called the client to terminate the relationship, to which he said something unprintable but wonderfully inventive. That quote quickly became the team motto and is still being trotted out as a joke in internal sales meetings.

5. **The prima donna client.** Success and failure should be a shared experience. When you and the client achieve a desired outcome, it should be celebrated as a team effort. And, when something goes awry, there shouldn't be any finger-pointing on either side. Each accepts responsibility for his or her part in what went wrong and quickly resolves the issue. Rarely is a mistake one-sided but if it is (and all on you), accept responsibility immediately and resolve the issue. If a client is continually parading your joint success as his or her own singular success while at the same time foisting all the blame on you for failures, your relationship is one-sided and can never be good for you, no matter how profitable.

Firing a client may mean a short-term hit to the organization's profits, but it's critical for the long-term emotional health of your team and the company. Firing a client now not only frees up time for you to spend on more profitable clients, it also provides a boost of morale internally. When you step up and fire a bad customer, you win everyone's trust, loyalty, and respect.

Especially your own.

COLLEEN'S POWER TIP #10: SET YOUR OWN MINIMUM PROFIT PER CLIENT

Supermodel Linda Evangelista famously said that she would "not roll out of bed in the morning for less than ten thousand dollars." It was a smart business move on her part. Ten thousand dollars was her minimum profit per shoot. Your Sales Radar must also have a minimum profit, a minimum profit per client. This is the number, expressed in either revenue or margin, that you will not work for less than (or as the queen might say, "the number for less than which you will not work"). Clients above this minimum can either stay as service accounts or be reclassified as growth accounts. Clients below it must be fired.

Resellers will often state their minimum profit as the margin they make between the buying and selling price; product companies, as the margin between the manufacturing costs and the selling price; and service companies base their minimum on the project fee or daily rate minus the cost of the employee. You can also keep it simple and base your minimum profit on the revenue size of the project. Whatever way you choose is fine as long as you implement the practice daily—no exceptions!

As an added bonus, if you start tracking the minimum profit on your current clients, you will find yourself also starting to use it in your client Attraction phase and avoid bringing on new unprofitable clients in the future.

. . . .

Now that you have classified your accounts and have determined which ones to cut, you are ready for Growth. Let's turn our attention to the positive activities in the Growth state of engagement on the Sales Radar: growing sales to current customers so they can contribute to your Nonstop Sales Boom.

CHAPTER 10

Entering the VORTEX: How to Build a Path to High Engagement and New Opportunities

IN CHAPTER 9, we focused on segmenting our customer base according to potential for growth, and identifying and removing from our customer base unprofitable customers with no potential for growth.

In this chapter, we will focus on growing the three customer segments—service, growth, and key accounts. Each segment does not require a separate growth strategy, because the core strategy is the same for all three segments: More engagement means more business. The deeper your relationship with the customers in those segments, and the more people you know within the customer organization, the more likely that you are going to perceive and create sales opportunities because you understand the client's needs and potential needs. Similarly, you are much more likely to be approached with sales opportunities by clients who trust you and know what you can offer.

As shown in Figure 10–1, developing the depth and the breadth of your customer relationship means a higher level of engagement between you and your customer. As a result, your service and your growth accounts will move toward the key accounts quadrant, and your key accounts will move farther into the sweet spot in the northeast corner of your matrix. The result of this movement is more revenues for all three types of accounts. (Remember, your maintenance accounts are already maxed out, so we're not going to talk about them in this chapter.)

Once you have a close and productive relationship with as many people connected to the customer as possible, the next step is to exploit those contacts with targeted discussions, interactions, and activities that have the best chances of leading to new sales.

In the first part of this chapter, we will focus on deepening your current relationships and multiplying your contacts throughout the customer organization to give you the maximum opportunity to make new sales. In the second part of the chapter, we will introduce the VORTEX Framework, with components and activities that will transform relationships and new contacts into sales opportunities.

Figure 10–1. The Sales Leader Classification Model Moves Northeast

INCREASE YOUR RELATIONSHIP VALUE: FROM PERSONAL TO CORPORATE RAPPORT

To be fully engaged with your customers, you need to develop three kinds of rapport:

1. **Personal rapport:** The goal here is not to talk about your kids, but to show the customer that you see him or her as more than a conduit to money.

2. **Business rapport:** With this type of relationship, the customer sees you as a resource committed to his success, and not just a supplier of products or services.

3. **Corporate rapport:** Corporate rapport is a mindset in which you view your customers as more than the individuals with whom you have a relationship.

Figure 10–2 illustrates how building the three rapports increases the value of the relationship. You are now more committed to your customers, and they to you. There is more mutual trust and respect, which might have been there before, but not as intensive.

Figure 10–2. Three Levels of Rapport

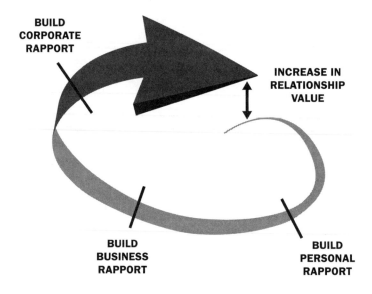

BUILD CORPORATE RAPPORT

INCREASE IN RELATIONSHIP VALUE

BUILD BUSINESS RAPPORT

BUILD PERSONAL RAPPORT

Let's see how to improve the three types of relationships listed above.

Build Personal Rapport

The development of personal rapport is perhaps one of the most well-known and traditional sales techniques and I will not go into detail in this book about how to build personal rapport. What is not often talked about, however, is the fine balance sellers must walk to enhance their personal rapport. You are not in business to gain friends! You are in business to develop trusting, profitable relationships for both you and your client. To do this you must *balance your personal relationship* with the client with *your transactional relationship.*

When you call on a client, is the conversation always about reordering, upgrading, or writing a check? If so, you're heavy on the transactional communication and constantly asking for money, which will wear on the client and erode personal rapport.

Instead of focusing only on transactions with each call, build in personal communication. Show the clients you care about them. But let's be clear, I'm not talking about conversations about kids, holidays, and hobbies. Modern, sophisticated buyers see right through that. Leave these to social occasions, conferences, and networking events. What is important during a business meeting (or call) is showing the client you remember your last conversations.

ENGAGED SELLING:

Personal rapport requires a balance of transactional and personal communication.

Start your conversations with:

> ➤ "When we spoke last you . . ."
> ➤ "I was thinking about what you said last week and . . ."
> ➤ "I know you were away in Bermuda last week . . ."
> ➤ "I remember that X was important to you . . ."

These statements show the client that you have been listening, and whenever clients feel listened to, your personal relationship with them is enhanced. Enhancing your personal relationship is the first step to Growth.

You will find excellent resources on how to build personal rapport at www.nonstopsalesboom.com.

Build Business Rapport

Today's client requires a deeper relationship with you than ever before: business rapport.

Establish yourself as a resource for your clients. Introduce them to potential clients or employees. Put them on a client advisory panel, asking their opinion and input, which will give them an intrinsic sense of ownership and investment in your company and product. Provide research and benchmarking to show them how they are performing relative to others in their markets and conduct business reviews to showcase your knowledge of their business and your understanding of their goals; offer ideas about how they can reach those goals faster. Ensure that your company and you as an individual are participating in thought leadership conferences, professional development, and other reputation-building activities. (Even better, invite them to co-present with you highlighting a joint success.)

When companies hire me to conduct exit interviews of the clients they have lost, two-thirds state clearly that they leave *because they feel their previous seller had become indifferent to their needs.* You can't grow business in a client that leaves you. And I know you are *not* indifferent to their needs. Chances are, you are just not showcasing your interest and involvement. Once a month or more, work on business rapport with those clients you are actively trying to grow. Schedule a mailing, a call, or a meeting where you highlight your business acumen relative to their business and your Sales Radar will be filled with Growth opportunities.

I was attending a large sales meeting with over 350 sellers from a multinational bank. On stage was the chief financial officer from its largest client discussing his ideal relationship with the bank. He said, "You think that you are doing me a favor by coming in to see me every six months to update me on my accounts. But I need you here every month educating me on what's going on at the bank, in the worldwide investment markets, and in my accounts. I am extremely busy. How am I supposed to keep up with the information and sort out what's important if we are not sitting down to talk each month?" The room went silent as it had never occurred to these sellers that their clients saw meeting with them regularly as an asset.

Build Corporate Rapport

Don't underestimate the power of not only having a good relationship with your main point of contact at an organization, but also having excellent rapport with other people within the client. With the amount of turnover in most companies, it's a mistake to assume that a great and loyal contact within the organization will necessarily equate to a secure relationship with the client.

A few years ago a client of mine was managing a multimillion-dollar staffing services contract. The customer was the marquee key account for our client, but problems cropped up when their main contact, the vice president of human resources, was forced out of the company quickly, and quite unpleasantly. Let's just say she was escorted out of the building and her key pass was shredded immediately! When the new vice president was hired, she did a complete review of services. And, because our client had not developed any corporate rapport, and was associated with the old regime (which had been poisoned internally), there were no additional relationships to turn to, and no advocate fighting on their behalf. Not one other employee of the customer stood up and said to the new vice president that our client's services were necessary to do their jobs; no executives considered them integral to the company (or even knew about them). As a result, they appeared as "just a vendor," and lost a million dollars of their contract to a competitor within three months of the new executive taking over.

A salesman with a large multinational client of mine once managed a key account for his company. This key account was worth a million dollars in current revenue with growth potential of several orders of magnitude. The salesman's relationship with the chief operations officer (COO) was sound and since this COO made all the decisions in the account, the salesman felt he had no need to develop other contacts. I distinctly remember him telling me, "Don't worry, Colleen. The COO loves me; I have this account sewn up."

Shortly thereafter the COO left (with no warning) and was replaced by an outsider whose first job was to review all vendor relationships. The seller did not have any allies in the account who reported to the new COO. Nor did he have any allies at equal executive levels to the COO. As a result, no one fought internally on his behalf. And so, as this seller was also tied to the old regime, he was easily replaced and a million dollars of current business plus the future potential evaporated in two months. That seller was never able to recover the account or find the revenue in new accounts. He left the company within a year.

You can't build a Nonstop Sales Boom by only having one contact in each account—no matter how powerful that contact appears to be. Luckily for you situations such as those above are easy to preempt. While you can never know when your buyers will leave, get fired, or go through mergers and acquisitions, you will mitigate your risk by building and maintaining multiple relationships. And in doing so, you will grow your business at the same time!

While it's wonderful to have a quality relationship with each of your clients, don't underestimate the value of quantity. People move on; give yourself the insurance of having established a reputation in multiple areas of your client's organization.

Traditional salespeople only pay attention to personal rapport and in doing so create the boom–bust cycles

ENGAGED SELLING:

Relationship Quality + Relationship Quantity = Ensured Growth

of sales results we discussed in Chapter 1. Perpetual sales boomers pay close attention to all three rapport types, resulting in a Sales Radar full of new opportunities for growth (and commissions)!

CONNECTING THE CORPORATE PLAYERS

Smart sales leaders work hard at connecting corporate players within their clients as a way of enhancing corporate rapport and ensuing growth. To connect corporate players effectively you must develop multiple contacts inside your accounts, create a community of advocates inside your best clients, and then connect them with their peers inside your own company. This is what leads to internal referrals and new opportunities.

Simply creating relationships without the connection is like building railway stations without connecting tracks or houses without streets. The connectivity makes for railroad systems and neighborhoods—the whole being greater than the sum of the parts.

Think of this process as *infiltration*. It's about building a community. When done well, a corporate community will win you a broad base of support throughout the organization, while building a library of knowledge about how that client's business operates (e.g., who makes decisions, what are their strategic objectives, what is their business plan for the future). Infiltration is about more than mining a corporate hierarchy for influential decision makers. It's about becoming an insider, not just a partner. Every point of contact has value. Every conversation is a good conversation—whether it's with a CEO or a gatekeeper. Insight comes in many forms, and each contact you make in that corporate community plays a role in the sales process. You will never lose business by forming too many of these relationships, but you're sure to lose business if you create and connect too few of them.

ENGAGED SELLING:
There is no such thing as the wrong contact; the more corporate contacts you have the stronger the corporate relationship is.

Some examples include:

> ➤ A VP of strategic accounts for a consumer credit company created a private, corporate community on LinkedIn connecting the 40 members on his team who manage the client with over 200 contacts on the client site. The daily communication and

transparency of this community helped to maintain and grow a $45 million per year account with a major investment company.

➤ Top sellers at a medical devices company take their executive team on the road for a series of day long meetings with the executives of each of their biggest hospital clients once a year for a day of planning. They call these events "client days" and spend three-quarters of the time reviewing the client's goals and objectives combined with an industry overview. Only the end of the day is focused on the seller's business, showing a product roadmap and discussing those new innovations that are in alignment with the client's objectives. This is a unique approach because most sellers simply show up and present what they want first, rather than listening to their client's future plan and then tailoring their presentation on the fly to meet the client's needs.

➤ U.S.-based feed, seed, and fertilizer manufacturers routinely host meetings bringing together salespeople, agronomists, product specialists, and executive leadership from their company to meet with the sellers, buyers, agronomists, and leaders of their retail clients.

➤ The VP of enterprise sales for an office supply chain creates an internal user group at each of his biggest clients. What this means is that he connects the department heads for all the departments and divisions that are buying from him. This internal community creates two benefits for the buyer. One, they are able to see how others are using the product to be more effective, and two, they are able to create an internal buying group that helps to streamline purchases and create savings on bigger orders. The seller benefits by getting internal referrals more easily because the internal user group actively encourages other departments to join. As well as benefitting from larger orders—bringing greater revenue and saving his company money in delivery costs—the seller is creating buyer loyalty ensuring that the competition doesn't make inroads.

> ➤ An executive in the paper business at Supremex connected corporate players to create emotional communities with his best clients and vendors each year, making sure that his sellers, sales leaders, and plant managers were all included in community-building and developing relationships with the buyers and users of their product. (You see, I come by my focus honestly. This recently retired executive is my dad.)

MULTIPLYING CONTACTS IN CUSTOMER ORGANIZATIONS: THE ISO RELATIONSHIP MATRIX

The previous section talked about deepening current relationships through personal and business rapport, and broadening relationships throughout company clients through corporate rapport. In this section, we're going to talk more specifically about how to multiply your contacts in an organization. You must first begin with four questions, listed below with the reason for their importance:

1. **What departments are affected by my product or service besides the one I sold to originally?** This question is important because if your project affects other teams, you should meet them and find out what success or challenges you are causing the other groups. Perhaps a sales or retention opportunity will be found in meeting these teams.

2. **What departments do my buyers work most closely with?** This question is important because if your buyer works closely with other departments or divisions these could be ISOs for you. For example, marketing and customer service departments often roll out client management software after a sales department has done so, because they work closely together and see the benefit of sharing a single source of data.

3. **Who does my buyer report to and who is his or her direct report?** This question is important because you need to have

access to the future power, backup power, and ultimate power for the best ISOs. What if your buyer leaves?

4. **Who is using the product?** This question is important because getting to know the users of your product or service will allow you to build relationships with future buyers as well as to receive testimonials and case studies to use internally.

Once you have the answers to these four questions you can create an ISO Relationship Matrix (as shown in Figure 10–3) to help you identify whom to meet and then develop strategies on how to meet them. In each box you should have the name and title of the person you want to meet.

As you can see, this matrix is a modified organization chart focused only on those departments or divisions that are relevant to your buyer and your potential to grow or maintain the account.

Add as many departments or divisions as you need for the most complete matrix of the account you are managing. You might have six rows across and five down or two across and four down, depending on the complexity of your account and scale of your product. Don't worry about

Figure 10–3. ISO Relationship Matrix

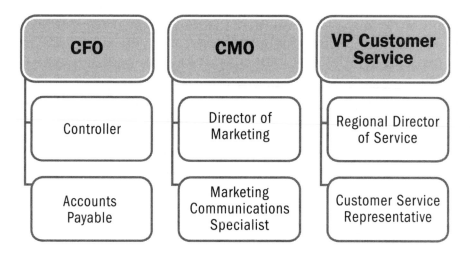

the size of the matrix. Only worry about the accuracy of the matrix based on the goals you have for the account.

If you wish to download extra working copies of the ISO Relationship Matrix you can do so from www.nonstopsalesboom.com.

If your matrix is full of titles and no names, this is your cue to sit down and work with your few (or only) contacts in the account to fill out the details. Once you have the information documented, ask for their help in making the introductions. A simple question such as "Can you help me with an introduction?" or "Can I tell them that I work with you?" will work for you to receive the green light to call the new contacts.

ENGAGED SELLING:

One is a dangerous number in sales.

OWN THE NEW RELATIONSHIP BEFORE INTRODUCING OTHERS INTO IT

As the seller on the account, the accountability for the relationship and its growth stops with you. As such, after you have identified each new contact in your account and asked for an introduction, meet with them yourself, first. *You must own these relationships before you introduce others from your company.*

Of course, if your managers, leaders, or teammates from other departments have been engaged with the client during the Attraction and Participation states, encourage these relationships to continue, but also deepen them by developing your own relationship with these contacts.

Never allow yourself to be cut out of a relationship inside the accounts you manage. This will erode your Sales Radar view and reduce the number of ISOs you can create and see.

Only after you have met each new contact personally should you take the time to match your new contacts with additional contacts inside your company. Creating this high level of infiltration deepens corporate rapport, protecting your account from erosion to the competition and putting you in the best position to grow. Some examples of doing this include:

1. You develop a relationship with the COO, the director of operations, and three warehouse managers during the Participation state of your Sales Radar. After implementation, you ask for a tour of one of the facilities and take along your manager as well as a technical support lead from your office. During the tour you meet with five warehouse employees who are all using your new resource planning software.

2. Your initial buyer is the owner of a small business and during the project kickoff you meet the comptroller and the sales manager. During a project status meeting you bring your customer service contact for the client and a specialist to meet the employees most affected by the project, and you bring your manager to meet the business owner and their leadership team.

3. A long-standing client of yours has new opportunities to grow because it has just opened offices in several new international locations. You arrange for a meeting to include your existing executive contacts as well as their new managers from the overseas divisions, and include team members from your company who are fluent in the foreign languages native in the new acquisitions.

4. A client of yours has been bought by the competition. You have a great relationship with a vice president who has been let go and a manager who is staying. You ask the manager for a referral to the new vice president and take your vice president along to build a peer-to-peer relationship.

Never underestimate the power of the peer-to-peer relationship in building corporate rapport. I once had a buyer at a major motion picture

ENGAGED SELLING:

The ethical aspect of creating deep, multilayered relationships is worth mentioning. If you leave your company or are absent for a long period, the client is not abandoned.

company tell me, "If you want our vice president of Legal at this meeting you'd better bring your president. He simply won't work with anyone below him." While I didn't like the attitude, I took that directive to heart, and bought a ticket for my president to make the flight. We dealt with the vice president of Legal together and in that one meeting closed a multi-million-dollar incremental sale with our client.

THE VORTEX FRAMEWORK: TRANSFORMING RELATIONSHIPS INTO SALES

In the first part of the chapter, I've described how to improve the quality and the quantity of your relationships with your customers and customer organizations. You have multiplied your contacts so that even many of your service accounts and growth accounts are now on the path to becoming key accounts. But you must now push hard to transform all of the contacts and relationships you've developed into new sales from current customers. The VORTEX Framework can guide you in this quest. It consists of a set of components that will inspire a variety of sales activities, some of which are featured later in the chapter.

When I survey buyers, 70 percent of them tell me that consistent and relevant information from their sellers is critical to their making a buying decision. In digging deeper, they define "consistent" as one or two times a month and "relevant" as being important to them personally and/or professionally related to their exceeding their goals.

Knowing this, I am constantly amazed at the number of sellers who do nothing to encourage Growth within their own customer list.

Your Growth potential is only as high as your clients' perceived quality of your relationship with them. To improve this perception and grow each account you must *transition your thinking* from "*managing an accounts list*" to "*building a relationship with my client.*"

You will create a profitable relationship with your customers using the following VORTEX components:

- ➤ V is for variety.
- ➤ O is for occurrence.
- ➤ R is for reliability.
- ➤ T is for truth.
- ➤ E is for engaging.
- ➤ X is for excellence.

Let's take a look at these components one by one.

Variety

Recent studies from the Information Marketing Association show that your current clients can tolerate up to 200 contacts per year before they will consider you a stalker—as long as you provide a variety of touch points. For the record, I am not suggesting that 200 is the right number for you. I use this extreme study to show you that you probably are not doing nearly enough. Most companies we survey on behalf of sellers want to hear from them between 12 and 52 times a year.

The reason customers can withstand up to 200 touches per year is because smart salespeople know to mix up the media types they use to contact their customers. You can't call a customer 200 times a year without getting on the do-not-call list. You can call, email, mail, and fax; send them to your web store; use audio and video; attend networking events, trade shows, and fundraisers; make in-person sales calls; use article placements in trade journals; and send gifts and advertising specialties. To increase the number of opportunities in your Sales Radar you must increase the kinds of media you use to reach out to your clients in order to increase the frequency with which you reach out to them.

Occurrence

How often are you in touch with your clients? Regardless of whether 12 or 52 touches are appropriate for you, don't let the number cloud my real message to you: You are likely not doing enough. In my work, most companies and sales professionals feel that if they reach out four times a year, they are stalking the client. Personally I believe that 26 is the minimum number of touches required each year for a truly profitable relationship.

Using component #1, variety, you can build strong relationships with your clients by delivering valuable information on a regular basis using a variety of media types. Once every two weeks will not be overwhelming. I mentioned Donald from The Placement Office earlier in this book. He executes VORTEX flawlessly. He reaches out to his clients every two weeks using in-person meetings, mail, and the telephone.

Reliability

All 26 touches should be sent on a regular schedule. Your customers will come to expect them and, hopefully, look forward to them. You might consider sending a monthly email newsletter, combined with a bimonthly hard-copy newsletter at two-week intervals. You could advertise a free monthly webinar or teleclass for your clients on product training or business topics complementary to your products. You could schedule a client advisory meeting for key accounts every four or six weeks. Trust is built with consistent behavior over time. Consistently and reliably delivering your message to your clients will demonstrate you can be trusted to deliver what you said, when and how you said it. This will lead to growth. Clients don't like surprises; they like results.

In order to build a relationship with your clients you must maintain constant contact with them without lapse or interruption. What do you think would happen to the relationship with your spouse if you unexpectedly didn't come home one night, and didn't call, didn't email, didn't text-message, and then arrived home again unexpectedly three months later? When you don't call your friends for weeks at a time, does your relationship grow stronger or weaker?

I have often thought that the sales relationship is similar to the dating or courting relationship. Regular contact at consistent intervals is key. You can't build a personal relationship without regular communication. Likewise with business relationships. If you don't call, your clients will build a relationship with someone else (i.e., your competitor) who does. Use a reliable scheduling system and never miss a meeting. Donald's clients are so tuned into his schedule of contact that his best clients now call if a touch point is late or missing. This loyalty has led to year-over-year growth every year for the six years I have been working with Donald and his team.

Truth

Truth is as important as variety and reliability. Whatever you send, discuss, or do has to be true of you and your company's brand. It has to provide real value. Don't just "pitch" your clients each time you reach out to them. Share valuable ideas, industry data, your favorite books on business, and your thoughts on articles they might find useful that can help them grow your business—while showcasing the true "you" of you and your company. For example, Harley Davidson's owners in North America receive road atlases with highlighted scenic motorcycle trips. Luxury retailer Kate Spade publishes restaurant and sightseeing tips in its staff's favorite cities, and Costco publishes a business-focused magazine for its corporate members.

Another truth? Remember that you are selling to a fellow human being, not a faceless corporate entity.

Engaging

Be entertaining and friendly, yet professional. Your clients want to have fun; they want to laugh and they want to enjoy doing business with you. Your relationships will not grow if you are miserable to be around. Which airlines command the most customer attention during the preflight safety announcements—those on Southwest and WestJet, or those on the traditional airlines such as American, United, Air Canada, and US Airways? Southwest and WestJet are more engaging because they make the announcements fun and friendly while still being professional.

Make sure that every contact attempt you make is worth opening, reading, and acting on. A banking client of mine recently sent 30 invitations to an art auction to his 30 best customers. It was a fun event sponsored by his bank that showed a more human side to their business. All 30 said no, but six proactively asked for follow-up appointments because they wanted to revisit their portfolios and add new services.

Excellence

Clients want to be associated with winners, with people who excel at everything they do. So always look and act the part. Your materials must be top-notch, your conversations on trend, and your appearance that of a top seller. An easy way to accomplish this is to always have success stories to share. When you are sharing with your clients (in writing or conversation) how other clients like them have succeeded, you are explicitly giving them new ideas to benefit their business as well as implicitly showing them that you are a success. The more good they see you doing in the market, the more they will want to be a bigger part of your community.

So, what else do we need to know? As defined by www.dictionary .com, a vortex is "something regarded as drawing into its powerful current everything that surrounds it." And this is how you want your customers to react to you. When you create a vortex you draw toward you everything you touch, and, combined with the power of referrals (discussed in Chapter 13), those people your clients reach out to will also be drawn in. Thus, your network and circles of influence are expanded and the power of the vortex is increased.

Using the six VORTEX components as a guide, I have provided some ideas in Figure 10–4, ideas that other Engage clients are using today. No need to follow slavishly; this list is to get you started thinking about what VORTEX activities would be suitable for *your* clients. Keep in mind that not all accounts are created equal in terms of their Growth potential, which is why I have suggested some activities for key accounts that you might not provide to a service account.

Figure 10–4. VORTEX Activities

VORTEX Activity	Account Type			
	Service Account	Growth Account	Maintenance Account	Key Account
Electronics newsletter	✔	✔	✔	✔
Business review	✔	✔	✔	✔
Site visit	✔	✔	✔	✔
Lunch-and-learn events	✔	✔	✔	✔
Monthly status call		✔	✔	✔
Tour of your facility or open house		✔	✔	✔
Executive introductions		✔	✔	✔
Invitations to industry-hosted events				✔
Introductions to new vendors			✔	✔
Peer-to-peer meetings			✔	✔
Research papers		✔	✔	✔
Free training (virtual or in-person)		✔		✔

Using the chart as a guide, a seller of enterprise software to large organizations might have the following VORTEX plan:

Month 1: A handwritten thank-you card is sent in the mail within three days of the purchase. The client is added to the company newsletter and the first issue is sent.

Month 2: A site visit is arranged for all of the implementation team to visit the client's site and meet the key players. At the same time a kick-off meeting could be conducted to ensure the project starts smoothly.

Month 3: An updated research paper that was conducted by your association is sent to the client with highlighted sections that you think will be most interesting to the client.

Month 4: Your company's quarterly newsletter is sent containing new product announcements, client success stories, and company news. This could be sent to your buyer but also anyone in the account who could benefit from its content. Don't be shy in asking your contacts (especially those in your ISO matrix) if they want to be subscribed!

Month 5: You invite the client to tour your facility and meet the developer who is working on the client's installation.

Month 6: You host a lunch and learn which individuals in your client's office are best suited to introduce other departments to your solution.

Month 7: Your company's quarterly newsletter is sent containing new product announcements, client success stories, and company news.

Month 8: You host your first business review of the progress to date and document any red flags. At this meeting you also lay out the plan for what is coming.

Month 9: You invite the client to be your guest at an industry event. You introduce the client to their peers at other similar companies and ask to have your client featured in the next company newsletter.

Month 10: Your company's quarterly newsletter is sent containing new product announcements, your client success stories, and company news.

Month 11: You organize peer-to-peer meetings between your executive team and the client's executive team in order to build relationships and strengthen the corporate rapport.

Month 12: You have a one-year anniversary business review meeting to summarize the year and plan for the next 12 months.

A word about this plan: Remember my personal belief in a 26-touch minimum? I haven't abandoned it. The plan above is a guide that doesn't include project deliverables such as the weekly status report during the implementation phase, or the training sessions for additional staff.

The beauty of developing a VORTEX plan like our software vendor's is that you only have to think of the activities once and then simply execute them each month. I suggest keeping a log of the activities in your client file so you can see what's been completed and what is still to be delivered. Once you've created the VORTEX plan, immediately schedule the time to complete each task in your calendar each month. If you don't schedule the time, you will not execute on your plan! (The best sellers we work with create an annual schedule in their calendars so that none of the VORTEX activities are missed.)

WHERE THE MAGIC HAPPENS

You want your customers buying from you because they have a stronger relationship with you than any other provider and because it's clear to them that you deliver more value. When your clients think to come to you first even if it is less convenient, or they feel guilty about dividing allegiance, and they readily refer you to others, you have created a VORTEX relationship. You will have more permission, more tolerance, and more acceptance of your promotions and offers when you have achieved this VORTEX relationship. The by-product of this is, of course, a Nonstop Sales Boom.

Growth of your current accounts is critical to creating a Nonstop Sales Boom and here's why. Most businesses have an average closing rate of about 25 percent. So, for every four new opportunities that come their way, they close just one of them. And that's not too bad. The problem, however, is that those same businesses tend to lose half of their customers every five years. That kind of churn, if it's not supported by an incredible influx of new business, can make it exceedingly difficult to grow.

Stronger businesses, on the other hand, close deals at a stronger clip—around 33 percent, or one of every three opportunities that cross their paths. But their customer retention rates are better, too—generally in the neighborhood of 70 percent. As a result, those companies possess stronger leverage and can grow their business more profitably.

Truly breakthrough companies—those that create Nonstop Sales Booms—are even more remarkable, but not because their closing ratios on net new business are any better. In most circumstances, that ratio is still around 33 percent. But here's where the magic happens: Those businesses boast *client retention rates* of about 95 percent, and they're able to efficiently drive profitability by selling *new products and services* to those existing clients every year.

COLLEEN'S POWER TIP #11: THE POWER OF THE BUSINESS REVIEW

A business review meeting, the second activity listed in the VORTEX Activities chart (Figure 10–4), is one of the best tools I have found for growing clients. At a minimum you should be conducting them twice a year for maintenance, key, and growth accounts and once a year for your high-potential service accounts. For the multinational clients I work with business reviews are held quarterly due to the complex nature of the projects and massive size of the accounts.

A property and casualty insurance company once told me that they had their agents do annual business reviews for the biggest 20 percent of their corporate accounts once a year at the end of the policy year. They bragged that this was industry standard but they were ignoring the link between not being in front of their clients often enough and two troubling trends in their overall business.

> ➤ Trend one: The competition was doing a midyear meeting in an effort to take the business and they were being successful 50 percent of the time.

> ➤ Trend two: 100 percent of these key accounts were shopping around for the best rates each year, causing the sellers to have to work harder to close the sale and discount rates to keep the business.

When we increased the cadence for the business reviews to quarterly for the top 10 percent and biannual for the top 25 percent, midyear policy replacements from the competition stopped and clients' shopping behavior was cut in half.

Business reviews are critical to Growth because they ensure you are in front of the client more often than the competition, building deeper relationships with increasing numbers of people and delivering them value beyond the expectations of the project.

A business review is *not* a sales meeting. And this is precisely why it is such a great tool for growth. Business reviews are your opportunity to have a value-based discussion focused on the client's needs and interests in four areas.

1. The current levels of value (tangible and intangible) that the client is receiving from you now and how that value compares to the expectations that were set at the start of the relationship. In other words, are you performing below, at, or above expectations?

2. What the future holds for your client. What are the client's strategic initiatives for the next year?

3. What your company is planning for the year that the client needs to be aware of. This is your chance to share product and service enhancements, expansion plans, or other key initiatives relevant to the client's relationship with you.

4. The industry in general. This will allow you to showcase your expertise in the client's business and industry by sharing insights from your unique vantage point. Specifically, what trends do you see coming that the client needs to either leverage or de-risk for?

Business reviews must be attended by your buyer as well as any key stakeholders and project participants. This is also your opportunity to add new relationships by using your ISO Relationship Matrix to identify people you have not met and inviting them to the business review. You will find that it's easier to both get new contacts to meet with you the first time, and get your clients to refer you internally to other people, when you are requesting they attend a group meeting. Simply put, meeting in a group is less threatening than meeting one-on-one with a salesperson!

Your business reviews should also include key resources from your company. This could be a project lead, an executive, your manager, the head of customer support, or specialists. Whoever you choose, make sure you never outnumber the client! Doing so turns the mood of the business review from a conversation to an inquisition quickly. Plan effectively by knowing who from your client will be attending and then identify the appropriate people from your company based on the agenda and stature of the participants, using a three-to-one ratio. Three of them and one of you.

A typical business review agenda might cover the following topics:

> Review the objectives of the current project and progress to date. Quantify and share success based on the goals set for the project.

> Share wins. Don't expect that people are sharing good news internally on their own. You must be that conduit of all successes related to your relationships inside the account as these successes will ultimately lead to more projects and/or Leverage (which we will be discussing in the next chapter).

> Address any missteps and the process you used to resolve them. Confirm that everyone is satisfied with the corrections and no lingering issues remain.

> Introduce or reconnect your top managers to the customer.

> Meet and get to know other important customer contacts.

> Discuss industry trends, research and market analysis, and benchmarks that your client might be interested in.

> Set goals for the upcoming year.

Use business reviews consistently, and see the value of your client relationships increase and your ISOs multiply.

. . . .

Having learned in Chapter 9 how to determine which of your existing customers can be most productive for you, in this chapter we explored ways to deepen and enhance your relationships with them—because that is how you will get the most out of the Growth state on your Sales Radar. And that's really the essence of the discussion in these two chapters. You cannot create a boom by only selling new business each year. Nonstop Sales Booms require a balance: selling both to new clients and growing your existing accounts. In sales, that can be admittedly hard to do; after all, it's more fun and exciting to bring a new client into the fold than simply nurture long-term relationships with existing clients. Yet, nurturing those relationships and selling more to existing clients is the key to sales efficiency and profitability.

In Part 5 we turn to the final quadrant on your Sales Radar, Leverage. We begin in Chapter 11, with a discussion about Leverage and how a well-managed client will help you grow more easily.

PART V

LEVERAGE

THE LAST STATE OF CLIENT ENGAGEMENT in your Sales Radar is Leverage—your secret sales force. The Leverage state is when you have developed your client relationships to such a high level that they are now creating opportunities for you through referrals, advocating on your behalf with testimonials, and providing case studies and references for others to learn from. In this way, those in your client base that have reached the Leverage state become an adjacent sales team.

While the word "leverage" has a modern, technical air to it, in actuality leveraging contacts is an ancient art, honed in the teaming bazaars and marketplaces that have existed since the dawn of commerce. In Chapter 11, we explore the core concept that has always been and continues to be at the heart of flourishing marketplaces: a sense of community. The greatest leverage comes from clients who feel that they are part of your community—and that you are part of theirs. In chapters 12 and 13, we look at two of the most potent tools for leverage, testimonials and referrals, respectively.

CHAPTER 11

The Borderless Bazaar: Creating a Sense of Community with Your Clients

AS WE MENTIONED IN CHAPTER 2, today's marketplace is in the midst of a profound transformation in how sales are generated and sustained, and nowhere else is that more apparent than in the changing relationship between sellers and buyers.

Gone are the days of pure transactional selling. Buyers don't wait for you to come to them anymore. Instead, they seek what they are looking for. When they're prepared, they choose to do business with those who best meet their needs. More than ever, *the strength of communities determines how successful you'll be in positioning yourself in the minds of your buyers as that top pick.*

That's why the Leverage state is centered on community building.

History can teach us something valuable about communities. Think back to when you were young and you were enchanted by Ali Baba, Aladdin, and Sinbad the Sailor of *One Thousand and One Nights*. Commerce in the ancient world of that book took place in the merchants' bazaar. Bazaars were the places that lay the foundation for the modern marketplaces we know today. Part of their power was in their community structure.

ENGAGED SELLING: The larger and more active your client communities are, the more of the best new prospects you will be able to attract.

Being part of a bazaar meant that sellers shared what they knew and pooled their resources, as did their customers—banding together into a connection-rich network selling goods and services. Just like the changed landscape of today, this was good news for current clients and new buyers. Whether they needed a merchant, a craftsperson, a food seller, or a banker, someone could confidently connect them to what they were looking for. This was the origin of the referral process, testimonials, and word-of-mouth marketing. From the beginning of history, merchants have been leveraging their connections to find new business.

In other words, success at the bazaar hinged on the relationships forged in the marketplace from these networked communities. The structure of the ancient bazaar matches what I'm seeing in the marketplace today. Today's selling and buying communities are where relationships get forged. And, to be part of a community requires that you and your client collaborate on communicating value, to help the market grow. In doing so, you expand the community and attract new prospects.

Think about it this way: *Building communities helps you to leverage your current clients to find new buyers.*

OCCUPY SPACES AND CREATE COMMUNITIES

Today's bazaar is *without borders*. This means that buyers all over the world can find what they are looking for in spaces where people congregate. I'm talking about *spaces* rather than *places*! Spaces don't occupy a fixed location, nor do they have limits on who can join or what they can contribute. Spaces can be created online. They can be found in professional associations. And they can be forged in the content that you create for others, addressing topics that people are thinking about. By occupying spaces, what you are doing is creating a sense of kinship and shared purpose among current clients and allowing them to communicate your value to prospects that are also present in the same space.

Choose the spaces where your clients prefer to congregate.

In cyberspace, for example, the Flyer Talk forum is a unique and very active group of frequent fliers from all over the world. People communicate with the forum administrators and others directly about airline policies, programs, seat sections, and destinations. They share pictures, thank-yous, and, of course, complaints. And they tend to associate with others who are clients of their preferred airline. Most importantly, those who love their airline and frequent flier program use this forum to fervently defend their airline of choice, convincing others to join in as well. Because this is a community of peers, all frequent fliers, participants trust the other members' recommendations and are more likely to do business with new airlines based on recommendations and testimonials. As a frequent flier myself it's the first place I go for research on a new route I might be flying or when having to choose a new airline. The feedback on the forums has a direct influence on my choice of route and carrier.

In a live environment, Salesforce.com's Dreamforce Conference has grown to be the "must attend" community event for sales operations for clients of Salesforce.com and for prospects. Once a year, thousands of current clients, as well as prospective clients wanting to learn more about the product, take over San Francisco for this user conference that features best practices from sales thought leaders, exceptional sales teams, and Salesforce.com. They have created a unique physical space as a world's best learning and networking environment for all sales operations professionals whether they are Salesforce.com clients or not.

Dreamforce has developed a cultlike status within the sales community and many potential customers attend as part of their research and due diligence because they know that they will be able to speak personally with current Salesforce.com customers to receive real-life examples about whether the software is as good as the "sellers say it is." This community event works to convert prospects because prospects feel they are in control, learning about the software on their own terms rather than being "sold to."

Communities establish a sense of permanency and socially tested credibility that resonates with prospects. They provide the potential for a Nonstop Sales Boom because they create a steady flow of new prospects that are already predisposed to want to do business with you based on the recommendation of your current clients. There are two different communities you need to develop to fully leverage your clients.

TWO BASIC COMMUNITIES: KNOWLEDGE-BASED AND EMOTION-BASED

The concept of community is built around common values and needs fulfillment. While we can probably cite scores of community possibilities (profession-based, hierarchy-based, affiliation-based, and so forth), the knowledge-based and emotion-based communities will prove vital to your success, and will fill your Sales Radar beyond all others.

Knowledge Communities: United by Information and Experience

Information and field-tested insights are highly valuable commodities in today's marketplace. People have a hunger for good ideas, and that's why it's important to share what you know. I don't just mean you personally. Sharing what you know applies just as much to groups of people *adjacent* to your sales organization, such as customer support, marketing, product development, and professional services. Today, many businesses are building knowledge communities to better engage their clients and generate loyalty while also enticing prospects to research and ask questions about their products.

Knowledge communities are spaces where clients can go to learn more about the products they own and how to use them for maximum value. They are also spaces where a prospect can interact with a product before buying. The best knowledge communities contain testimonials and use case studies from real clients showcasing to everyone how the most successful companies are implementing the solutions. They can also include training videos, how-to guides, live discussion, video testimonials, online streaming of live events, and live meetings.

Some companies, for example, software as a service (SaaS) businesses, such as Infusion Software and Salesforce.com, house their knowledge communities in a secure area on their website to control access. They limit premium learning materials to clients only. In these closed-door communities company specialists regularly post videos, publish case studies, develop white papers and e-books, and announce product updates and events—all designed to help software users gain maximum value from their system.

ENGAGED SELLING:

Communities can be common gathering grounds where your best clients can help sell your best prospects.

Besides providing exceptional access to the best information, knowledge communities have a secondary value to you, and your clients. They enhance both the tangible and intangible value we discussed in Chapter 8. Tangible value is enhanced because the documents and training are helping clients use the products more thoroughly and thus gain a higher return on investment, and intangible value is enhanced because these value offerings are not available to the public.

While keeping your knowledge community behind closed doors might not seem like the right way to leverage clients, it is in fact a smart strategy for lead generation. Why? Because when current clients are treated as exclusive insiders and receive exclusive benefits they become more successful. And, when they achieve success they communicate more passionately about you publically. Infusion and Salesforce both benefit from a very passionate public constituency of clients that they can leverage to attract new prospects because this constituency advocates on their behalf every day.

Think of your knowledge community as a library or repository of information to ensure the highest value is extracted from your products. Today, the content that you generate for your knowledge community has more than just new-release shelf appeal. It also creates a valuable catalogue backlist—just like a publisher. The more you add to your knowledge backlist—especially if you post your content online—the more valuable the information becomes for your audience today and in the future. Massive knowledge repositories are attractive to your community of clients because they have instant access to the information they need to be more effective.

Ideally, knowledge communities offer the *opportunity for clients and prospects to interact with you as well as each other.* You can begin by doing all, many, or some of the following—and more.

Host a regular webinar on best practices, announcements, or advanced skills related to your product. These can be recorded and distributed for ongoing use. Consider interviewing a top client during each of the sessions and have them share their knowledge with the attendees. These webinars can be hosted by various experts in your company such as trainers, product specialists, customer support, or the leadership team.

Conduct a series of regional meetings. Before it was bought, restaurant point-of-sales software company Posersa hosted six annual meetings across the country to train its best clients on how to use its system more effectively to generate more restaurant sales. The events were free and provided a chance for clients to interact with each other as well as with company experts to learn to use their systems more profitably. Further, these elite clients were also taught how to attract new diners and grow their business. Finally, in attendance were a small selection of key prospects invited by the local sales team. At these meetings they had the chance to interact with both the clients and the experts presenting.

Client knowledge forums are an-

ENGAGED SELLING:
Whenever you have the chance to introduce your best clients to your best prospects the results are increased sales.

other type of knowledge community required to create a Nonstop Sales Boom. For example: InfusionSoft, a CRM (Customer Relationship Management) software company, hosts a support forum for clients to learn about and resolve issues with their software; car enthusiasts attend forums hosted by the manufacturers to discuss enhancements and performance; agroscience companies participate in Ag chat forums to discuss issues around world food supply and grain prices. These communities (forums) are critical to new client attraction because potential buyers are more likely to believe the words of another client than they are a salesperson. My mentor Alan Weiss has perhaps the most effective and dynamic forum in the world for his particular constituency of consultants and professional services providers (AlansForums.com). He has extended this to the mobile world with an app, AlansWorld. One way leverage is achieved in these communities is that existing customers encourage prospects to participate in their programs by discussing the success they have had. You don't create a knowledge community without your ongoing, active involvement. It's better for you to be a part of the conversation than separate from it.

Enhancing Knowledge Communities with Expertise

No matter what line of work you're in, you've been honing your professional skills throughout your career and have built up a library of know-how. Multiply that by the number of people in your company and you're looking at an incredibly deep pool of expertise. On top of that, there are experts outside of your company—consultants, speakers, trainers, authors, and other corporate executives—who complement the work you do and whom your clients find compelling. This expertise enhances your knowledge community by broadening their scope and increasing the value your clients receive from their relationship with you

For example, speakers at the 2013 Dreamforce Conference for Salesforce.com users included Sheryl Sandberg of Facebook and Deepak Chopra. In 2012 Tony Robbins spoke at the event. These are experts outside of the company whom Salesforce.com users care deeply about. They are also celebrity speakers whom prospects are drawn to.

Other examples of using experts in knowledge communities include:

> Bankers inviting accountants to speak at an event with clients and prospects present.

> Agricultural retailers inviting state agronomists to discuss success on client farms with prospective clients.

> A feed company partnering with a local veterinarian to discuss equine health for thoroughbred breeders.

> A manufacturer partnering with a business coach to help their resellers run more profitable businesses.

> A staffing company interviewing a consultant on teleseminar, webinar, or seminar applications.

> A shipping company holding a seminar for its customers and prospective customers and inviting a customs and brokerage specialist to speak.

The experts in your communities can also be your clients, giving them the opportunity to share their expertise and even to talk about how they have benefitted from doing business with your organization. Prior to the 2010 Vancouver Winter Olympics, Workopolis (an online jobs database) was awarded the contract to recruit the volunteers for the games. They showcased this work in a case study and invited their client, the vice president of human resources for the Olympics, to speak at a series of cross-Canada events. I attended the event in Ottawa along with over 300 of their clients and prospective clients. What made this event unique was that the room was filled with executive-level buyers (from clients and prospects) who stayed late to engage with the hosts and the speakers. As a result, new prospects entered the Sales Radar and existing client relationships were strengthened, making it easy for the sellers to build community, identify ISOs, and leverage the account for more referrals and testimonials.

Expertise complements knowledge. It adds proof to the promise of good ideas. That's why experts help nurture client relationships. They enhance trust, proving your competence and adding value so you can build loyalty and leverage your clients profitably.

View yourself *not* as the center of the knowledge universe, but as an enabler, leveraging the universe of knowledge to reach your clients, improving their condition and enhancing your value to them, and to get them talking to your best prospects.

ENGAGED SELLING:

Don't just tap into communities, create them to your specifications.

Emotional Communities: Connections of the Heart

Emotion-based communities provide affiliation and support through common bonding and experiences. Many soldiers, athletes, even students often consider their initial training a "boot camp" or ordeal, which they later take common gratification from ("Remember when we had to go on that 20-mile hike in the rain?" "Do you remember the incredible credit load that first semester?" "We used to train preseason in 105-degree heat"). Personally I notice that my husband, Chris, has a much tighter bond with his college classmates from the small military college he attended than I do with mine (I went to an enormous liberal arts university)— no doubt because of their unique shared experience.

Organizations such as Salesforce.com, Apple, Southwest Airlines, or Ben & Jerry's have formed these emotionally based communities through distinctive involvement of their client base and a manifest demonstration of listening and interacting.

As we know, people (clients and prospects) line up for hours and blocks just to get a new Apple product before others, and the store sends out coffee and donuts while they wait. The other day I walked by a lineup so large I just had to go in to see what was new . . . and potentially buy something! That is the power of leverage. Apple's Genius Bar is a fantastic example of becoming emotionally involved even in the face of an offering's dire technical problem.

Southwest Airlines customers write letters to the airlines' president thanking them for their in-flight experiences. Ben & Jerry's diehard fans drive out of their way to tour the production facilities in a small Vermont town, and Salesforce.com users share success stories publically at the Dreamforce Conference about their switch to cloud-based CRM.

Emotional engagement creates commitment, not merely compliance. When you design the Apple computer online (as people once designed the Dell computer), there is a personalization. Auto companies provide "configurators" that allow the customer to experiment with various color combinations and options online. Airlines provide personal recognition cards for their best customers to present to their favorite employees.

Most important, emotional communities create evangelists, which is a highly visceral and voluntary undertaking. Like Paul on the road to Damascus, they are suddenly stunned by a new insight, and can't wait not merely to share it, but to convert others. (This is why you should "seed" all hosted events and presentations with your delighted clients.)

Creating evangelists is exactly what the Leverage state is about. The more evangelists you have in the market, the more leverage they create for your business. By evangelizing, not only do they help create loyalty with your existing clients, they attract new clients through word of mouth and the power of their referrals. As a result, these evangelists attract increasing numbers of new prospects into your Sales Radar.

Emotional communities also give you the power of the benefit of the doubt. They forgive errors, mistakes, and omissions. That's why Apple's iPhone can have antenna problems without losing sales, but US Airways is blamed for everything from conspiracy to incompetence when one of its flights is delayed or canceled.

CREATE A COMMUNITY OF PEERS

Leverage is further strengthened when you create a community of peer groups by connecting small groups of clients who can help each other succeed. Create a community of peers composed of clients from separate companies who can talk about how they have solved challenges, or how you have helped them make more money, save money or time, or retain their employees.

You can bring peers together in many ways. It can be as simple as taking two clients to lunch so they can meet and talk about their businesses together. Or hosting an advisory group or a user forum specifically with complementary clients (not competitors) in the room. You can bring a small group together to share best practices or case studies, each person underlining the advantage of doing business with you and perhaps even doing business with each other.

Where possible, try to connect peers who could benefit from knowing each other because they might be able to do business together. You will increase leverage, which will lead to referrals, when you retain current clients for a long time. And, what could be better at helping you retain clients than when they credit you for helping them expand their business or find a new partner?

Recently, an Engage client in industrial sales purchased a table for a local high-profile fundraising event. He invited the CEOs of his seven biggest customers to join him at the table and they were able to network with each other. After the event he reported to me that it was a bigger success than anticipated because although they all were CEOs of local companies in similar markets, none of them had ever happened to meet personally. My client had created that opportunity. The connections made at the event strengthened the seller's community and led to direct referrals to many other—and widely disparate—CEOs with whom these powerful clients thought he should be doing business.

Another Engage client in the business products market makes it a habit to have lunch each week with two clients who don't know each other but who should. By connecting his clients he creates a small but powerful community that his clients can leverage to create more value in their markets and that *he* can leverage to more referrals, more testimonials, and ultimately more sales.

These corporate peer connections are invaluable for business to grow.

When you facilitate them among your best clients either internally among themselves or externally with partners you create leverage that converts into a Nonstop Sales Boom.

Smart, successful companies today recognize the power that results from bringing people together. They don't settle for sales teams who operate in isolation. They create communities where everybody can learn from each other and gain from that expertise.

ENGAGED SELLING:

Learning through your auspices creates credit that accrues directly to you.

WHY COMMUNITIES MATTER MORE AND MORE

So why do communities matter so much now? Because just like in those ancient bazaars of the classical world, buyers today are looking for more than a transaction: They want to do business with people who can offer knowledge and insight in addition to their products or services, knowledge that will ensure the greatest success in the shortest period of time. The success your clients are demanding can only be achieved if you take the time to build communities. That means putting client needs first: helping them learn and grow and delivering value above and beyond what your product or service provides.

Leverage is created through their success. Success attracts success. Only by making your current clients successful do you attract the best and most interested new prospects.

Consider the following case study, which reveals the power of leveraging community and relationships.

A few years ago, Engage Selling Solutions began working with a small-business telecommunications manufacturing company. At the time their business model hinged on having their clients interact only through their reseller network, and never with the manufacturer directly. As a result, product development stagnated because there was no opportunity for actual users to provide feedback or make suggestions for new features.

Any changes to product were made slowly, in reaction to market changes rather than based on client request. With help from Engage, this company decided it was time to do things radically differently.

A senior executive within the firm spearheaded a bold initiative to create a client-focused community. Doing this meant confronting one of their biggest fears—that their clients would just use this new forum as an opportunity to complain about what was wrong with their product.

Instead, three interesting things happened. First, the clients began offering suggestions about product features, leading to entirely new applications that had never been considered before. Second, the company suddenly and unexpectedly found themselves with a wealth of success stories as their customers began to share with them and with each other all the ways that they were using their product. Third, the firm's clients became deeply loyal, not just because they felt their input was valued, but also because they had a new sense of personal ownership in the new direction of the firm. *The outcome of this community and relationship approach was immediate.* Referrals skyrocketed, leading to increased sales; and sales boomed nonstop quarter after quarter for several years.

Amazing things can happen when you embrace change as an opportunity to work differently from the past. Find ways to build your own communities. Think about how you can become a trusted part of that borderless bazaar in the marketplace today. Where is your location in the souk?

Return on Customer Relationship: The Value of Clients Beyond What They Buy

Are your communities working to create a Nonstop Sales Boom for you? You can tell by annually measuring your return on client relationship (ROCR).

So what is this ROCR?

ROCR is the true worth of clients beyond simply what they buy. When you calculate this worth and track whether it is growing or shrinking over time you will know if you have achieved leverage or not. Here are the factors that you should consider when determining your ROCR:

1. **Total sales.** This is the easy one and often the only thing sellers measure. While it's easy to calculate, it only shows a small portion of the client's true value. You need to calculate the total value of the client's original order plus all the incremental sales you have made to them over the years.

2. **Referrals.** What is the value of all the business they have referred you to? A customer who provides direct referrals for your company multiplies the effect of their purchases. For example, if a customer refers two other customers—whom you didn't have to pay for to acquire—then they can be worth three times their original sale, boosting their ROCR. Don't be surprised if you find that the value of the referrals is higher than the total value of the client's own purchases. I have a client I work with in Louisville, Kentucky, who has only spent $10,000 with Engage directly. But, he has referred over $250,000 of new business to me over the last five years. I consider him a key account! Client retention is the key to repeat referrals. When a seller closes on a piece of business, he or she makes two sales—one is the immediate check and the other is referral business. Too many sellers don't pay attention to retention and never completely reap the rewards of the second sale.

3. **The value of the customer's brand.** While references are the most powerful selling tool that any company has, they are even better if your client has a powerful, well-respected brand. When Marriott became a client of mine at PS Software, their value to me soared because they brought a powerful brand to our client list in a targeted market (major hotel brands) that we wanted to pursue. We actively promoted our work with them and quickly received interest from other hotel chains because of Marriott's strong brand. At the same time, I was also managing Enron. Their ROCR dropped like a stone when their company was rocked by scandal and investigated by the U.S. Department of Justice that same year. The reputation of your client is critical to creating community. Great

clients want to be around other great clients. And, if prospects believe that if you are adding value to already well-respected companies in the market then you will be able to add value to them as well.

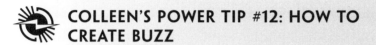

COLLEEN'S POWER TIP #12: HOW TO CREATE BUZZ

The power of your client's brand has a direct effect on the value of the buzz the client can create for you in the marketplace. "Buzz" or advocacy can be defined as the power for a well-known client to act as a reference, providing testimonials or referrals that make it easier for you to sell. They shorten your sales cycle, ensuring profitability.

Figure 11–1 is a diagnostic that shows your success at creating the best ROCR for each customer. When you plot your clients on the chart based on their retention rate and referral generosity you can see clearly what the ROCR is for each client: high, low, or nonexistent.

Figure 11–1. The Return on Client Relationship Matrix

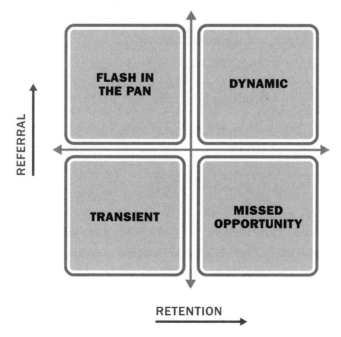

Working clockwise from the top left of Figure 11–1:

1. If you have a client with low retention but high referrals you have a *flash in the pan*. This is because the client buys quickly, refers quickly, and then moves on. While you might have a few months or a year of profitable activity it dies off quickly, leaving you an empty space in your Sales Radar.

2. If you have high retention and high referral you have a *dynamic* client with the highest ROCR. If this client also has a strong brand, then this is a platinum client! These clients buy from you often, refer business when you ask, and also refer proactively on their own.

3. If you have a client with high retention and low referrals you have a *missed opportunity*. In these cases you have a very loyal client who is not referring. While there may be some very rare cases where the client wants to maintain confidentiality, in most cases I find the reason these missed opportunities exist is because the seller is not asking for referrals. When was the last time you asked your most loyal clients for referrals?

4. If you have a client with low retention and low referrals you have a *transient client*. They buy from you, keep to themselves, and move on. These clients never become part of your community, stick to themselves, and offer no opportunity for leverage.

Take some time now to diagnosis your top 10 clients. Where do they fit on *your* ROCR matrix?

Understanding your clients' ROCR and where they fit on your ROCR matrix will help you understand how much leverage each client is providing you. For example, clients with high ROCR and who sit in the *dynamic* quadrant of the matrix are your best referral sources. They are those who speak most generously about you and whose success is likely to be shared publically with your prospects. These are the clients who are most willing to advocate on your behalf and fill your Sales Radar with hot new opportunities. These clients need to be rewarded.

Clients that sit in the *missed opportunity* quadrant are those who can be identified for future leverage. They are willing and able to provide referrals, but you have not fully unlocked their leverage potential! Identifying this group of clients is powerful because you can now put plans in place to ask for referrals and solicit case studies.

On the other hand, with your *transient* and *flash in the pan* clients your ROCR matrix shows you clearly those who are never going to be valuable beyond their initial sale. Perhaps, these are not the right types of clients to be attracting in the future. Look at this group closely. Are there commonalities among the clients? Is there a pattern emerging that proves a certain demographic is not the right demographic for your Sales Radar?

. . . .

Selling successfully in today's tough market is critical to your long-term success. Balancing your sales and service efforts in all four quadrants of the Sales Radar so you place emphasis on both new clients as well as retaining and growing existing ones will make selling a lot easier. This is what creates a Nonstop Sales Boom.

Throughout this book we have talked about what it takes to build up your Sales Radar. Beyond methodical steps what this is really about is building a *community* where you help make a difference in the lives of your customers and share those successes publically with your market. Leveraging your current clients in turn ensures you will grow your business.

Remember that growth doesn't happen unless you've made a difference to your clients!

Communities blossom where trust is earned and added value is revealed steadily. They are the glue that binds our sales efforts. Work hard to achieve this and your Sales Radar will reward you many times over with a Nonstop Sales Boom.

In Chapter 12 we will look at what is perhaps the most valuable tool in the Leverage state on your Sales Radar, the testimonial.

Testimonials: Your Greatest Leverage Tool

LEVERAGE IS NOT POSSIBLE without testimonials. In order for you to leverage your customers, they *must* be willing to speak openly about their success with you, engage with other key prospects, and be willing to help you attract new prospects onto your Sales Radar. Testimonials are so important that I am dedicating an entire chapter to this subject.

First, let's talk about why testimonials are so effective. Consider the story of legendary businessman W. Clement Stone. He built what would one day become a multibillion-dollar empire by selling burial insurance policies door to door for pennies a day during the Great Depression.

There's no denying that Mr. Stone's knack with people was a big part of his success. And he also had a little something extra—a binder over-flowing with testimonials from his community of clients. Legend has it that that binder never left his side when he was knocking on all those doors. There was a good reason for that. It was chock full of stories—and not just happy accounts from people who were satisfied. It also told painful stories about how people had lost houses, husbands and wives to misfortune . . . and how *relieved* they were that, thanks to him, they had signed on the dotted line long ago, and now were covered. In my opinion this binder was an early version of the emotional communities we discussed in the previous chapter. After reading stories out of that binder, it's hard to imagine how *anyone* could ever say no to him!

He went on to found Consolidated Insurance and develop a personal worth of over $450 million.

That's the amazing power of testimonials. They work because they reaffirm for others what the others already know is true. They work because they *leverage a client's experience into a prospect's future.*

As a sales professional, you take pride in the work you do (and I can say that with confidence about each and every one of you reading this, because you've already invested in this book!). When you meet with prospects, it's likely that you talk about all the great things that you do for your clients. You might also talk about how often you go the extra mile because service matters to you. But let's face it: You don't become successful and stay that way for long if all you ever do is talk about the sizzle without showing the steak.

That's where testimonials come in. They back up what you say with what noted psychologist Robert B. Cialdini, in his book *Influence: The Psychology of Persuasion* (Collins Business Essentials, 2006), calls "social proof." If we drill down a little deeper into human psychology, we also learn that testimonials have amazing persuasive powers. That's because they touch on both the fact-based and emotion-based motivators that drive people to buy things. They reaffirm that your claims are credible and that your services are the real deal. They validate the feelings that a prospect has for you. And they do so with a message that is unmistakably authentic and sincere.

When you combine all those motivators together, it helps you make a very convincing case to prospects. That way, you can say, "Don't just take *my* word for it, have a look at what my customers say. . . ." It deepens the confidence that people will have in your message and it can dramatically reduce the barriers you face in closing that sale.

W. Clement Stone understood this—and that's precisely the insight that you can get working for you in your Sales Radar, no matter what you're selling.

Let's examine how best to find those testimonials within your client base and leverage them to fill your Sales Radar with new prospects.

KEEP YOUR EARS OPEN WIDE

Alan Weiss, who has worked with me on this book, recalls a time he visited the vet with his dog. He saw the *Merck Manual* on the counter and told the vet that Merck was a large client of his.

"Do you know," said the vet with wet eyes, "that Merck has done more for animal health over the past decade than any other company on earth?"

When he next appeared before the AgVet (Merck's animal health division) sales force, he told that story, and the room was absolutely quiet. Surprised, he later asked the vice president what had happened.

"All we hear," he said, "are stories of how we missed a shipment or produced a bad side effect. We never really hear this. It's inspiring, and that one story will last all year for our team's motivation."

How often are *you* sharing customer success stories with your colleagues?

Success stories are great motivators, but they also are a source of your greatest sales tool: testimonials. When you're talking to your customers on the phone, does anyone ever share with you a little story about how they were able to make great use your product or service? Check your email. Has anyone ever sent you a note just to say "Thanks for the great work" on that last job you did for them? Have you ever received glowing feedback from a client who responded to a survey that you sent out? Each of those is a testimonial, just waiting for you to act on it. The team at Kinnser Software is tuned into each of their customer's conversations. As soon as one of them shares a success story they respond with thanks, a compliment, and "Can I quote you on that?" As a result they have a group of customers affectionately known as the "Kinnser Army" who are ready, willing, and able to step in and help close new prospects on a daily basis. And that brings me directly to my next point.

NOTHING VENTURED, NOTHING GAINED

As our friend W. Clement Stone once famously said, "If there is something to gain and nothing to lose by asking, by all means ask!" When a client says great things about you, about your work or the products you sell, give him the opportunity to turn that praise into a testimonial. Simply ask: "I'd really love to share your success with others. Would that be okay?" People generally like to be helpful to other people, but they'll rarely think to give you that all-powerful testimonial unless you ask. Here are some great ways to acquire testimonials—and make effective use of them:

Contact your passionate newer customers. Get on the phone and call your newest customers. No matter which industry you serve, the most passionate praise you'll find for your work and the service tends to come from customers with whom you have only recently started doing business. Andy Sernovitz, the author of *Word of Mouth Marketing: How Smart Companies Get People Talking* (Greenleaf Book Group Press, 2012), explains why: Your new customers are the ones who are most excited about having found you. Follow the lead of Audi. Less than 30 days after a new car purchase an Audi representative calls to confirm that the customer is happy with the purchase and to ask for feedback on the dealership. If that feedback is positive the surveyor asks if that information can be shared.

Contact your wise and insightful repeat customers. Your repeat customers, while perhaps not as excited because they are used to the great service you give them, provide prospects with important insight about what makes your product or service worth buying. Make a point of calling up people you've been doing business with for a long time and ask them why it is that they call on you. The answers you get will

ENGAGED SELLING:

Ask clients to take their iPhone and make a quick, casual 30-second video testimonial. These are worth their weight in platinum.

often include a great sentence or two that can be added to your testimonial collection. Again, all you have to do is ask.

Make it easy for people. One of the most common comments you'll hear from clients when asking for testimonials is, "Well I'm really not much of a writer, so it's hard for me to put it in words." The real power of testimonials comes from the fact that they're not polished, that they're authentic and from the heart. A marketing vice president I know quite well recently shared with me his secret about how he addresses this issue in his business.

> I borrowed an idea from John Caples—one of the great copywriters of the 20th century. When asking a client for a testimonial, he'd simply say, "Finish this sentence in twenty-five words or less: I really like (product/service/person) because . . ." This really works because it gets right to the point about the feelings people have for you, for what you do, and for what you're selling.

And here's your fallback position: Show the client or customer other client endorsements and testimonials as an example. That should set the table for them.

Do unto others. Write testimonials for others in your client community and those whose services have impressed you. This creates reciprocity, and sends an important message to everyone about the high standards you have not only as a supplier, but as a buyer, too. Social networking sites such as LinkedIn are handy tools for doing this. (Please note that I am not suggesting you use the LinkedIn "endorsement" function. That I find useless and annoying. Instead, use the functionality that lets you actually write a testimonial for the client, supplier, or partner.) You will find that they will return the favor with glowing references for you too.

Make testimonials noticeable. As you build your collection of testimonials, you'll need to find a place where new prospects can read them. Fortunately, you have a lot more choices than W. Clement Stone did back in the Depression. Not only can you put them all in a binder to show prospects, you can also include testimonials in other products and most won't cost you much more than a few minutes of your time. Here are some examples:

- ➤ Create a special web page devoted to testimonials. Check out www.shedshop.com/testimonials/index.html as a best practice.

- ➤ Look for opportunities to include sample quotes from your collection and feature them in steady rotation on the main page of your website.

- ➤ Include a new testimonial on the signature line of every outbound email.

- ➤ Feature testimonials prominently in your knowledge community.

The possibilities for publishing testimonials are endless and the potential benefits to your sales record can be quite amazing.

Make your expertise ubiquitous. Your prospects should see proof of your expertise everywhere, from social media to events, sales strategies, and other approaches to the marketplace. This can be part of the ubiquitous prospecting approach we discussed in Chapter 4. Seeing you everywhere within their market draws customers to you. By providing exposure outside the traditional sales process, you introduce prospects to your solutions and your team in the places they trust and frequent; this is an excellent opportunity to build rapport, trust, and proof of expertise.

Stuck for ideas on where to place testimonials? Use the following text on all printed or digital material: "Clients say the following about (*name of team member*)" and put it:

- ➤ In the biographies of all members of the sales team the management team, and the board of directors

- ➤ On the "About Us" segment on your website

- ➤ In customer forums or discussion groups

- ➤ At the beginning or end of your client profile page

- ➤ After your signature on letters and emails

- ➤ On each internal page of your website down the left-hand or right-hand margin

- ➤ On the slides used in sales presentations

> ➤ In all marketing and e-marketing releases

Visit www.nonstopsalesboom.com for an additional 25 ideas.

Thank your customers regularly. When you ask for a testimonial, you are battling with numerous other competing customer priorities. By thanking them (sincerely!) for taking the time to act on your request, your customers will treat your request with higher priority. And when you receive the testimonial, be old-fashioned; send a handwritten thank-you note!

THREE MUST-HAVE TESTIMONIAL TYPES

With written testimonials there are three versions you want to include in your materials. The good news is that you don't have to get three testimonials from each client. You just need to know how to chop up a testimonial effectively to create the format you need. Here are some examples you can consider for your business:

Variation 1: A Full letter

Always strive to receive a full-letter testimonial from your client. Once you have a full letter you can break it into smaller chunks to use in a variety of ways. A full-letter testimonial should include:

> ➤ Client's letterhead
>
> ➤ A full, personal signature
>
> ➤ Title
>
> ➤ Full contact information
>
> ➤ Details about the program you offered
>
> ➤ Quantifiable results

Here is an example from one of our clients:

ABC STAFFING COMPANY

June 1, 2013

Re: Increased Sales Through Coaching, Mentoring, and Training

Dear Colleen:

In the first four months of 2013, we hired Colleen Francis and Engage Selling Solutions to work with a number of our sales professionals with 1 to 10 years' experience. It was an enormous success. In fact, the success of the program can be seen through our actual results, with sales up 22 percent over last year.

On a weekly basis, Colleen worked closely with each individual on:

- Setting achievable goals
- Turning larger objectives into smaller activities
- Building their confidence level
- Honing their negotiation skills and dealing with discounting
- Choosing better language and tone
- Asking for business
- Creating stronger meetings
- Overcoming hidden objections
- Increasing follow-up and after-sales service

This high-impact coaching program has been felt throughout our organization. Our sales team is asking for continued or future coaching ideas and support. They expressed a comfort in working closely with an impartial, outside specialist who could offer new ideas or repackage existing ones. In addition, they heard feedback from a different angle or approach and were better able to accept suggestions for improvement.

The investment in mentoring and coaching programs can be significant; in the case of Colleen and Engage Selling, the investment was more than worth it. I would highly recommend their programs, and more so, their program delivery and effectiveness.

Should you require clarification or have questions, please contact me at (613) 230-1111, ext 111.

Bob Smith
President
ABC Staffing Company

And remember, one of the best ways of getting a letter like this is to draft it for the customer! Don't be shy—you are helping her out by saving her time. So give her a call, ask a few questions, and ask the customer if you can send her some text based on the conversation to be used in a testimonial letter. Customers will almost always say yes!

Variation 2: A Paragraph Testimonial

You can leverage this full-letter testimonial by creating a shorter, one-paragraph version that would be suited to marketing materials or websites. Choose the most powerful and quantifiable points in the letter to create a powerful paragraph. It's okay to string together a few sentences from various parts of the testimonial letter as long as all the words came from your customer!

Always include the name, title, and company of the client to complete your testimonial.

> In the first four months of this year, we hired Colleen Francis and Engage Selling to work with a number of our sales professionals with 1 to 10 years, experience—and with enormous success. In fact, the success of the program can be seen through our actual results, with sales up 22 percent over last year. Our sales team is asking for continued and future coaching ideas and support. While the investment in mentoring and coaching programs can be significant, in the case of Colleen and Engage Selling, it was more than worth it. I would highly recommend their programs, and more so, their program delivery and effectiveness.
>
> Bob Smith, President, ABC Staffing Company

Variation 3: A Brief Testimonial

Sometimes short, snappy testimonials are best. In the one- or two-sentence format you can use testimonials in email, on websites, or as the footer in your proposals. To make the best use of this format choose only the objective and metrics-based comments from the letter. Editing is okay as long as you don't change the client's intention or thoughts in the letter. It's always best to seek approval from your client on any changes you make, just to ensure he is comfortable with the changes.

We hired Colleen Francis and Engage Selling to work with a number of our sales professionals, which was enormously successful, as seen through our actual results, with sales up 22 percent over last year.

—Bob Smith, President, ABC Staffing Company

To make the best use of your testimonials be sure to start with the letter format. You can then leverage the letter into various other formats to use in diverse media and sales situations.

Prospects believe clients first and you second. This is a key reason why testimonials are critical to creating a Nonstop Sales Boom. When you create communities that are talking openly and passionately about their success with you, where people are learning from each other, you create success that others want to be associated with. In doing so you will be able to attract more prospects into your Sales Radar through the buzz that is generated as well as referrals.

COLLEEN'S POWER TIP #13: FIVE PROACTIVE TACTICS FOR COLLECTING TESTIMONIALS

When it comes to collecting testimonials, you must take an active role in their collection. Just placing a form on your website or making one call after the sale and waiting for clients to respond will not deliver the results you want. Instead, develop a process for regularly collecting feedback; this will provide a systematic way to gather testimonials. Such a process would include the following practices:

Build requests into your standard process. A simple fact is that the more people you ask for testimonials, the more you will receive. And the easiest way to do that is to *ask each and every one of your customers.* You'll want to think about the appropriate time frame for them to have experienced the product to ensure that they can talk about results—the key to an effective testimonial. One consulting client of mine trained everyone on the sales and service teams to ask, "Can I share your success with others?" during their post-sales process. This ensured the client was asked for a testimonial up to three times in a six-month period. How well do you think this worked? Nearly *75 percent* of their clients allowed testimonials to be used.

Don't hesitate to ask again. Many clients we work with assume that customers don't respond to testimonial requests because they aren't happy. More often than not, it's because they are simply very busy and don't have time to provide the feedback being requested.

So if a customer doesn't respond to the testimonial request, don't hesitate to ask again. And again. I'm not suggesting that you unleash a torrent of requests, but periodically asking for that feedback will help the customer by providing opportunities to respond when it is a better time for them. (This is no different from selling. An initial no or a lack of response never sends top sellers running away; it motivates them to return.)

Make it easy for customers. Make it easy for clients to give you feedback by using an online form or a quick telephone questionnaire. Just make sure it's easy to find and/or use. Dell support represents a best practice at www.support.dell.com to follow. It offers various ways for Dell users to interact

> **ENGAGED SELLING:**
>
> Purchases of desserts and after-dinner drinks rocket up to 25 percent from just 5 percent when the server simply asks, "Would you like one of our fine desserts and after-dinner drinks?"

with the support team, leave feedback, and rate the service including questions and options, such as:

> ➤ How likely are you to return?
> ➤ How likely are you to recommend Dell to others?
> ➤ A 1–5 ranking of the webpage and Dell in general

This feedback form can be accessed anywhere on the site. Not only is it easy to use, it shows clearly that Dell is interested in your feedback and not hiding from its clients.

Don't be afraid to reach out in person. Online or telephone collection, of course, is not your only option. If you have a chance to see your customers in person, there is no better way of getting feedback. Simply put, it's much harder to say no to someone who stands in front of you and directly asks for a testimonial. And, if you have your handy smartphone or camcorder, it's a perfect chance to capture video. The best sellers I work with make a regular habit of soliciting feedback from their new clients every few months. As a result they always have a batch of fresh testimonials to use as marketing material and proof of performance in sales meetings with new prospects.

If you don't see your customers in person, then why not pick up the phone? Especially for those customers who you know have had great results, a quick phone call can capture the information for a great testimonial. The key here is to make it easy: Ask questions that would form the basis of a testimonial, write it up on the customer's behalf, and send it to her for her quick approval. Here's a hint: To avoid telephone tag, encourage clients to leave the testimonial on your voice-mail system in case you're not immediately available.

. . . .

Clients believe clients first and you second. That is why testimonials and case studies are the single most important tool in your Leverage state. In Chapter 12 you saw that the smartest sellers are those who build testimonial collection into the ongoing management of all clients so that current client success can be leveraged into new prospect attraction. In doing so, they ensure that their Sales Radar is always full of the best new prospects.

Next we explore the power of referrals. In Chapter 13 you will see how to solicit the best referrals from your best customers that will lead you to your Nonstop Sales Boom.

High-Powered Leverage: How to Get the Most Referrals to the Best Prospects

A HIGHLY LEVERAGED CLIENT is one you can count on to provide referrals, unsolicited and solicited. Referrals are critical to creating a Nonstop Sales Boom because they fill your pipeline with high-quality opportunities at no cost whatsoever. At a recent conference, I was speaking to sales managers and business owners, and the topic of referrals came up. The sales leaders in the room expressed frustration that their teams weren't asking for referrals, despite the fact that everyone on the team knew that the quality of a referred lead is *far* superior to that of a cold lead.

According to a number of different clients, a cold lead, or an inbound lead from a random source, has a closing rate between 25 percent and 30 percent, as you learned in Chapter 3. In contrast, you double your success with a referred lead, which traditionally has a closing rate of 50 percent.

Given that kind of power, you'd think that everyone out there would be making good use of referrals, right?

No, not right.

Very few businesses capitalize on word of mouth from their existing customers. I've found this to be the case in my discussions with groups during Engage sales training exercises, and I'm not alone. Business guru Tom Peters recalls how he once polled executives at a workshop and asked them what percentage of their customers were giving their businesses all they could, including referrals. He was stunned by the answer: "I knew they would be quite a bit lower than 100 percent but I've found that most executives estimate that only somewhere between 0 and 25 percent of customers are giving them all the business they could. The numbers are even lower for referral sources" (www.tompeters.com/dispatches/010491.php).

Understanding why you hesitate to ask for referrals will help you overcome the problem (yes, *problem*) and boost your sales.

Two issues keep sellers from asking for referrals: fear and ego. As a salesperson, you face rejection on an almost daily basis, so it may come as a surprise that fear of rejection would play a role in your reluctance to ask for a referral. It's ironic, but in fact, the last thing we all want is another opportunity to be rejected! Asking a client for a referral opens up potential refusals and negative feedback, and as a result, you avoid what you may see as an unnecessary step in the sales process.

Sellers also typically have big, healthy egos. We're trained to believe that we can sell in the face of adversity—in fact, we have to in order to be successful. We believe that our method is the best, and we can sell on our own without anyone's help. The concept of sellers as lone hunters means that we're reluctant to ask for a referral, because a referral is asking for help—a potential sign of weakness. Not many people understand this issue, which seems counterintuitive—because it is!

I know this issue well because, as a junior sales rep, I fell into the ego trap. I didn't want to ask for referrals, because I didn't want customers to think I was desperate for new business. The reality was, I was desperate for new business. It's an unfunny Catch-22, and it's important that you get past this hurdle if you plan to have a Nonstop Sales Boom.

In order to help get past your fear and ego, I suggest you focus on referrals as an *institutionalized* sales strategy during the Leverage state of your Sales Radar. That means creating a process that you follow each time you make a sale. I have provided a sample workflow in Figure 13–1 that a software client created for his referral program. Notice that the client is reminded *seven* times for a reference in three different formats and is rewarded for his help.

Another systematic way to get past the fear of referrals is to have a referral blitz, a referral campaign, or a referral contest. Many Engage clients motivate their sales teams to get referrals through healthy competition, prizes, and financial incentives, or just accolades for having the most referrals in the business. They use this approach quarterly and they see two distinct benefits. One, they increase their referrals, and two, they open the door for more business to the client they called. Either result is welcome.

Figure 13–1. Referral Strategy

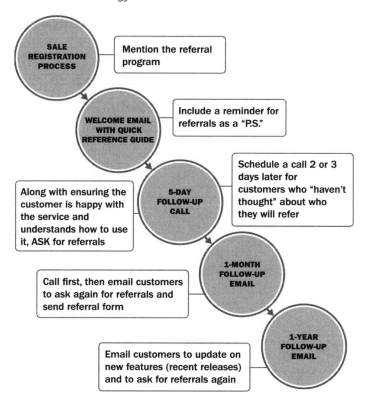

At the end of the day their Sales Radar is full of new opportunities and a Nonstop Sales Boom can be created.

COLLEEN'S SEVEN SECRETS TO REFERRAL SUCCESS

Referrals are personal acts of trust. If you want to increase your referral rate, you first have to examine how you conduct yourself on a daily basis. What have you done to deserve referrals? The business results you provide clients are not the only thing driving their willingness to give you referrals. Equally important is how likeable and deserving you are personally.

High Regard = High Referrals

Like everything else in sales, there is no magic "likability" bullet that works to build trust every time with every client to gain more referrals. However, the following are my top seven ways to prove to your clients that you are deserving of their referrals. Executing this list well will ensure you receive referrals—even when you don't ask for them!

Reward Your Current Advocates

Once a year, trace your new clients back to their roots to see who was responsible for all the additions to your client base. Odds are, you'll find between 5 and 20 primary referral sources, ranging from current clients to friends, partners, and suppliers. This is the client community we discussed in Chapter 11.

Provide some new value at least quarterly to these referral sources—your best advocates—to stay in the forefront of their minds. Send them an article or video that you think they will enjoy. Place a call to tell them you were thinking about them and share a business or personal success tip relevant to them. Invite them to lunch or breakfast, or—best of all—provide them a referral for *their* business.

For example, Hugo, a financial services consultant in Saudi Arabia, shared with me that only 10 percent of his business came from referrals because of the very private nature of his superwealthy clients. We started an "advocate program" for him, with a concrete set of tasks and a calendar: He started to meet his only referral sources for breakfast twice a year and arranged for books, articles, and newsletters on their preferred topics to be sent regularly. Within one year Hugo's referrals grew from 10 percent to 50 percent of his new business annually. He may not have increased the number of his sources, but he sure got a lot more out of the few he had.

What Hugo did for his advocates was perfect. He delivered value. Whatever you send has to be of value to them, not simply an advertisement for you. If you help them grow, trust me, it won't take long before they'll return the favor and help you grow, too.

ENGAGED SELLING:

Reciprocity in referrals is very powerful. Give and you shall get.

Help Your Clients

An insurance agent I work with doubled her referrals in one month simply by asking the following at the end of every client meeting: "How can I help you?"

Many of your clients will be genuinely surprised by this question, because no salesperson has ever asked them before. That's why your follow-up question is equally indispensable: "You've helped my business grow by becoming part of our community. I'd like to help your business grow, too. Who is an ideal prospect for me to introduce you to?"

At a networking event you can do this as well. Rather than showing up looking to meet new clients for your business, look around the room to see whom you can connect. When you connect them, your likability goes up and two people now think you are more deserving of referrals.

In my own business I make it a habit of introducing people to my network of professional advisors. In the summer I arrange golf tournaments with my accountants and invite potential clients for them to play in our foursome. In the winter I invite groups of clients who I think need to meet each other to private events, fundraisers, or dinner. By making sure my clients have a steady stream of referrals from me, I ensure that I receive a steady stream of referrals from them.

Think Value

Referrals happen only when you provide value to your customers beyond the products they buy from you. I saw a great example of this recently when I was on a wine tour of Ontario's Niagara region. I noticed that many winemakers were almost as eager to tell me great things about other wines produced in the area as they were about selling their own wine. At first, I found this odd. Why would they take time to sell me on their competition? After I returned home, I noticed how that helpful gesture had shaped my behavior. Not only did I buy more from those generous winemakers, I specifically mentioned them to friends who were visiting the area. Moreover, I noticed that I was most eager to make a return visit to those wineries who gave me all the great tips and I actively sought out their wine in our local stores. Their added value to me (outside of the great Pinot Noir I bought) drove increased sales from me, and my friends. There's good karma in providing exceptional value.

Be *the* Expert

Clients don't want to associate with salespeople. They want to associate with experts who can help them personally or professionally. One way to show your clients you deserve more referrals is to become that expert. You can do this by actively speaking at industry conferences, or at workshops or teleconferences. Writing case studies or publishing the ones written for you by a marketing team also helps to develop your expertise. Being active in the marketplace as an advocate for customers' issues positions you as an expert focused on client success.

Finally, you can become an expert by associating with experts. For example, Engage clients in the global forwarding business routinely hold workshops for their clients and invite customs and international experts to speak. The sellers in the room are experts by association. Engage clients in the animal health business associate with both veterinarians and breeders. By introducing their clients (breeders) to these expert veterinarians, the sellers become even more trusted by their clients. Engage clients in corporate banking routinely have specialized accountants speak at their conferences on succession planning, valuations, and cross-border finance. In doing so they increase their referrals because the corporate CEOs invite their friends and colleagues to attend these events.

Think Free

Free offers are timelessly powerful. I've benefitted from this firsthand, not just as a consumer but as a business owner. For example, I have a client who recently referred me to someone in her organization. To show my appreciation, I sent a free ticket to a much-sought-after Engage event. One software company I work with offers a free training session for staff once a referral is secured and another offers one free month of its software for every new customer referred to its business. Even corporations that are not allowed to accept gifts are allowed to accept reduced fee or free professional services if they benefit the company and not an individual.

Another great example comes from a client in the hospitality industry. She sends free gasoline cards every time she receives a referral (and you can well imagine how greatly this was appreciated when gas prices skyrocketed to $4 per gallon). Included with the card was a little note that said, "You filled up my tank, now it's my turn to fill up yours."

Little things—gestures that don't cost a fortune—go a long way toward cementing a great business relationship.

Celebrate!

Most businesses send holiday cards, which have become passé simply because everyone is doing it. If you want to stand out and be remembered by your clients, why not try something a little different? In addition to, or instead of, sending cards out each December, mix a few of the ideas listed below into your annual calendar. These ideas may sound corny but they will all work to increase your referrals. I know because I didn't just dream up a list for this book; these ideas have all been implemented by businesses that I've worked with that have a strong record of referrals. Clients like to do business with people who treat them like people, are fun to be around, and who recognize accomplishments and celebrate with them. Pick the ones that resonate best with you and your clients. Regardless of the market, your clients will appreciate the attention and reward you with valuable leads and introductions.

> Mike in financial services sends annual thank-you cards on the anniversary of your doing business together.

> Donald, who owns an advertising agency, sends Valentine's Day candy baskets with the message "We love having you as a client."

> Todd in corporate lending sends Thanksgiving cards or food baskets. If the company can't accept gifts he sends the basket on its behalf to a food bank or Meals on Wheels charity in its local town—and makes sure the client is acknowledged.

> Susan in the feed manufacturing business sends birthday cakes or cards on clients' birthdays. For very large clients (and by special request) sometimes she makes her famous homemade fudge.

> Chris sends St. Patrick's Day cards with a note about "being lucky to have them as a client."

> Doreen in outsourced lead generation has sent orange and black candy in cards at Halloween.

> Casey in my office receives gifts from our suppliers including cupcakes on Administrative Professional Day. (As well as something from me!).

> Gen in the ships services business invites his best clients to a private event during national holidays in Japan. These are held at the Norwegian embassy because Gen's company is Norwegian, adding a unique and first-class element to the event.

> Paul in global forwarding hosts New Year's celebrations (feasts and parties) in Hong Kong.

> Suzanne in pharmaceutical sales works with her healthcare and hospital clients to volunteer with them on a local project in the community. While many industries have laws and rules against

receiving benefits from suppliers, foundations and community associations are always happy to accept volunteer time.

> Kevin in heavy equipment sales sends dinner to his clients during harvest.

> Jeremy in enterprise software sends congratulations to his clients when he knows they've completed something significant in their personal or professional lives such as celebrating a business anniversary, earning a black belt in karate, or being listed as one of the best employers to work for in their city.

Be World Class!

You will receive more referrals simply by being the best, from your client's perspective, at what you do. Here is one way to ensure that happens. After the Participation stage is complete say to your clients, "One of the ways I know I'm doing a good job for my clients is when they tell others about me. I know that only happens when you think I am providing world-class service to you. What would world-class service mean for you?"

ENGAGED SELLING:

All selling is human-to-human selling. Show people you care about them as human beings and they will reward you with loyalty, advocacy, and referrals for future business.

Start this process with a customer review system that gauges your client's path to purchase, and his current needs or concerns (see Figure 13–2). In many ways, this is an intelligence-gathering process that will allow you to better understand who your customers are, why they buy, and what their current and future pain points are. You can use this information to better serve your current clients, but also to identify new opportunities that this client can refer you to.

Within the first 30 days of acquiring and onboarding new customers (immediately following the Participation state), ask the following questions:

> What prompted you to buy our product or service?

> ➤ Why are you continuing to do business with us?

> ➤ How is our product helping you?

> ➤ How can we best serve you going forward?

> ➤ What contacts inside our company would you like to have access to?

If you uncover any immediate concerns address them right away. The benefit of making this call within the first 30 days after a purchase is that you can quickly resolve any issues. If there are no issues to resolve, take action on the steps the client sees as the best way forward, and make the introductions the client requested. Doing so will increase the trust your client has in you and therefore the referrals she sends.

Now that you know the secrets for making yourself more deserving of referrals let's look at the big mistakes sellers make asking for them.

AVOID THESE CLASSIC MISTAKES WHEN ASKING FOR REFERRALS

To receive referrals you must ask for them correctly. Making the following mistakes (every one of which I have witnessed firsthand) will cost you referrals and of course future revenue.

Figure 13–2. Customer Survey Success

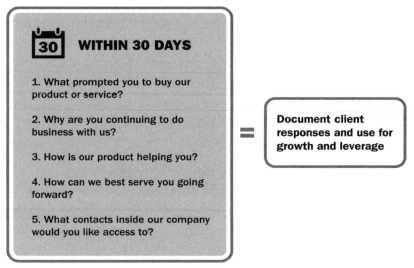

Don't Ask Too Soon

The worst time to ask for a referral is when you're still at the point-of-sale stage in the sales cycle. If the ink isn't even dry on the deal, odds are good that your new client hasn't yet formed a complete opinion of you and your company. Besides, asking for a referral as the sale is closing makes you look greedy, selfish, and not very deserving. Success in sales is about building and maintaining relationships. Making the sale is just the start of that relationship. In a sense, it's a relationship that is much like a marriage—a lot of work needs to be done to keep that relationship working well. Romance people properly.

Give your customers time. Don't ask for a referral until the client has received a positive benefit from working with you and your company. It's only acceptable to ask after a product has been delivered or installed and the client has told you he is satisfied.

Remember, All Referrals Are Personal

People refer business to you not for business reasons, but for personal reasons. While the service you provide is professional, when a client recommends your service to someone she knows, it becomes a very personal act. The referral demonstrates a high level of trust in you, and that's not to be taken lightly. It also represents a level of risk for the referrer—her advice is on the line. Therefore, it's important that any referral program you develop is based on the idea that you value your customers as people first—not as revenue centers. I call this *human-to-human selling.*

Show Your Thanks

Forgetting to say thank you is a big mistake . . . so big that it's cringe-worthy. Think about it for a moment. If a client makes the decision that you deserve a referral, and you miss the opportunity to thank him for that gesture, you risk shutting off that referral pipeline, perhaps permanently.

When it comes to referrals, there are in fact two instances where a thank-you is in order. First, thank your client when he refers your name to a friend or colleague. Send a card or call to express your appreciation. Do *not* send an email. A card is personal and it sits in someone's hand, making it memorable in a way that email simply

ENGAGED SELLING:

Referrals can be evergreen if you nurture them.

can never be. The second time to express thanks is when that new referral buys from you. A small token of thanks can again be as simple as a hand-written note or a phone call. Or, depending on your industry (where regulation and corporate policy will allow it) you might consider inviting the client to lunch or sending him a small gift. The key is to make a gesture that says, "I really appreciate you thinking of me."

Be Persistent, but Don't Overdo It

There is a fine line between persistence and stalking! When you initiate a referral program, it's important that you be judicious in how often you reach out to your existing customers. Once every 30 days is a good rule of thumb, using a combination of calls, emails, and marketing. (Remember the VORTEX component *variety*?) While you might not ask for referrals in each of these communications you can mention your referral program or share stories of a new client who came to you from a referral.

In a monthly newsletter that a restaurant equipment seller sends he thanks his referral sources publically. This sends the message that he is open for referrals, and as a result he receives two to three referrals a week.

If you communicate less than every 30 days with your clients it's too easy to lose that top-of-mind position in the marketplace. On the other hand, if you try sending tokens of appreciation—or calls or even emails— to a client once a week, you definitely run the risk of being perceived as a stalker.

Be Specific

A component of an effective referral program needs to include asking your customers if they know someone who could benefit from the products or services you are selling. However, it's important that you be specific. It's simply not enough to ask, "Who else do you know in your organization?" or to say in passing, "If you know anyone else who needs my services, don't hesitate to pass my name around." It's too easy for the person to whom you're speaking with to say, "Gosh, no one comes to mind right now, but let me think about it and then I'll be sure to pass your name along." You can guess what happens next. That client goes back to the office, handles 25 calls and the mountain of tasks in her inbox, and before the day is over, she's forgotten about your request.

It's perhaps the *very* best method to mention a name: "I know you're a colleague of Maryann Foster, and I'd love to meet her. Can you introduce us?"

If you ask a general question you are asking the client to do all the work for you and, as a result, get limited or no referrals. The best sellers ask for an introduction to a specific person, and always get it! Here is how it works:

HOW TO ASK FOR A REFERRAL	
GENERAL (WRONG WAY)	**SPECIFIC (RIGHT WAY)**
Do you know anyone who could benefit from my services?	I would love to meet the CEO of the company next door. Do you know him?
Could other departments in your company use this product?	Your VP of sales, Bob Smith, would be a great fit for us. Can I tell him you and I do business together?
If you think of any other people I should meet, let me know!	I noticed that you have an IT director for Canada. Do you mind if I contact him next week?
Who else do you know?	Your European division would likely have the same issues as you did when we started talking. When I call them next week can I share your success with them?
Can you refer me to . . . ?	I'll be calling Bob Smith next week. Can I share your success with him?
I would like to meet others like you.	I will be calling your colleague Susan Chan next week. Can I tell her we do business together?

TWO WAYS TO ASK FOR A REFERRAL

There are two ways to ask for a referral. Most sellers only use the first, but perpetual boomers use both. The first is to ask *directly*. For example:

> ➤ "Bob, can you help me with an introduction to Susan?"

> ➤ "Margaret, I'd like to meet Frank in the technical department. Can you introduce me?"

> ➤ "Sally, are you okay with me telling the finance director we do business together?"

> ➤ "Alan, can I share your success with the VP of sales?"

In each of these specific requests I am asking for permission for something or asking the client to help with the referral. In a high-trust relationship you should receive a yes to all of these requests but there is always a chance the client will say "No" or "Let me think about it." This could be an indication of one or more of three things:

1. She doesn't know the person you are requesting to meet.
2. She doesn't trust you.
3. You have a customer service problem that is unresolved.

If the reason for the "no" is #1 above, ask for a different introduction. If it's #2 or #3, find and resolve the issue first before pressing for the referral.

The second way to ask for a referral is to simply *tell* the client what you're going to do before you do it, rather than *ask*. This can increase the likelihood of the client agreeing to your request. It works like this: First, decide whom you are going to call in advance of your meeting and schedule the call in your calendar. Next, meet with your client and use one of the following scripts:

> ➤ "Bob, I'll be calling Mary in purchasing next week. Can I tell her we do business together?"

> ➤ "Ann, I have a note to call Chris, your CFO, next week. Can I share your department's success with him?"

The difference between the two approaches is subtle but powerful. In the "tell then ask" approach you are telling the client first that you are making a call. This makes you sound like an insider, as someone who already knows the potential new contact. When the referral source feels like you might already have a relationship with the person you are calling, it's much easier for him or her to say yes to the request.

 **COLLEEN'S POWER TIP #14: WHERE CAN YOU FIND REFERRALS?**

A fully leveraged client offers referrals to two groups: those inside his company to other buyers, divisions, or departments; and those outside his company to friends, family, business associates, and suppliers. Figure 13–3 displays these relationships.

Figure 13–3. Referral Sources

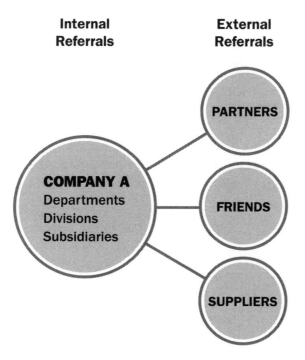

To determine to whom you want to be referred, do some homework first. Make a list of your top 25 prospects. Now ask yourself *where the links exist between your best clients and your best prospects.* These become the key links in your referral supply chain. Where there is a link, call your existing client and ask for one of two kinds of referrals, inside referrals or outside referrals.

To find the best *inside referrals* use the following four steps:

> **Step one:** Work from your client's organizational chart. If you don't have one, ask for one or find one online.
>
> **Step two:** Sit down with the client to review the organizational chart with names and titles. Engage client Mark reports that when faced with blank spaces on an organizational chart his clients pick up the pen and start filling in spaces.
>
> **Step three:** Decide whom you want to meet. You can either decide quickly in that meeting or take the organizational chart away for more research. Either is fine as long as you eventually get to step four.
>
> **Step four:** Ask for a specific introduction. "Bob, you mentioned Andy is the VP of sales for South America. Do you mind if I call him next week?" Or "Sarah, I'll be calling Mark next week in your finance department. Can I tell him we do business together?"

Outside referrals involve somebody in a different company than you're currently working with. These are the sources connected to but outside the company that you saw in Figure 13–3. Let's say your targeted prospect works for IBM, a company that currently supplies your customer in a different field than yours. Your request could sound like this: "Stephen, I'm looking to meet the VP of sales at IBM. Do you know her?" If your client says yes, then you follow up with: "Would you be able to help me with an introduction?" The key word is "help." It's an incredibly powerful word and using it in your request will almost always get you a satisfactory reply. Or, if you have done your homework and are ready for the "tell then ask" approach, say, "Stephen, I'll be calling Pat Smith, the VP of sales at IBM, next week. Do you know her?"

Treat referrals as something you obtain from clients *as a rule*—not as an exception. They are vital to creating your Nonstop Sales Boom. Not only do they help attract new customers, but they also help you broaden your network and maintain the loyalty of your leveraged customers. Current clients who refer new business to you consistently tend to *stay clients for a longer period of time.* They either want to stay because their entire network is in your community and/or because you have become a trusted and pervasive supplier to their organization.

I suspect over the next years we will see an even greater disparity in results between making cold calls with and without referrals. The perceived risks associated with buying from a stranger in the minds of buyers aren't going to go away, and as a result, people are going to be more prone to sticking with who they know. Referrals keep you in the "know and trust" category in the minds of buyers.

It's important that you balance your need for referrals against the tolerance of your client. The last thing you want is to be so persistent about asking for referrals that you look like you are begging. Nobody trusts a desperate-looking or -sounding salesperson! On the other hand, you must be persistent and consistent and find subtle ways to remind your clients that you are always open to receiving referrals and new prospects.

. . . .

Creating a referral strategy with clients in the Leverage state based on the principles outlined in this chapter will help you find the right balance of prospects for your Sales Radar. You'll never hurt a relationship, and you'll build a community of buyers to help you create a Nonstop Sales Boom.

Your personal Sales Radar is now complete. With that, it's time to turn our attention to your organization. In Chapter 14 you will learn how to activate and optimize your Sales Radar throughout the sales organization to ensure that it is working to create your Nonstop Sales Boom.

CHAPTER 14

Organizational Imperatives: Supporting and Enabling the Sales Radar

EVEN WITH THE BEST INTENTIONS, the Sales Radar can be sabotaged by an organization's strategies, processes, and structures. In this chapter, which is largely addressed to managers and the executive suite, we review some of the organizational imperatives required to ensure that your Sales Radar is fully functional. Specifically, we look at how companies can avoid undermining its Attraction, Participation, Growth, and Leverage efforts and initiatives by:

> Managing their talent to encourage and reward the right behaviors

> Implementing a rigorous process to manage and monitor the sales pipeline effectively

> Developing the right sales and product development strategies that give the organization the greatest flexibility and opportunity to serve more customers

> Installing an organizational structure that encourages and facilitates cross-functional collaboration

When its talent, processes, strategies, and structure are aligned with its revenue and sales goals, an organization will be able to take full advantage of the myriad sales opportunities that appear in all four quadrants of the Sales Radar.

TALENT: CREATING AND COACHING HIGH-PERFORMANCE TEAMS

There are four talent imperatives that top-performing companies consistently implement:

1. Enforcing a high-performance culture
2. Aligning compensation with goals
3. Nonstop training and coaching
4. Nonstop recruiting

Enforcing a High-Performance Culture

Top-performing organizations manage their teams to ensure 80 percent or more are hitting targets (and poor performers are coached up or out quickly). In a typical sales organization 10 percent of salespeople overachieve, always exceeding their target. Another 20 percent underachieve dramatically and are considered "dead wood." And 70 percent are average, performing inconsistently and regularly missing their quotas. Perpetually booming companies, on the other hand, build an entire team of top performers. To do this, *they get rid of their average, not merely their underachieving.* Their tolerance level is far below what most companies will endure. I call this "Finding the best, removing the rest."

For example, some sellers tend to repeat what they prefer doing *regardless of what is actually required to exceed their targets.* When interviewing sellers last year for a new business, I was told by one candidate: "I don't make cold calls anymore. I've done my

ENGAGED SELLING:

Sales managers who do not enforce high performance are the worst performers of all.

time. Cold calls are beneath me." Refusal to do the work necessary for this business cost that salesman a job opportunity. In your business it could be costing you a Nonstop Sales Boom. Make sure that your sellers are doing the job required of them, not only the job they want to do. And if they think anything is "beneath them," it's time to let them go.

Alignment of Compensation with Goals

Your teams will do what you pay them to do, which I realize is not exactly a conceptual breakthrough. Yet, many organizations forget this and continue to pay their sellers out of alignment with the behaviors they expect. For example, a hotel's sales team does not get paid for repeat bookings from existing customers. As a result, they ignore their current clients in favor of new clients. The hotel's general manager can't understand why repeat business is lower than industry averages! If you pay a seller more for new sales than repeat sales, the momentum will be to coach toward new client development rather than cross-selling to the existing customer base. To create a Nonstop Sales Boom you must align compensation with the exact behaviors you want your sales team to complete.

For example, I know of a software sales VP who noticed that all deals over a million dollars were being ignored or disqualified in the pipeline. He later learned that his team's compensation was clawed back on all deals over a million because the company had to involve other team members and departments to help close the sale. As a response, the sellers simply ignored the big deals and worked on achieving their full quota on smaller deals that they were going to be paid full commissions on. As soon as the compensation plan was changed, the sellers' behavior was corrected, a team-selling model was adopted, and revenue soared to 25 percent over target in one year.

Nonstop Training and Coaching

Last year a client recalled his first sales job to me. He was told, "Here is your order pad and here are the keys to your truck. Don't come back until you have an order."

Selling is a learned skill and sellers must be trained and coached regularly, like any other professionals. What do Lebron James, Usain Bolt, Sydney Crosby, Andy Murray, and Phil Mickelson all have in common? They are sports professionals at the top of their game who report to training on time, every time. The research on coaching and training is conclusive. According to CSO Insights, the win rate of firms that spend less than $1,500 per year per rep is 47 percent whereas the win rate of firms that spent between $1,500 and $5,000 per rep is 52.2 percent. Making the same point in their blog article entitled "The Dirty Secret of Effective Sales Coaching," Matthew Dixon and Brent Adamson noted that their SEC study, which involved thousands of sales representatives, saw sustained improvement of up to 19 percent in the performance of sales representatives who received quality coaching (blogs.hbr.org/2011/01/the-dirty-secret-of-effective).

Here's a story that vividly demonstrates the importance of coaching. In 2011, the vice president of sales of an office furniture company discovered that his installation team was routinely criticizing the products being installed (and using colorful derogatory language, no less), *in front of their clients.* They had not been hired for their customer service skills nor were they trained in customer retention. As a result, growth opportunities were lost because trust was eroded and perception of the product diminished before the installation was even complete. When the installers were trained and coached in sales and service skills, customer retention and growth soared and the company has been able to sustain a Nonstop Sales Boom for the past two years.

Nonstop Recruiting

Too often business leaders settle into complacency when their teams are performing well and they stop recruiting, or it falls by the wayside when there's too much else on their plates. But, it's essential to constantly have recruiting on your to-do list for three important reasons:

1. **People leave.** No matter how well you pay your team, or how well

they seem to be performing, one thing's always certain: Turnover happens. Whether it's someone winning the lottery, moving because of a spouse's promotion, or getting a better offer somewhere else, some of your employees will inevitably move on from your company. And as their manager, you'll be the last to know, so don't be caught in a bind when one of your key team members gives notice.

2. **People underperform.** Traditionally, sales teams fall into a pattern: Twenty percent hit well above their target—they are your high performers; 60 percent hit their target fairly consistently—they are your workhorses; and another 20 percent underperform or are too new to measure. You always want to have the option to replace your bottom 20 percent with better performers, and you won't have any options if you're not actively recruiting.

3. **Your team will grow.** Even in the best-case scenario—where all of your team members are overperforming and you're hitting it out of the park in your market—it's time to start attacking new markets. And at that point, you'll need new salespeople to go after those markets.

ENGAGED SELLING:

ABR = Always Be Recruiting

ALIGNING PROCESSES TO BE SALES-RADAR READY

The fundamental process imperative to create a Nonstop Sales Boom is to implement a *rigorous, objective sales forecast and performance measurement system.* Too many organizations today don't have a standard sales process that they use to monitor a seller's progress and lead conversions. At the same time, I am still shocked how many sellers don't embrace and use their sales process and CRM database to manage their day. It's just not possible to create a Nonstop Sales Boom in a disorganized or ad hoc sales environment.

Here are two examples of the hazard of not having rigorous processes in place. A newly minted sales VP with a quarterly target of $750,000 in revenue told me that her team routinely finishes the first month of the quarter with only $150,000 in the pipeline and that 80 percent of the team achieve their targets with opportunities that never make it into her forecast. She has no idea where these leads come from, how long they take to close, or what happens to them when they don't. Her pipeline and the opportunities inside it are invisible to her. As a result, she can't re-create a successful month, replicate the best sellers' behaviors, or coach for top performance. When she has success, she has it by accident. Nonstop Sales Booms can only be created on purpose.

Executives within another company insisted that their sales team knew what their closing ratio was supposed to be. On further investigation, it became obvious that this expectation was anything but clear to that team. One seller interviewed "thought" his closing ratio was 50 percent; he obviously underperformed prospecting activities because he was unaware that the actual figure was closer to 30 percent. While sellers may not like the fact that their closing ratios are actually lower than they think they are, knowing the real number is the only way to improve performance and create a Nonstop Sales Boom.

The best sales organizations build their sales process, from prospecting to closing, on the sales pipeline as described in earlier chapters of this book. However, they don't make the mistakes that underperforming companies and sales teams make with the pipeline. I am constantly amazed at how much this powerful tool is mismanaged. Before we continue on to strategies, however, let me revisit one of the fundamental ways to ensure that your sales pipeline is an objective monitoring and forecasting tool: using the pipeline to measure *percentage of sale completed* and not *probability of close.*

ENGAGED SELLING:

The facts might not always be pretty, but knowing them is the only way to create a Nonstop Sales Boom.

We covered this in detail in Colleen's Power Tip #2 back in Chapter 3, so I'll only quickly mention the point here again. Probability of close is a subjective measurement that requires sellers to make a judgment about their chances of making a sale. It requires interpretation, reflects bias, and is easy to abuse. When sellers think that moving an opportunity through the pipeline increases its probability of close, they're less likely to use that pipeline accurately. They will hold back on moving deals into fully qualified stages until they are convinced that they will close, limiting the opportunities they put into the pipeline in the initial stages because they don't want to use the pipeline to track deals that they might lose. They arbitrarily change the probability percentage to match how they "feel" about the opportunity.

Change your pipeline management from "probability of close" to "percentage complete" and you will correct this long-term destructive behavior.

CHOOSING THE RIGHT SALES AND PRODUCT DEVELOPMENT STRATEGIES

Companies and their executives often make top-level decisions that substantially hinder the success of their own sales organizations. These decisions concern both sales and product development strategies. Nonstop Sales Boom companies, on the other hand, will be both *flexible* and *consistent*. This sentence may appear contradictory, but it isn't.

Implement Flexible Sales Strategies

Far too many people wrongly believe that one sales approach trumps all others. For example, if the company is focused on growth of market share, it might wrongly assume it should only be focusing on client acquisition at the expense of managing its existing client base. As a result, the sales leaders will reorganize the team, the goals, the territories, and the compensation plans to focus on new sales *while the existing customers are ignored.*

But sales strategies will need to change quickly in response to the markets, and an organization needs to have multiple sales strategies depending on the needs of its market and the products that are being launched. To fully optimize your Sales Radar you must avoid the myopic view that "one size fits all." Ensure you adopt a strategy that is flexible enough to meet the needs of clients in all states of engagement.

Manage Product Lines Consistently

Nonstop Sales Boom companies do not fall into the trap of becoming overly reliant on one product at the expense of others. For many traditional businesses this is counter to the autonomy many sellers believe they need to operate successfully; they feel they need to be able to choose what parts of the portfolio to focus on. In reality, all this "choice" does is provide an excuse for the seller to not line up with the go-to market strategy of the sales leadership. For example, companies that launch new products into an existing market and do not set separate targets and compensation for these new products run the risk of their sellers either ignoring the new products because the older ones are easier to sell or abandoning the older products to focus on the new products exclusively. The first option ensures the product launch will be a failure; the second creates a large bust in sales in the existing market, market erosion of the product, and dissatisfaction in the existing customer base. Too often, sellers' unwillingness to sell both product lines in parallel is used as an excuse to avoid learning about new product lines and to stay in their comfort zone. This is particularly dangerous when considering how to deliver new products to existing clients—a key strategy for booming companies.

For example, one telephone service provider gave up trying to attract new clients and instead focused all its resources on protecting its base (no names please). As a result, it lost market share as it refused to listen to the market, innovate, and diversify. Sales teams ignored marketing departments, and engineering sat in isolation working on making the current solutions better rather than being open to the market's demand for a new solution. By operating on a "not-to-lose" basis rather than playing to win, this business created a perpetual bust in its sales results.

CREATE A COLLABORATIVE ORGANIZATIONAL STRUCTURE

Some organizations have a culture that prizes one aspect of the sales process above all others. For example, large organizations often have a culture of "silos." The sales department doesn't talk to the business development, marketing, customer service, and account management departments. As a result, leads passed from marketing do not always align with the current sales strategy, and account managers are not briefed by sales regarding the client's buying process. Do you remember Trend Micro's innovative office plan, where sales and field marketing shared a space, from Chapter 4? This doesn't happen to them. A large, well-established high-tech company admitted to me that it lost a $500,000 order from an existing client because the engineering department managing the account didn't trust the consulting team to handle it, nor did they want to pass it to the sales team. *Your Sales Radar will not function fully in an entrenched silo culture.*

Of course there are exceptions, and some types of companies do focus on structure with sales and marketing working together to track opportunities before and after the sales pipeline. These include early-stage companies, such as technology start-ups, which focus on meeting with contacts and prospects before an opportunity is identified because they are learning the market and must focus on identifying *new* opportunities, opportunities that might not even have existed in the past. In some cases marketing and sales are often a joint responsibility of a single executive; this executive pays attention to both the finding and the closing of deal. I consider this a plus.

Sadly, companies that focus singularly on one aspect of the sales cycle also tend to alienate the few customers they do win because they do not have a Sales Radar in place to grow and leverage an existing customer base. They have not planned for success.

At the opposite end of the spectrum, some traditional businesses twist their structure to focus on account management rather than actively generating new business, because they think there is limited room to grow and they want to protect their existing base from eroding. In this case sales, marketing, and customer service are not working together to give clients what they need. Instead they are making decisions in isolation from the market, based on what they would rather do.

Here's another example of how a silo culture will create a sales bust. The marketing department of a billion-dollar software company in charge of generating leads for the sales team created a lead generation system to find, nurture, and convert leads to sales-ready status. This is a common structure for large organizations. The trouble was that the sales leaders took a hands-off approach to marketing's lead generation process, even though it affected their team's performance directly. Definitions for "sales-ready lead," "qualified opportunity," "accepted lead," and "rejected lead" were created in isolation from the already established sales process and without agreement from the sales leadership team. Without participation from the sales VP, the marketing group had dramatically overestimated the criteria for a sales-ready lead, resulting in a process that was far too rigorous for most leads to pass through. In turn, this process delivered too few leads for the sales team to hit its targets. In addition, leads that did make it through the process were often rejected by sales because by the time the nurturing process was completed they were either not the right fit, or too old to be considered actively sales-ready. As a result hundreds of new leads were lost each month.

 **COLLEEN'S POWER TIP #15: BRINGING YOUR ORGANIZATION TOGETHER**

The Sales Radar will not function at 100 percent effectiveness in a siloed organization. Here are five tips to help bring your company together to create a Nonstop Sales Boom using the Sales Radar:

1. Have marketing teams and sales teams work together to transform product "features and benefits" into "client results and testimonials."

2. Communicate wins internally, to ensure that the entire company is aware of high-profile clients.

3. Insist that sales operations data be included in key decisions, allowing sellers to make decisions based on data, not on gut.

4. Be sure that proposal writing is a team effort between a proposal team, sellers, and the client, ensuring proposals that are in perfect alignment with the customer's objectives.

5. Have research and product development work together with sales and meet customers directly, ensuring that product enhancement and new releases are in alignment with what the clients need. (Here's a true—and pathetic—story: I once sat in on a sales meeting where the sales team and development teams were fighting about "what the customer really wanted." The development team had not talked to the customer in over 12 months because the sales team didn't think they could add value to the discussion. This company had not made the new sale in more than six months.)

CREATING AND MAINTAINING YOUR NONSTOP SALES BOOM

Any radar system has to discriminate between friend and foe, threat and opportunity. Your Sales Radar should be highly sensitive to *all* opportunities, and not just the ones directly in front of you! Tunnel vision is for moles.

The "air traffic control" of your Nonstop Sales Boom isn't meant to avoid collisions but rather to *create* encounters with high-potential buyers and referrals. Your radar set—and your future—are based on a 360° view of the world of opportunities, as opposed to a narrow glimpse.

Add to this your new ability to move freely and quickly with your buyers in all four states of client engagement and you're able to do something the air traffic controller is not able to do: land the plane.

But you can land the business!

Index

INDEX